BEST of the BEST from GEORGIA

Selected Recipes from Georgia's FAVORITE COOKBOOKS

BEST
of the BEST
from
GEORGIA

Selected Recipes from Georgia's
FAVORITE COOKBOOKS

EDITED BY
Gwen McKee
AND
Barbara Moseley

Illustrated by Tupper England

QUAIL RIDGE PRESS

Recipe Collection © 1989 Quail Ridge Press, Inc.

CONTINUED

COPYRIGHT

CONTINUED

Somethin's Cookin' in the Mountains © 1984 Soque Publishers; *Southern Seafood Classics* © 1988 The Southeastern Fisheries Association; *Southwind Cuisine* © 1987 Doreen Mac Adams; *The Stuffed Griffin* © 1976 The Utility Club; *A Taste of Georgia* © 1977 Newman Junior Service League, Inc.; *A Taste of the Holidays* © 1988 Dot Gibson Publications; *Tea-Time at the Masters*® © 1977 The Junior League of Augusta, Georgia, Inc.; *Temptations* © 1985 Junior Service League of Rome, Inc.; *Traditionally Wesleyan* © 1985 The Wesleyan Business Club; *Tullie's Receipts* © 1976 Atlanta Historical Society; *Unbearably Good!* © 1986 Americus Junior Service League; *Vincent Russo Seafood Cookbook* © 1984, 1988 Vincent Russo; *Windsor Academy Cookbook* © 1988 Ponder's, Inc.; *You Are The Boss in the Kitchen* © 1979 Ursula's Cooking School.

ISBN 0-937552-30-5
First printing, September 1989 • Second, August 1991
Third, August 1993 • Fourth, October 1995 • Fifth, January 1999
Sixth, February 2000 • Seventh, March 2001

Library of Congress Catalog Card Number: 89-60780
Manufactured in the United States of America
Designed by Barney and Gwen McKee
Chapter opening photos and cover photo courtesy of
Georgia Department of Industry and Trade, Tourist Division

Library of Congress Cataloging-in-Publication Data

Best of the best from Georgia: selected recipes from Georgia's favorite cookbooks / edited by Gwen McKee and Barbara Moseley: ilustrated by Tupper England.

p. cm.
Includes index.
ISBN 0-937552-30-5
1. Cookery--Georgia. I. McKee, Gwen. II. Moseley, Barbara.
TX715.B4856379 1989
641.59758--dc20   89-10205

QUAIL RIDGE PRESS
P.O. Box 123 • Brandon, MS 39043
1-800-343-1583
E-mail: info@quailridge.com
Website: www. quailridge.com

The Georgia peach is the most famous commodity in the state. Its lovely blossoms appear in mid-March and the fruit is available from June to August.

CONTENTS

Georgia is a land of mountains and valleys, swamps and seashores, peaches and peanuts. It is the state where Presidents Jimmy Carter was born, Woodrow Wilson grew up, Dwight Eisenhower played golf and Franklin D. Roosevelt died. Throughout the state, antebellum homes that escaped Sherman's wrath still welcome visitors to take a step back into the days of "Gone With the Wind." Many famous people were born in Georgia--Flannery O'Connor, Martin Luther King, Jr., Burt Reynolds, Ty Cobb, and Ray Charles to name but a few. And many more have moved to Georgia, to be a part of this beautiful, thriving state."

And Georgia certainly has a rich food heritage brought about in some part by its bounty of fresh fruits and vegetables, with its most popular commodities being peaches, peanuts, and Vidalia onions. Its 100 miles of Atlantic shoreline affords a superb seafood selection. So cooks have always had an abundance of available "homegrown" ingredients with which to create their special Georgia recipes.

In *Best of the Best from Georgia*, seventy-one of the leading cookbooks within the state lend some of their favorite recipes to demonstrate the wonderful food heritage that exists in the state today. Savannah Red Rice, Brunswick Stew, Vidalia Onion Pie, and Southern Peach Cobbler are but a few of the traditional favorites.

We consider it a privilege to have met so many lovely people who are the authors, editors, and publishers of the contributing cookbooks to this Georgia edition. Their communication, cooperation and assistance are very much appreciated and will be remembered.

Each contributing cookbook has its own unique features and flavor, and we have attempted to retain this flavor by reproducing the recipes as they appear in each book, changing only typeset style for uniformity. A complete catalog of these cookbooks begins on page 309. We do beg forgiveness for any books that might have been included that we inadvertently overlooked.

We are very grateful to the food editors of newspapers across the state, particularly Louise Dodd of the *Macon Telegraph,* who recommended local cookbooks for inclusion; to the book and gift store managers and personnel who cheerfully and thoughtfully lent their knowledge of popular books in their area; and to the many, many kind Georgians we met along the way who eagerly told us about the cooking and traditions of their state.

Our sincere thanks go to the Georgia Tourist Division for their assistance and use of photos and information; and to Dot Gibson who shared her vast cookbook knowledge with us, and further lent her time and talent in writing the foreword; and to our favorite illustrator, Tupper England, who has a knack for capturing the spirit of the state in her lovely drawings; and to Shiela Musgrove, who cheerfully did all she was asked—and then some—to help move this tremendous project along.

We are extremely pleased to share these outstanding Georgia recipes from prized Georgia cookbooks. Our travels all over the state convinced us that these people know how to cook! The proof is in the pudding, so we confidently and proudly invite you to treat yourself to a taste of "the best" from Georgia.

Gwen McKee and Barbara Moseley

FOREWORD
By Dot Gibson

Our cooking is part of our heritage. No matter who we are or where we are from, the cooking of our mothers, grandmothers, and friends has become a part of our lives. Those special recipes from our childhood days—grandmother's turkey and dressing, mother's pecan pie, or those favorite cookies—all bring warm and happy memories. If we are lucky, these recipes have been written down for us so that we can pass them on to our children and grandchildren.

In my years of working with cookbooks and the interesting people associated with them, I have come across many who *read* cookbooks from cover to cover. I am often told, "I take cookbooks to bed and read them like novels." I once met a lady in an airport who said she always brought a cookbook to read on the plane because it took her mind off her fear of flying. Cookbooks were once "just recipes" but today with pictures, stories, and personal comments, they afford us a glimpse into a local culture as they share their special recipes and their heritage with us.

I have lived in Georgia all my life and am proud of the many beautiful cookbooks from our state. It is interesting and exciting to have a sampling of these lovely books in one volume. Perhaps you will even find a few of the old familiar recipes you wish someone in your family had written down for you. *DG*

Dot Gibson is president of Dot Gibson Publications of Waycross, Georgia, a distributing company of regional and community cookbooks. Widely known in the cookbook world, she has written and published eleven books and is an independent cookbook consultant.

CONTRIBUTING COOKBOOKS

The Abbey Cookbook
Adventures in Healthful Cooking
Atlanta Cooknotes
Atlanta Natives' Favorite Recipes
Atlanta's Pet Recipes
The Bachelor's Cookbook
Betty Talmadge's Lovejoy Plantation Cookbook
Boarding House Reach
Cherries Galore
Cooking in the New South
Cooking with Tradition
Cooklore and Recipes of Ireland
Country Cakes
Country Cookin'
Country Cupboard Cookbook
Crab Chatter
Culinary Classics
The Dapper Zapper
Educated Taste
Encore
Famous Recipes from Mrs. Wilkes' Boarding House
Fancy Foods and Flowers
Feast and Fellowship
Flatlanders Cook Book
Foresters' Favorites
The Frances Virginia Tea Room Cookbook
Frederica Fare
From Mother With Love
Georgia Entertains
Georgia On My Menu
Georgia's Historic Restaurants and Their Recipes
Golden Isles Cuisine
Good Cookin'
Gottlieb's Bakery 100 Years of Recipes
Guess Who's Coming to Dinner
Head Table Cooks

CONTRIBUTING COOKBOOKS

The Historic Roswell Cook Book
The Holiday Hostess
The Hors D'Oeuvre Tray
Lasting Impressions
Little Bit Different!
Look Mom, I Can Cook
Macon Sets a Fine Table
The Market Place
The Original Vidalia Onion Cookbook
Peachtree Bouquet
Perennials
The Pirates' House Cook Book
Potlucks & Petticoats
Puttin' on the Peachtree
Quail Country
Ramblin' Chefs from Georgia Tech
Recipes from The Olde Pink House
Savannah Collection
Savannah Style
Second Round, Tea-Time at the Masters®
Simply Scrumptious Microwaving
Somethin's Cookin' in the Mountains
Southern Seafood Classics
Southwind Cuisine
The Stuffed Griffin
A Taste of Georgia
A Taste of the Holidays
Tea-Time at the Masters®
Temptations
Traditionally Weslayan
Tullie's Receipts
Unbearably Good
Vincent Russo's Seafood Cookbook
Windsor Academy Cookbook
You Are the Boss in the Kitchen!

Appetizers

One of the many restored old homes depicting the beauty of Savannah's historical past.

Orange Blush

1 (6-ounce) can frozen orange   4 tablespoons sugar
 juice concentrate, thawed   16 ounces club soda
1 cup cranberry juice   Mint for garnish

Combine orange juice concentrate, cranberry juice, and sugar. Chill. Just before serving, stir in club soda. Pour over crushed ice in goblets. Yield: 6 servings.

Bear in Mind: Add sprigs of fresh mint or lemon balm to each goblet. For extra zip, add vodka.

Unbearably Good!

Orange Yogurt Drink

3 large oranges, thinly peeled   3 tablespoons honey
3 cups lowfat (2%) milk   About 18 cracked ice cubes
1 1/2 cups lowfat orange yogurt   Garnish, as desired, (optional)

Tear orange into sections and remove seeds and membrane. Put orange, milk, yogurt, and honey into electric blender. (*Note:* To keep blender from overflowing, make in 2 or 3 batches.) Process until mixture is smooth, adding ice a little at the time through hole in lid until desired consistency is reached. Serve in frosted glasses, garnished with a piece of fruit or mint leaves, if desired. Makes 6 servings. No cooking required.

Cal.-230 Pro.-8g Fat-4g Carb.-45g Fib.-.6g Sod.-102mg Chol.-20mg

Adventures in Healthful Cooking

Summertime Citrus Tea

6 tea bags
4 cups boiling water
1 (6-ounce) can frozen orange
  juice (or limeade)
  concentrate, thawed and
  undiluted

1 (6-ounce) can frozen lemonade concentrate, thawed and
  undiluted
10 cups water
1 1/2 cups sugar

Steep tea bags in boiling water, about 5-7 minutes; discard tea bags. Add remaining ingredients. Serve over ice. Yield: 1 gallon.

Cooking with Tradition

Coffee Punch

2 quarts strong coffee
1 pint cold milk
2 teaspoons vanilla extract
1/2 cup sugar

2 quarts vanilla ice cream
1/2 pint whipping cream
Ground nutmeg

Combine coffee, milk, vanilla, and sugar; chill. Break ice cream into chunks in punch bowl just before serving; pour chilled coffee mixture over ice cream. Whip cream; spoon into mounds on top of punch. Sprinkle with nutmeg. (This mixture may be made 1 day ahead.) Serves 15-18.

The Stuffed Griffin

Autumn Punch

1/2 gallon apple juice
1 1/2 quarts cranberry juice
2 cups water

1/4 cup brown sugar
2 cinnamon sticks
1/2 teaspoon whole cloves

Combine all ingredients. Bring to a boil. Lower heat and simmer 30 minutes. Yield: 1 gallon.

Smells wonderful and tastes great. Perfect for holiday open house. May be kept warm in crockpot.

The Market Place

Hot Tomato Bouillon

1 can condensed tomato soup
1 can beef broth bouillon
1/3 teaspoon prepared
  horseradish, wet
1 dash Tabasco sauce

1 cup water
Dairy sour cream or un-
  sweetened whipped cream
1 tablespoon sherry (optional)

Simmer all but cream and sherry 5 minutes. Add sherry. Add cream just before serving to float on top of cup. Serves 6.

Atlanta Natives' Favorite Recipes

Chatham Artillery Punch

8 liters white rum
4 liters gin
4 liters rye
4 liters brandy
3 gallons rosé or Catawba wine
1 pound green tea, steeped
  overnight in 2 gallons cold
  water and strained

2 quarts maraschino cherries,
  drained
2 pounds pineapple chunks -
  fresh is best
5 pounds light brown sugar
Juice of 3 dozen lemons
Champagne

Mix all ingredients except champagne in a large, clean plastic trash can with lid. Cover and store in a cool place for a minimum of 2 months—it only improves with age. Serve in a punch bowl with a large block of ice. Add champagne to taste; 1-2 bottles per punch bowl. Also good mixed with orange juice and/or club soda for a lighter drink, or sipped straight as a liqueur. Make sure each cup contains some fruit, but by no means feed it to your children. This is the most subtly lethal punch you will ever drink. Three glasses and you're out!

Note: Perhaps you could make this a neighborhood project, or save your old wine bottles, bottle it, and give as Christmas presents. You say you don't want to make 10 gallons of punch? Oh, all right, here's a reduced version--

2 liters rum
1 liter gin
1 liter rye
1 liter brandy
3 bottles rosé or Catawba wine
1/4 pound green tea in 2 quarts
  cold water

2 cups maraschino cherries
1/2 pound pineapple
2 1/2 cups firmly packed light
  brown sugar
Juice of 9 lemons

The Pirates' House Cook Book

Resaca is the name of the battle site which initiated General Sherman's "March to the Sea." With his 60,000 Union troops, he destroyed an estimated $1 million in Georgia property. Augusta was spared, it is said, because he had loved a girl who lived there.

Planter's Punch

2 ounces light rum
1 ounce Myers dark rum
6 ounces orange juice
6 ounces pineapple juice
1/2 ounce grenadine
Ice

1 ounce banana liqueur,
  divided
2 orange slices, lime slices,
  pineapple spears, and maraschino cherries for garnish

Combine the rums, orange juice, pineapple juice and grenadine in a shaker with ice; shake well and strain into 2 hurricane glasses. Top each glass with 1/2 ounce of banana liqueur and garnish with an orange slice, lime slice, pineapple spear and maraschino cherry.

Recipes from The Olde Pink House

Lime Tree Cutter

2 ounces rum
1 ounce brandy or Cognac
1/2 ounce gin
2 ounces frozen limeade
  concentrate

1 ounce frozen orange
  concentrate
1/2 ounce Orgeat Syrup (an
  almond flavored syrup)
1/3 cup crushed ice

Combine all ingredients and mix in a blender until smooth. Serve at once. Serves 1.

You Are The Boss in the Kitchen!

Frozen Peach Daiquiri

1 pint frozen fresh peaches
3 packets daiquiri mix
9 ounces cold water

6 ounces golden rum (preferred
  over clear or "white" rum)

Cut frozen peaches into chunks and put into blender—or food processor—then add the water, rum, and daiquiri mix. Blend at high speed until smooth. Makes 4 "normal" drinks. Frozen peaches preferred as then no ice or ice cubes are needed in the drink. Serve with jalapeño dip and corn chips.

Head Table Cooks

Tipperary Dew

1 part Irish whiskey   1 part Italian type vermouth
1 part green chautreuse

Stir with ice in jug and strain. Give every man his *dew.*

Cooklore and Recipes of Ireland

Lady Killer Cocktail
(After dinner drink)

1 cup chocolate ice cream 2 ounces apricot liqueur
1 ounce whipping cream   1/2 ounce vodka
2 ounces Cognac or brandy

Blend ingredients together until smooth. Serve at once or keep in freezer in blender and blend again before killing! Makes 2 servings (1 for the lady and 1 for the killer).

Note: This drink was a true "lady killer." One of my students once made a double recipe of this and filled it into a thermos for him and his date to take that night to the drive-in movie. He told me that by the time the main feature was on, his date was deep asleep!

You Are The Boss in the Kitchen!

Coffee Liqueur
Homemade Kahlua

1/3 cup instant coffee   1 fifth vodka
3 1/2 cups sugar   3 tablespoons plus 1 teaspoon
2 cups water   vanilla

Combine coffee, sugar and water. Heat until dissolved; cool. Add vodka and vanilla. Pour into half-gallon glass container. Age 2 weeks. Use as is for Kahlua or serve mixed with milk.

A Taste of the Holidays

Smoked Salmon Dip

1 (4-ounce) package smoked
 salmon
1/4 cup chopped onion
1 (8-ounce) package cream
 cheese, softened
1/2 teaspoon fresh lemon juice
1/4 teaspoon pepper

1 tablespoon milk
1 teaspoon sliced scallion
3 teaspoons red caviar, drained
 and divided
Scallion greens to garnish

Combine salmon, onion, cream cheese, lemon juice, pepper, milk, and scallion in blender or food processor. Process until smooth. Gently fold in 2 teaspoons caviar.
Cover. Refrigerate at least 2 hours. (May be prepared 2
days before serving.) Garnish with remaining 1 teaspoon
caviar and scallion greens. Serve with crackers.

An elegant appetizer to begin an evening. Yield: 2 cups.

Second Round, Tea-Time at the Masters®

Special Crab Dip

1 (8-ounce) package cream
 cheese, softened
1/4 cup light cream or milk
2 teaspoons lemon juice
1 1/2 teaspoons Worcestershire
 sauce

1 clove garlic, minced
Dash salt and pepper
1/2 pound white crabmeat

Beat cream cheese; gradually add cream and beat until
smooth. Stir in remaining ingredients and blend. Chill.
Makes about 1 1/2 cups.

Crab Chatter

Hot Crabmeat Dip

1 (8-ounce) package cream
 cheese
1 tablespoon milk
1 (6 1/2-ounce) can Alaskan
 King crabmeat
2 tablespoons finely chopped
 onion

1/2 teaspoon cream-style
 horseradish
1/4 teaspoon salt
Dash pepper and Worcestershire sauce
1/2 cup slivered almonds

CONTINUED

CONTINUED

Have the cream cheese at room temperature, and combine with the milk. Add the crabmeat (drained well) with the onion and horseradish, salt and pepper. Blend well. Spoon into an oven-proof dish, and sprinkle slivered almonds on top. Bake for 15 minutes at 375°. Serve hot with sesame seed wafers.

Foresters' Favorite Foods

Crabmeat Dip

1 stick butter
1 (8-ounce) package cream
  cheese
1/4 cup minced onions
1/2 teaspoon salt
1 pound white crabmeat

Let butter and cream cheese soften at room temperature, blend together over low heat; add onions and salt. Stir in crabmeat and mix thoroughly. Remove and serve in chafing dish along with crackers.

For microwave owners, you can save lots of time by melting cream cheese and butter at full power for 3 minutes.

Vincent Russo's Seafood Cookbook

Crab Maire

4 green onions, chopped
1/2 cup chopped parsley
1/2 cup butter
2 tablespoons flour
1 pint half-and-half
1/2 pound Swiss cheese,
  grated
1 tablespoon sherry
Salt and pepper to taste
1 pound crabmeat

Sauté green onions and parsley in butter. Stir in flour; add half-and-half cream to make sauce. Add all other ingredients except crabmeat. Cook over low heat until cheese is melted. Add crabmeat and heat. Place in chafing dish and serve with melba toast rounds or toast points. Yield: 50 servings.

Quail Country

Crab and Shrimp Dip for Chafing Dish

2 (8-ounce) packages cream
  cheese
1 (16-ounce) carton sour cream
1 can cream of mushroom soup
2 tablespoons lime juice
1 cup mayonnaise
Red Hot to taste
3 tablespoons paprika
2 teaspoons pepper

Salt to taste
4 green onions and tops,
  finely chopped
1/2 cup parsley, chopped
1 pound coarsely chopped
  shrimp (cooked)
6 ounces king crab, torn in
  pieces

Mix cream cheese, sour cream, mushroom soup, lime juice, mayonnaise, Red Hot to taste, paprika, pepper, salt; heat until warm. When ready to serve, fold in chopped onion, parsley, shrimp, and crabmeat.

Serve hot from a chafing dish with Triscuits, Wheat Thins, etc.

Head Table Cooks

Crabmeat Canapés

6 ounces shredded crabmeat
1 cup mayonnaise
1/2 teaspoon lemon juice

1/4 cup chopped Vidalia onion
1 egg white
Ritz crackers

In a small mixing bowl, combine crabmeat with mayonnaise and season with lemon juice. Add chopped onions. Beat egg white until stiff (not dry) and fold in crabmeat mixture. Place approximately 1 teaspoon crab mixture on each Ritz cracker and cook 45-60 seconds on high in microwave, or until heated thoroughly. Serve immediately. Yield: 25 canapés.

The Original Vidalia Onion Cookbook

Artichoke Dip

1 (14-ounce) can artichoke
hearts
1/2 cup mayonnaise
1 teaspoon Worcestershire

1-2 teaspoons onion, grated
3 slices cooked bacon,
crumbled
Red pepper, garnish

Drain, then mash artichoke hearts with fork. Combine with remaining ingredients. Chill. Before serving, sprinkle red pepper on top. Serve with bland crackers or melba rounds. Yields 1 cup.

Should be made a day ahead.

Tea-Time at the Masters®

Daffodil Dip

1 (8-ounce) package cream
cheese
1/2 cup mayonnaise
1/2 cup parsley (fresh and
snipped)
2 tablespoons chopped or grated
onion

1 clove garlic, minced
1 tablespoon anchovy paste
Dash pepper
1 hard-cooked egg

Soften cheese and add all ingredients except egg yolk. Mix well. Sprinkle egg yolk on top for garnish. Use raw vegetables such as cut celery, radishes, broccoli, sliced turnips, squash, and spring onions. Can be mixed in blender.

Fancy Foods & Flowers

Pizza Dip
Outstanding!

1 (8-ounce) package cream
  cheese, softened
1 (14-ounce) jar pizza sauce
1/3 cup onions, chopped
1 1/2 cups mozzarella cheese,
  grated

1 (6-ounce) can ripe olives,
  drained and chopped
2 ounces sliced pepperoni,
  chopped
Light corn chips

Preheat oven to 350°. Press cream cheese in bottom of 9-inch glass pie pan. Spread pizza sauce over cream cheese and layer remaining ingredients in order listed. Bake at 350° for 25 minutes. Serve with light corn chips. Yield: 8-10 servings.

Georgia On My Menu

Spinach Dip

1 (10-ounce) package frozen
  chopped spinach, thawed
1/4 cup fresh parsley, chopped
1/2 cup chopped onion
1 cup uncreamed cottage
  cheese (1%)

1 cup plain yogurt
1/2 teaspoon ground white or
  black pepper
1 teaspoon dry mustard
Tabasco to taste
1 teaspoon salt (optional)

Squeeze all liquid from thawed spinach. Place all ingredients into blender. Process on blend for 1 minute. Refrigerate until ready to serve. Serve with raw vegetables.

  Makes about 4 cups or 16 (1/4-cup) servings. No cooking required.

Cal.-27 Pro.-4g Fat-.5g Carb.-3g Fib.-.2g Sod.-146mg Chol.-2mg

Adventures in Healthful Cooking

Ginger Cream Spread

An original secret recipe from Mimosa Hall!

6 (8-ounce) packages cream cheese, softened
1 bottle Keiller imported ginger preserve

1/2 cup pecans
2 small jars Major Grey's chutney

Mix softened cream cheese and ginger preserve well. Place in 8-cup mold and freeze. To serve, unmold. Crumble pecans on top and surround with chutney. Serve with Carr's Wheatmeal Biscuits or other plain whole wheat crackers.

Note: Ginger preserve can be found in most supermarket fine food sections. Yield: 8-cup mold.

The Historic Roswell Cook Book

Vidalia Onion Spread

1 cup coarsely chopped Vidalia onions
1 cup Hellmann's mayonnaise

1 cup grated Cheddar cheese
Paprika

Combine onions, mayonnaise, and cheese. Pour into 1-quart baking dish. Sprinkle with paprika. Bake at 350° for 25 minutes. Blot with paper towel to remove excess oil. Serve hot with Triscuits. Yield: 6-8 servings.

Second Round, Tea-Time at the Masters®

Chipped Beef Spread

This party-dip recipe has been around for years, and seems to get better with age. It is always a hit at gatherings large and small.

1 (8-ounce) package softened cream cheese
2 1/2 ounces dried beef, shredded
1/4 cup finely chopped green pepper
1/4 cup finely chopped red bell pepper

1 medium onion, finely chopped
1/2 teaspoon black pepper
1/2 cup sour cream
3/4 cup chopped pecans

Mix cream cheese well with dried beef, green and red peppers, onion, and black pepper. Fold in sour cream. Spoon into casserole dish. Top with pecans. Bake at 350° for 20 minutes. Serve with crackers. Serves 8-10.

Savannah Collection

Cream Cheese and Chutney Canapé

1 (8-ounce) package cream cheese
1/4 cup chutney
1/4 teaspoon dry mustard

1 teaspoon curry powder
Toasted almonds, for topping
Pineapple half (optional)

Blend all ingredients well. Chill for at least 4 hours. Scoop out a pineapple half and fill with mixture. Top with toasted almonds. Serve with crackers. This is a quick recipe and may be made the day before using. Yield: 12 servings.

Cooking with Tradition

The 2056-mile Appalachian Trail originates at Springer Mountain, Georgia, and ends at Mt. Katahdin, Maine.

Cheese Caraway Nips

These keep well in a tin for drop-in company.

1 cup sifted all-purpose flour
2 teaspoons dry mustard (or
  more to taste)
1 teaspoon salt
3/4 cup sharp Cheddar cheese,
  grated

2 teaspoons caraway seeds
1/3 cup shortening
4 tablespoons water

Preheat oven to 450°. Combine flour, mustard, salt, cheese, and caraway seeds. Mix in shortening. Sprinkle with water. Form into two balls. Sprinkle with additional flour and refrigerate until firm. Roll out as thinly as possible. Work quickly to keep dough cold. Cut into strips and place on ungreased cookie sheet. Bake for 7-9 minutes. Yield: 4 dozen.

Temptations

Chilies and Cheese Bake

Serve hot and bubbly—hold on a warming tray.

1 (4-ounce) can chopped green
  chilies
2 cups (8-ounces) Longhorn or
  sharp Cheddar cheese, shredded

1 egg
1 tablespoon water

Heat oven to 350°. Spread undrained chilies evenly in a 9-inch pie pan. Sprinkle grated cheese over chilies. Beat egg with water until blended, then spread over cheese. Bake 15-20 minutes until cheese is hot, bubbly, and lightly browned. Serve with corn chips. Hold on warming tray so cheese stays soft. Serves: 8-10.

Lasting Impressions

Plains Cheese Ring

Former First Lady Rosalyn Carter is given credit for making this addictive spread popular. It's said that it was one of Jimmy's favorites and was always on the Carter family's holiday table. It can be served with a meal, but also makes a great addition to an appetizer table. You will be pleasantly surprised at the way the unlikely ingredients interact.

1 pound sharp Cheddar cheese, grated, then allowed to soften
1 cup chopped pecans
1 cup mayonnaise
1 small onion, grated
Black pepper to taste
Dash cayenne
Strawberry preserves

Combine all ingredients except preserves. (A food processor works well and eliminates the need to chop ingredients.) Place in ring mold, greased with a little mayonnaise. Chill. When ready to serve, unmold. Fill center with preserves. Serve with buttery crackers. Serves 8-12.

Savannah Collection

Boursin Cheese—Home Style

8 ounces whipped butter
16 ounces cream cheese
2 cloves garlic
1/2 teaspoon oregano
1/4 teaspoon basil
1/4 teaspoon dill weed
1/4 teaspoon marjoram
1/4 teaspoon black pepper
1/4 teaspoon thyme

Place cream cheese and butter in large bowl of an electric mixer or food processor. Beat at high speed till smooth and fluffy, stopping motor often to scrape down sides of bowl with a rubber spatula. Add remaining ingredients and continue to beat until well combined. Pack into containers and allow to mellow for at least 12 hours in refrigerator before serving. Serve cold with crackers.

Note: To prepare in advance: if wrapped airtight, this will keep for 2 weeks to a month. Do not freeze.

Feast and Fellowship

Fancy Cheese Ball

1 (8-ounce) package cream cheese, softened
8 ounces Roquefort cheese, softened
8 ounces Cheddar cheese, softened
1/2 cup green onion with tops, chopped
3/4 teaspoon garlic salt
2 tablespoons paprika
2 tablespoons chopped bell pepper
2 tablespoons chopped green olives
2 tablespoons chopped pecans
2 tablespoons chopped fresh parsley
2 tablespoons cooked, crumbled bacon
2 tablespoons chopped black olives
2 tablespoons chopped pimiento

Combine all cheeses, onions, and garlic salt. Mix well and shape into a large ball. Mark ball with a knife into 8 sections (like a beach ball). Fill each section with one of the garnishes: paprika, bell pepper, green olives, pecans, parsley, bacon, black olives, and pimiento. Yield: 40-50 servings with other hors d'oeuvres.

Bear in Mind: Use red caviar and parsley at Christmas. Use red and black caviar for a Georgia Bulldog Party. Substitute your own school colors.

Unbearably Good!

Crusty Havarti

1 (7-ounce) round, creamy Havarti cheese or Brie cheese	3 frozen patty shells or 1/2 sheet frozen puff pastry
1 tablespoon Dijon-style mustard	Water
	1 egg, lightly beaten

Spread top of cheese with mustard. Set aside. Arrange patty shells close together in triangle. Moisten, touching edges with water. Pinch together. Roll dough out to 9-inch circle. Place cheese in center of circle, mustard side down. Gather pastry edges over cheese. Moisten edges and pinch together. Place on greased foil in shallow baking pan, seam side down. Brush all over with beaten egg. Roll scraps into design and arrange on top. Chill 30 minutes. Preheat oven to 375°. Brush again with egg. Arrange foil closely around side of cheese. Bake for 15 minutes. Brush again with egg. Bake 15 minutes more, or until golden brown. Cool 30 minutes on rack. Serve warm as an appetizer with fruit.

Note: This recipe comes from the Danish Cheese Association. Substitute sautéed, chopped mushrooms for mustard if desired. Serves 4.

Cooking in the New South

Cheese Rolls

Cut crust from slices of loaf bread (stack and use electric knife); roll each piece of bread flat with rolling pin.

COMBINE:

1 package grated cheese	2 teaspoons prepared mustard
2 teaspoons grated onion	1 teaspoon mayonnaise
1 teaspoon celery seed	

Spread small amount of above mixture on bread, roll up, dip in melted butter. Bake these at 400° or broil until brown. Can be used for luncheon bread or hors d'oeuvres. Can be prepared, dipped in butter, and kept in freezer and then browned when needed.

Atlanta's Pet Recipes

Pizza Bread

3 eggs
3 teaspoons dried oregano
3 tablespoons grated Parmesan
  cheese
2 loaves frozen pizza dough,
  thawed

2/3 pound pepperoni
1 round of provolone, cut in
  half and shredded

Beat together eggs, oregano, and Parmesan. Set aside. Roll bread dough into 2 8x14-inch rectangles. Spread with egg mixture, reserving 3 tablespoons. Layer pepperoni and cheese on top of egg mixture. Roll up jelly-roll style. Place seam-side-down on baking sheet; seal ends of roll. Baste with reserved egg mixture. Bake at 350° for 20-30 minutes. Yield: 2 loaves. Bake on pan that has sides!

The Market Place

Marinated Broccoli

1 bunch fresh broccoli
2 (5 3/4-ounce, drained
  weight) cans pitted black
  olives, drained

Bleu cheese, crumbled
1 (8-ounce) bottle Italian
  dressing
1 pint cherry tomatoes

Blanch broccoli in boiling water 2 minutes. Drain. Plunge in ice water. Drain. Combine broccoli, olives, and cheese. Toss with dressing. Refrigerate overnight. Just before serving, cut tomatoes in half and toss with other ingredients. Yield: 8-10 servings.

Second Round, Tea-Time at the Masters®

Vegetable Sandwiches

3 carrots
1 cucumber
1 onion
1 bell pepper

1/4 teaspoon salt
1 (3-ounce) package cream
  cheese
1/2 cup mayonnaise

Grind vegetables and put in strainer. Press out all the juices. Mix with softened cream cheese and mayonnaise. Will spread 1 loaf of sandwich bread. Will keep in refrigerator for 5 or 6 days. Mellows with age.

Head Table Cooks

Toni's Open-Faced Cucumber Sandwiches

1 (3-ounce) package cream
  cheese, softened
1 tablespoon mayonnaise
1 tablespoon sour cream
1 tablespoon minced onion

Dash Worcestershire sauce
Garlic powder to taste
Salt and pepper
Cucumber, sliced
Sprig of fresh parsley

Cut out small rounds of bread with cookie or biscuit cutter. Mix all ingredients except cucumber till creamy. Spread on bread. Top with slice of cucumber and sprig of fresh parsley.

Macon Sets a Fine Table

Hi-Hat Mushrooms in Wine Sauce

Make lots of these for a large cocktail party.

16 medium-size mushrooms   1/2 pound sausage meat

Wash mushrooms. Remove and chop stems. Add these to sausage meat. Stuff the mushroom caps, rounding the sausage meat into a high crown. Bake in moderate oven, 350° for 30 minutes. Add mushrooms to sauce and heat till bubbly. Spear with toothpicks.

CONTINUED

CONTINUED

SAUCE:

1 (6-ounce) can tomato sauce
1/2 clove garlic, mashed to
  pulp

1/8 teaspoon oregano
1 cup white wine

Heat all ingredients together and add mushrooms to sauce. Easy. Do ahead. Yields 16.

Culinary Classics

Spinach Balls

2 boxes frozen chopped spinach,
  cooked and drained
2 cups herb bread stuffing mix
2 onions
6 eggs, beaten
3/4 cup melted butter

1/2 cup Parmesan cheese
1 tablespoon garlic salt
1/2 teaspoon thyme
1/2 tablespoon black pepper
1 tablespoon MSG

Mix cooked and drained spinach with all other ingredients. Roll into balls (makes about 70) and place on cookie sheets for freezing; after balls are frozen, remove from sheets and place in bags in freezer. Thaw 1/2 hour before baking. Bake for 20 minutes at 350°.

Flatlanders Cook Book

Kathleen's Vidalia Onions

12 small Vidalia onions, thinly
  sliced
2 cups water
1 cup sugar

1 cup vinegar
1/4 to 1/2 cup mayonnaise
1 teaspoon celery salt
Party rye bread

Combine first 4 ingredients. Marinate overnight in refrigerator. When ready to serve, drain and pat dry. Toss with mayonnaise and celery salt. Serve on party rye bread. Easy, must prepare ahead. Preparation time; 15 minutes. Serves 10-12.

Vidalia onions are indigenous to Georgia. A sweet regional onion may be substituted.

Atlanta Cooknotes

Zucchini Bites

4 small zucchini, unpeeled and
  grated (about 3 cups)
1 cup biscuit mix
1/2 cup onion, finely chopped
1/4 cup Parmesan cheese
1 tablespoon dry parsley flakes

1/2 teaspoon seasoned salt
1/2 teaspoon oregano
1/4 cup vegetable oil
4 eggs, slightly beaten
1 cup sour cream

Combine all ingredients. Pour into greased 13x9x2-inch pan. Bake at 350° for 30 minutes or until golden brown. Cut in 1-inch squares. Yield: 4 dozen.

The Market Place

Zucchini Zips

4 cups zucchini, thinly sliced
1 cup onion, chopped
1/2 cup butter
2 tablespoons parsley, chopped
1/2 teaspoon salt
1/2 teaspoon black pepper
1/4 teaspoon sweet basil
1/4 teaspoon garlic powder

1/4 teaspoon oregano
2 eggs, well beaten
8 ounces mozzarella cheese,
  grated
2 teaspoons Dijon mustard
1 1/2 (8-ounce) cans
  refrigerated crescent rolls

CONTINUED

CONTINUED

In a large skillet, cook zucchini and onion in butter until tender. Stir in parsley and seasonings. In a large bowl, blend eggs and cheese. Stir into vegetable mixture. Preheat oven to 375°. Separate dough into sections and press over the bottom and up the sides of an ungreased 9x13-inch glass pan. Spread this "crust" with mustard. Pour vegetable mixture evenly over the dough. Bake at 375° for 20-23 minutes. Let sit in dish for 10-15 minutes before cutting into bite-size squares. Yield: 8-10 servings.

Georgia On My Menu

Pickled Pineapple

2 (20-ounce) cans unsweetened pineapple chunks, well drained	3/4 cup vinegar
	Dash salt
1/2 cup juice from pineapple	15 whole cloves
3/4 cup sugar	1 cinnamon stick broken in two

Combine all ingredients except pineapple and simmer 10-12 minutes. Pour over pineapple in 1-quart jar with lid. Seal when cool and refrigerate a minimum of 3-4 days. Stores up to 8 weeks.

Delicious as hors d'oeuvres or as an accompaniment to meats.

Head Table Cooks

Savory Ham Balls

This has long been a favorite hot hors d'oeuvre. I have seen men scoop up the dredges with whatever crackers they could find.

1/3 cup fine dry bread crumbs
1/4 cup milk
1/4 cup catsup
1/4 cup minced onion
1 slightly beaten egg

1/4 teaspoon salt
Dash pepper
1 pound ground ham
1 pound ground pork

SAUCE:

1 cup apricot preserves
1/4 cup water
1 tablespoon Worcestershire
   sauce

1 tablespoon prepared mustard
2 tablespoons catsup
2 tablespoons vinegar

In large bowl, combine bread crumbs, milk, the 1/4 cup catsup, onion, egg, salt, and pepper. Add meats and mix thoroughly. Shape into about 5 dozen small meat balls. Place in 13x9x2-inch baking pan. Bake in 350° oven 25-30 minutes. Cool. Refrigerate or wrap and freeze.

To serve: Combine remaining ingredients in large skillet. Add meatballs. Cook, stirring occasionally, till meatballs heat through. Turn into blazer pan or baking dish; place over hot water to keep warm.

Encore

Hanky-Panky

1 pound ground beef
1 pound sausage
1 pound Velveeta cheese,
   chopped or grated
1 tablespoon oregano

1 tablespoon Worcestershire
   sauce
1 teaspoon garlic powder
1 loaf party rye bread

Brown beef and sausage together. Drain. Add other ingredients. Heat until cheese is melted. Spread on slices of party rye. Bake 350° for 10 minutes.

Educated Taste

Cocktail Meatballs and Sauce

2 pounds ground round steak
1 cup cornflakes, crushed
1/3 cup dry parsley
2 eggs
2 tablespoons soy sauce

1/4 teaspoon pepper
1/2 teaspoon garlic powder
1/8 teaspoon salt
1/3 cup catsup
2 tablespoons instant onion

MEATBALL SAUCE:

1 (16-ounce) can cranberry
  sauce
1 (12-ounce) bottle chili sauce

2 tablespoons brown sugar
1 tablespoon lemon juice

Combine all meatball ingredients and mix well. Roll into small balls, bite size. Place on ungreased cookie sheet and bake at 350° for 20-30 minutes. Pour off grease and set aside. Combine all sauce ingredients and heat until smooth. Pour over meatballs. Serves 20.

Golden Isles Cuisine

Nacho Platter

If your guests will be formally dressed, provide bibs!

1 cup sour cream
1/2 cup mayonnaise
1 (1 1/4-ounce) package taco
  seasoning mix
3 medium avocados, peeled
2 tablespoons lemon juice
1/2 teaspoon salt
1/4 teaspoon pepper
2 (10 1/2-ounce) cans jalapeño
  bean dip

1 cup chopped green onions
1 (4 1/2-ounce) can chopped
  ripe olives
2 cups chopped tomatoes
8 ounces sharp Cheddar cheese,
  grated
Nacho chips

Combine sour cream, mayonnaise, and taco mix. Refrigerate until chilled. Combine avocados, lemon juice, salt, and pepper in food processor or electric blender; process until smooth. Using large shallow serving dish or platter, layer in order: bean dip, avocado mixture, sour cream mixture, onions, olives, tomatoes, and cheese. Cover; chill thoroughly. (May be served without chilling, but flavors will not have had a chance to blend.) Serve accompanied by a basket of nacho chips for dipping. Must do ahead. Serves 20.

Perennials

Bacon Roll-Ups

1/4 cup butter
1/2 cup water
1 1/2 cups herb-seasoned
stuffing

1 egg, slightly beaten
1/4 pound hot pork sausage
2/3 pound sliced bacon

Melt butter in water. Remove from heat, stir in stuffing, then egg and sausage. Blend thoroughly. Chill for an hour. Shape into small balls. Cut bacon strips into thirds crosswise. Wrap bacon around dressing mixture and fasten with toothpick. Place on rack in shallow pan and bake 375° for 35 minutes or until brown and crisp. Drain on paper towel and s erve hot. Maybe made ahead of time and frozen before baking. Yield: 36 appetizers.

The Hors d'Oeuvre Tray

Chipped Beef Filling for Shells

1 (8-ounce) package cream
cheese, softened
2 tablespoons milk
1 (12 1/2-ounce) jar dried beef
1/4 cup finely chopped green
pepper
2 tablespoons dehydrated onion
flakes

1/2 teaspoon garlic salt
1/4 teaspoon pepper
1/2 cup sour cream
1/2 cup coarsely chopped
pecans
2 tablespoons butter
1/2 teaspoon salt

Combine and bake in an oblong pan at 350° for 20 minutes or cook on top of stove.

Note: This filling can be used as a dip, served with crackers.

Fancy Foods & Flowers

The nation's oldest and largest military park, Chickamauga and Chattanooga National Military Park, marks the site of one of the most important confrontations of the Civil War.

Pastry Shells

1/2 cup boiling water
1/4 cup margarine
Dash of salt

1/2 cup all-purpose flour
2 eggs

Combine water, margarine, and salt; bring to a boil over medium heat. Add flour all at once; stir vigorously using wooden spoon until mixture forms a ball, leaving sides of the pan. Remove from heat. DO NOT OVERCOOK. Add eggs 1 at a time, beating thoroughly after each addition; continue to beat until a stiff dough is formed. Drop by teaspoonfuls onto a well-greased cookie sheet. (This can be used in a pastry bag to form desired shapes.) Bake in preheated oven at 450° for 10 minutes; reduce heat to 350° and continue baking 10 minutes longer. Remove from sheet. Cool shells away from draft.

Note: Length of baking will depend on size; also ovens vary. Store in tight container. Shells can be filled with desired fillings. Yields 60-70 tiny shells.

Fancy Foods & Flowers

That Wonderful Crabmeat-Caviar Thing

1 envelope unflavored gelatin
Juice of 1 lemon
1 (8-ounce) package cream
  cheese, softened
1 (8-ounce) carton sour cream
1 medium onion, finely chopped

1 pound fresh crabmeat, picked
  over for shells
Red lumpfish caviar, as much
  as you can afford, but at least
2 (3 1/2-ounce) jars

Soften gelatin in lemon juice. Beat cream cheese and sour cream until smooth and stir in onion. Or chop onion in food processor, throw in cream cheese and sour cream and process until smooth. Melt gelatin and lemon juice over low heat. Stir into cream cheese mixture. Spread a layer of cream cheese mixture on the bottom of a glass bowl, preferably a straight-sided glass soufflé dish. Top with a layer of crabmeat. Spread another layer of cream cheese, then a layer of caviar. Repeat layers, ending with a solid layer of caviar. Serve with Bremner wafers or Carr's Table Water Crackers.

Note: This recipe is to die for; expensive, but worth it.

The Pirates' House Cook Book

Shrimp Mousse

Out of this world! Good served with crackers as an hors d'oeuvre or as a luncheon salad.

2 cups sour cream
1 pound cream cheese
1 cup mayonnaise
1/2 cup finely minced bell
  pepper
1/4 cup finely minced pimiento
1/2 cup chili sauce
1 teaspoon salt

1/8 teaspoon Tabasco
1 tablespoon Worcestershire
2 tablespoons gelatin
Juice of 2 lemons
1/4 cup cold water
6 cups cooked shrimp, chopped
  finely

CONTINUED

CONTINUED

Cream together sour cream, cream cheese, and mayonnaise. Add all seasonings and vegetables. Dissolve gelatin in water and lemon juice. Heat in a double boiler 5-10 minutes. Gradually fold this into cheese mixture. Add shrimp and blend very well. Pour into well-chilled (spray with a nonstick product) ring mold and chill overnight.

Frederica Fare

Shrimp Toast or "Kogi Chunkol"
This is a delicious Phillipino delicacy.

5 ounces water chestnuts,
  drained
1 pound raw shrimp
1/4 cup chopped green onion
  tops

2 teaspoons salt
1 teaspoon sugar
1 egg, beaten
15 slices very thin white bread
Bread crumbs

Purée water chestnuts, shrimp, and onions. Add salt, sugar, and egg. Spread paste on one side of each bread slice. Sprinkle with crumbs. Cut each slice into 4 triangles. Heat 1 inch of oil to "hot" (not smoking) and fry each triangle, shrimp-side-down, then brown on other side, (approximately 2 minutes on each side). Drain. May be frozen before serving; defrost, reheat at 400° for 5 minutes. Yield: 60.

Puttin' on the Peachtree

Hot Mustard Shrimp

1/3 cup red wine vinegar
1 teaspoon catsup
1/4 teaspoon horseradish
3 teaspoons hot mustard
2 minced cloves garlic
1/4 teaspoon salt
Dash pepper
1/3 cup oil
1 1/2 pounds shelled deveined
   cooked shrimp
Chives

In a large bowl, combine vinegar, catsup, horseradish, mustard, garlic, salt, and pepper. Blend in oil. Add shrimp. Chill. Serve in a bowl with toothpicks; garnish with chives. Serves 6.

The Hors d'Oevure Tray

Hidden Treasure

1 pound boiled shrimp, peeled
   and deveined
1 pint cherry tomatoes
1 (5 3/4-ounce) can pitted ripe
   olives, drained
1 (8-ounce) can whole water
   chestnuts, drained
1 (6-ounce) can whole
   mushrooms, drained
1/2 head cauliflower, broken
   into bite-size pieces
2 teaspoons dry mustard
2 cups mayonnaise
1/2 cup horseradish,
   drained well
1/2 teaspoon monosodium
   glutamate
2 teaspoons lemon juice
1/2 teaspoon salt

Toss shrimp and vegetables in large bowl. Mix remaining ingredients thoroughly. Pour sauce over shrimp mixture; toss again. Serve with toothpicks. Serves 12.

Peachtree Bouquet

Soused Shrimp

6 medium onions	1/2 teaspoon ginger
6 lemons	1 teaspoon whole black pepper
1 cup white vinegar	1 bay leaf
1/2 cup water	1/4 teaspoon hot sauce
4 teaspoons salt	1 cup vegetable oil
2 teaspoons sugar	3 pounds shrimp, cleaned and
1 teaspoon dry mustard	deveined

Slice onions thinly and set aside. Squeeze 1/2 cup lemon juice; slice remaining lemons thinly and set aside. Combine next 9 ingredients in a saucepan and bring to a boil. Lower heat and simmer for 5 minutes. Cool, strain, and add lemon juice and oil.

Cook cleaned, deveined shrimp just until pink. Drain and set aside. Layer shrimp, onion, and lemon slices in a large crockery or glass bowl. Pour marinade over and refrigerate at least overnight, covered. Serve shrimp with onions and lemon peel along with party rye or pumpernickel bread.

Georgia Entertains

Oysters Thomas

16-24 unshucked oysters	1/4 pound king crabmeat
4-5 slices bread, toasted	2 tablespoons butter, melted
2 green onions	2-3 tablespoons grated
1 sprig fresh parsley	Parmesan cheese

Preheat oven to 375°. Shuck oysters and leave on half shell. Finely chop toasted bread, onions, and parsley tops; mix together. Add crabmeat, butter, and Parmesan cheese; mix well.

Place oysters on jellyroll pan and bake until slightly curled. Remove from oven. Form crabmeat mixture into 16-24 thin patties; cover each oyster with a crabmeat patty. Return oysters to oven until slightly brown and hot through. Serve on folded napkins or plates. Yield: 4-6 servings.

Guess Who's Coming to Dinner

Spiced Pecans

1 egg white, slightly beaten	1/4 teaspoon allspice
2 tablespoons cold water	1/4 teaspoon cinnamon
1/2 cup sugar	1/2 teaspoon salt
1/4 teaspoon ground cloves	4 cups pecan halves

Preheat oven to 250°. Combine all ingredients except pecans, mixing well. Set aside 15 minutes. Add pecans and mix. Spread evenly on 2 greased cookie sheets. Bake 1 hour. Immediately loosen pecans from sheets. Store in an airtight container.

Easy, must prepare ahead, store in an airtight container. Preparation time: 20 minutes. Makes 4 cups.

Atlanta Cooknotes

Peppery Spiced Nuts

2 tablespoons butter, melted	Dash hot pepper sauce
1 pound pecan or walnut halves	1/2 teaspoon salt
2 teaspoons Worcestershire	1/8 teaspoon pepper

Preheat oven to 325°. In skillet sauté pecans in butter until hot. Add remaining ingredients. Arrange nuts in shallow pan and bake at 325° for 20 minutes. Yield: 4 cups.

The Hors d'Oeuvre Tray

Bread and Breakfast

One of Georgia's many lovely older homes offering bed and breakfast.
Macon.

Scrambled Egg Casserole

Relax and enjoy this one.

1 cup Canadian bacon, diced
1/4 cup green onion, chopped
4 1/3 tablespoons butter,
 melted
12 eggs, beaten

1 recipe Cheese Sauce
1 (3-ounce) can mushroom
 stems and pieces, drained
2 1/4 cups soft bread crumbs
1/8 teaspoon paprika

In large skillet, cook Canadian bacon and onion in 3 tablespoons butter till onion is tender but not brown. Add eggs and scramble just till set. Fold mushrooms and cooked eggs into Cheese Sauce. Turn into a 12x7-inch baking dish. Combine remaining melted butter, crumbs, and paprika; sprinkle atop eggs. Cover; chill till 30 minutes before serving. Bake, uncovered, in 350° oven for 30 minutes.

CHEESE SAUCE:

2 tablespoons butter
2 tablespoons all-purpose
 flour
1/2 teaspoon salt

1/8 teaspoon pepper
2 cups milk
1 cup American cheese,
 shredded

Melt butter; blend in flour, salt, and pepper. Add milk; cook and stir till bubbly. Add cheese and cook till cheese melts and sauce is smooth.

 Easy. Do ahead. Serves 8-10.

Culinary Classics

Florentine Eggs

8 hard-cooked eggs
1 (10-ounce) package frozen
  chopped spinach, cooked and
  drained
1/2 tablespoon grated onion
1 teaspoon Worcestershire
  sauce

2 teaspoons lemon juice
2 tablespoons butter, melted
Salt and pepper to taste
2 cups Medium White Sauce
Buttered bread crumbs for
  topping

Preheat oven to 350°. Slice eggs in half lengthwise. Remove and mash yolks. Combine yolks, spinach, onion, Worcestershire, lemon juice, butter, salt, and pepper. Mix well and fil egg whites. Place eggs in 8-inch square baking dish. Pour white sauce over eggs and top with buttered bread crumbs. Bake until bubbly.
Yield: 8-10 servings.

Bear in Mind: Add dash of cayenne pepper to white sauce for an extra kick.

MEDIUM WHITE SAUCE:

2 tablespoons butter
2 tablespoons all-purpose
  flour

1/4 teaspoon salt
1/8 teaspoon pepper
1 cup milk

In saucepan over low heat melt butter. Stir in flour, salt, and pepper. Cook and stir until mixture is smooth and bubbly. Remove from heat; stir in milk. Bring to a boil, stirring constantly; boil 1 minute. Yield: 1 cup.

Unbearably Good!

Babyland General Hospital in Cleveland, Georgia, is the birthplace of Cabbage Patch Kids and "Lil People."

Egg in a Nest

Bread
Egg

Butter

Cut a circle from the center of a slice of bread. Butter both sides of slice and circle. Place in frying pan on medium high heat and drop a little butter in the hole so egg will not stick. Crack egg and very carefully place in the hole. Fry for a few minutes until egg begins to set. Carefully turn and cook on the other side. The circle will toast in the frying pan while the egg is cooking.

Look Mom, I Can Cook

Plantation Casserole

2 cups croutons
1 cup sharp cheese, shredded
4 eggs, slightly beaten
2 cups milk
1/2 teaspoon salt
1/2 teaspoon prepared
  mustard

1/2 teaspoon onion powder
Dash pepper
8 slices bacon, fried crisp
  and crumbled

Preheat oven to 325°. In bottom of greased 10x6-inch baking dish, combine croutons and cheese. Combine eggs, milk, salt, mustard, onion powder, and pepper. Mix until blended. Pour over crouton mixture. Sprinkle bacon on top. Bake 55-60 minutes until eggs are set. This can be made the night before. Serves 6.

Macon Sets a Fine Table

Georgia has been nicknamed "the Empire State of the South," but is also called "the Peach State" and "the Goober State."

Blintz Casserole

Absolutely divine! Treat your football fans with this for brunch.

FILLING:

2 pounds ricotta cheese
2 eggs
1/4 cup sugar
1/8 teaspoon salt

1 lemon, juiced or 1/4 cup
  lemon juice
1 (8-ounce) package cream
  cheese, softened

BATTER:

1/2 pound margarine, melted
1/2 cup sugar
2 eggs
1 cup sifted flour

3 teaspoons baking powder
1/8 teaspoon salt
1/4 cup milk
1 teaspoon vanilla

Place all ingredients for filling in mixer and blend well. Set aside. Mix batter ingredients by hand and spoon 1/2 of batter into a greased 9x13x2-inch pan. Top this with filling—spreading, not mixing. Spread remaining batter over filling. Bake at 300° for 1 1/2 hours. Serve with fresh fruit and grilled Canadian bacon. Serves 12.

Puttin' on the Peachtree

Cherry-Sausage Brunch

1 (8-ounce) jar maraschino
  cherries
1 (13 1/2-ounce) can
  pineapple chunks
2 (8-ounce) packages
  brown-and-serve sausage
  links

4 teaspoons cornstarch
1/2 teaspoon salt
1/2 cup maple-flavored syrup
1/3 cup water
1/3 cup vinegar
1 medium green pepper, cut
  in chunks

Drain pineapple, reserving 1/2 cup syrup; cut sausages in thirds, brown in skillet, drain well. At serving time, blend cornstarch, salt, pineapple syrup, maple syrup, water, and vinegar in a pan or chafing dish. Heat to boiling, stirring constantly. Add cherries, pineapple, sausages, and pepper. Heat thoroughly, keep hot.

Cherries Galore

Grits and Cheese Casserole

4 cups milk
1 cup Speckled Heart grits*
1/2 cup butter or margarine
2 eggs, well beaten

1/2 teaspoon baking powder
1/4 teaspoon salt
1 cup grated Cheddar cheese

Preheat oven to 375°. Bring 3 1/2 cups milk to boiling point. Gradually stir in grits; cook over medium heat, stirring constantly, until thick, about 10 minutes. Remove from heat. Add butter; stir until melted. Stir in eggs, baking powder, salt, and remaining milk. Pour into 2-quart casserole. Bake, uncovered 30 minutes—then sprinkle grated cheese over top. Bake 15 minutes longer. Makes 6-8 servings.

*A good place to buy Speckled Heart Grits is Callaway Gardens' Country Store.

Country Cookin'

Overnight French Toast

This is a terrific breakfast recipe when you have house guests. Combine ingredients in the evening and bake the next morning.

1 loaf French bread
8 eggs, beaten
2 cups milk
1 teaspoon vanilla

1 1/2 teaspoons ground
  cinnamon
1/8 teaspoon salt

Slice French bread into 16 pieces (discard ends.) Beat remaining ingredients until frothy. Place bread slices in two 13x9x2-inch pans. Pour egg mixture over bread. Turn slices over to coat evenly on both sides. Cover pans with foil or plastic wrap and refrigerate overnight. Next morning place bread on cookie sheet and bake in preheated 450° oven for 5 minutes or until golden, turning once. Serve hot with honey or syrup. Serves 8.

Encore

Apple Pancakes with Cinnamon Cream Syrup

These fabulous pancakes with syrup are a snap to make. We think you'll agree they are among the best you have ever eaten.

APPLE PANCAKES:

1 egg
1 tablespoon sugar
1 tablespoon butter, softened
1 medium apple, peeled, cored, and quartered

1 cup evaporated milk
1 cup packaged pancake mix
Cinnamon Cream Syrup

Place egg, sugar, butter, apple, and evaporated milk in blender. Cover; process at low speed several seconds or until apple is chopped. Add pancake mix. Cover; process at high speed several seconds, until blended. Pour by 1/4 cupfuls onto preheated (400°) griddle or electric skillet. Cook until bubbles appear on top of cakes and underside is browned. Turn; brown on second side. (May transfer to electric hot tray for buffet service.) Serve hot with Cinnamon Cream Syrup. Yield: 15-20 pancakes.

CINNAMON CREAM SYRUP:

1 cup light corn syrup
2 cups sugar
1/2 cup water

2 teaspoons ground cinnamon
1 cup evaporated milk

In medium saucepan combine corn syrup, sugar, water, and cinnamon. Bring to full boil over medium heat, stirring constantly. Boil 2 minutes, stirring constantly. Cool 5 minutes. Stir in evaporated milk. Serve warm over Apple Pancakes.

Micronote: Place ingredients in large mixing bowl. Bring to boil on HIGH (5 minutes). Reduce power to MEDIUM; cook 2 minutes, stirring several times.

Perennials

Country Fried Ham Biscuits with Redeye Gravy

3 slices country ham, 1/4
  inch thick
1/4 cup coffee (or water)

1/4 teaspoon sugar
6 large biscuits

Fry ham on each side. Remove ham from drippings. Stir in coffee and sugar. Put ham back in gravy. Simmer till hot. Split biscuits open. Put in them ham and 1-2 teaspoons gravy each. If you can sit down to eat this breakfast, fill your plate with leftover biscuits and hot gravy—delicious! Serves 6.

Betty Talmadge's Lovejoy Plantation Cookbook

Rhett Butler's Biscuits

5 cups self-rising flour
1/3 cup sugar
1 cup shortening
2 packages yeast, dissolved
  in 1/4 cup lukewarm water

2 cups buttermilk
Butter, melted

Sift dry ingredients. Cut in shortening. Add yeast and buttermilk. Mix well. Chill 1 hour. Roll and cut. Set aside to rise 1 hour in warm place. Bake at 350° for 15 minutes. Brush with melted butter as biscuits start to brown. Continue to bake until brown. These can be made and refrigerated up to 10 days ahead.

Betty Talmadge's Lovejoy Plantation Cookbook

Applesauce Puffs

2 cups biscuit mix
1/4 cup sugar
1 teaspoon cinnamon
1/2 cup applesauce

1/4 cup milk
1 egg, slightly beaten
2 tablespoons vegetable oil

Combine first 3 items; add next 4 items and beat vigorously for 30 seconds. Fill muffin tins 2/3 full. Bake at 400° for 12 minutes. Cool slightly. Remove from tins.

Dip tops in 1/2 stick melted butter, then in mixture of 1/4 teaspoon cinnamon and 1/4 cup sugar. Makes 24.

Atlanta's Pet Recipes

Caramel Breakfast Rolls

Assemble ingredients and refrigerate overnight. Bake the next morning. I pop the rolls in the oven early Christmas morning, and they are ready with hot coffee by the time the last gift is opened!

2 (1-pound) loaves frozen
  bread dough, thawed
1 cup finely packed brown sugar
1 (5 1/2-ounce) package vanilla
  pudding and pie filling mix

1/2 cup butter or margarine,
  melted
1/4 cup milk or half-and-half
1/2 cup chopped nuts, divided
1/2 cup raisins, divided

Cut 1 loaf of dough into small pieces. Place them in a greased 13x9x2-inch baking dish. Combine brown sugar, pudding mix, butter, and milk, and mix well. Drizzle half of the liquid mixture over the dough pieces, then sprinkle with 1/4 cup nuts and raisins. Cut remaining loaf of dough into small pieces and place over first layer. Drizzle remaining liquid mixture over dough and sprinkle with remaining nuts and raisins.

Cover and refrigerate several hours or overnight. Bake at 325° for 50 minutes. The rolls tend to bubble over a bit when cooking. Place the baking pan on a sheet of foil or a cookie sheet to avoid a dirty oven. If rolls brown too quickly, place a loose sheet of aluminum foil on top. Serves 10-12.

Note: Maraschino cherries and crushed pineapple may be substituted for the nuts and raisins.

Encore

Banana Sour Cream Coffee Cake

1/2 cup chopped pecans
1/4 cup sugar
1/4 teaspoon cinnamon
1/2 cup shortening
1 cup sugar
2 eggs
2 1/2 cups cake flour

1 teaspoon baking powder
1 teaspoon soda
1/4 teaspoon salt
1/2 cup sour cream
1 teaspoon vanilla
1 cup mashed bananas

Combine pecans, 1/4 cup sugar and cinnamon; stir well and set aside. Cream shortening and 1 cup sugar until light and fluffy. Add eggs, beating well after each addition. Sift flour, baking powder, soda, salt; add alternately with the sour cream, then stir in the vanilla and bananas just enough to blend. Sprinkle half of reserved cinnamon mixture into bottom of a well-greased Bundt pan; spoon half of batter into pan. Sprinkle remaining cinnamon mixture over batter; then spoon balance of batter into pan. Bake at 350° for 40-45 minutes or until tests done.

Cool coffee cake 5 minutes in pan on a wire rack. Serve warm or cold. This cake slices perfectly...rates tops!.

Country Cakes

Caramel Breakfast Cake

1/2 pound Kraft caramels
1/2 cup hot water
2 tablespoons sugar

1/2 cup chopped pecans
1 can biscuits
1/2 cup melted margarine

Place the caramels and hot water in pan over low heat. Stir fast until the caramels are melted and smooth. Sprinkle the sugar over the bottom of a well-greased 9-inch cake pan. Sprinkle nuts on sugar and then pour on caramel sauce. Place the biscuits which have been dipped in the melted butter on top of other ingredients. Bake in preheated oven at 425° for 15-18 minutes. Flip out onto a plate and serve.

Windsor Academy Cookbook

Cinnamon Apple Muffins

2 cups flour
1/4 cup sugar
1/2 teaspoon salt
1/2 teaspoon soda
2 teaspoons baking powder
1 teaspoon cinnamon

2 eggs
1 cup buttermilk
1/4 cup oil
3/4 cup finely chopped
  apples

TOPPING:

2 tablespoons sugar

1/2 teaspoon cinnamon

Mix dry ingredients. Beat eggs with milk and oil. Add to dry ingredients. Add chopped apples. Blend just enough to mix. Fill well-greased muffin tins two-thirds full. Sprinkle small amount of sugar mixed with cinnamon on top of each muffin. Bake at 425° for 15-20 minutes. Makes 24 medium-size muffins.

Tea Room Notes: The cinnamon-sugar topping makes these muffins brown beautifully.

The Frances Virginia Tea Room Cookbook

Bacon Muffins

12 slices bacon
1 cup self-rising flour
1 cup self-rising cornmeal

1/4 cup sugar
2 eggs, well beaten
1 cup milk

Cook bacon until crisp; drain and crumble. Reserve 1/4 cup drippings. Combine flour, cornmeal and sugar. Add eggs, milk, and reserved bacon drippings. Stir just until moistened. Stir in crumbled bacon. Spoon batter into greased muffin tins and bake at 425° for 20-25 minutes. Yield: 12 servings.

The Market Place

Orange Sour Cream Muffins

6 tablespoons butter, softened
1 cup sugar
1 egg
1/2 cup sour cream
2 tablespoons + 2 teaspoons orange juice

2 tablespoons grated orange rind
1/2 teaspoon orange extract
1 1/4 cups flour
1/2 teaspoon baking soda
1/2 teaspoon salt
1/2 cup chopped pecans

Cream butter and sugar. Beat in egg. Fold in sour cream, orange juice, rind, and extract. Sift dry ingredients; add to orange mixture, blending well. Stir in pecans. Fill greased muffin pans 1/2-3/4 full. Bake at 375° for 12 minutes. Yield: 16-18 muffins.

Perennials

Peach Muffins

Perfect for ripe Georgia peaches; a summertime treat.

1/3 cup butter, softened
1 cup sugar, divided
1 egg
1 1/2 cups all-purpose flour
1 1/2 teaspoons baking powder

1/2 teaspoon salt
1/4 teaspoon ground nutmeg
1/2 cup milk
1/2 cup chopped peaches
1 teaspoon ground cinnamon
1/2 cup butter, melted

Preheat oven to 350°. Cream butter and 1/2 cup sugar. Add egg; mix. Combine flour, baking powder, salt, and nutmeg; stir flour mixture into butter mixture alternately with milk. Stir in peaches. Fill greased muffin cups 2/3 full. Bake for 20-25 minutes. Mix 1/2 cup sugar with cinnamon. When muffins are done, immediately dip tops into melted butter, then into cinnamon-sugar mixture.

Peachtree Bouquet

Poppy Seed Egg Bread

If making bread, why not make the best? This is it!

1/4 cup warm water (110-115°)
1 package active dry yeast
1/2 cup milk, scalded and
  cooled to lukewarm
1 tablespoon sugar
1 teaspoon salt
1 egg, beaten

1 tablespoon margarine,
  softened
2 3/4-3 cups flour
  (all-purpose)
1 egg yolk for glaze
Poppy seeds
Margarine, melted

In mixing bowl dissolve yeast in warm water. Stir in milk, sugar, salt, egg, and margarine. Add half of flour; beat with spoon until smooth. Using hand, mix in enough of remaining flour until dough handles easily and clears bowl. Turn out onto lightly floured board; knead until dough is smooth and blistered. Place in greased bowl, turn once to bring up greased side. Cover with damp cloth; let rise in warm place until double (about 1 hour). Punch down, let rise until almost double (30 minutes).

Turn dough out of bowl, divide into 3 equal parts. Roll each into a 14-inch strand. Place close together on a lightly greased baking sheet. Braid strands loosely (do not stretch). Tuck ends under securely. Brush with melted margarine. Cover with damp cloth; let rise until double (40-50 minutes).

Heat oven to 375°. Mix egg yolk with 2 tablespoons water. Brush braid with egg yolk glaze—sprinkle with poppy seeds. Bake 25-30 minutes until golden brown. Cool on rack. Yield: 1 loaf.

Note: To make a loaf, shape into loaf. Use a greased loaf pan (9x5-inches). Bake at 425° 25-30 minutes.

Lasting Impressions

Easy Beer Bread

2 cups self-rising flour
3 tablespoons sugar

1 (12-ounce) can beer, warm
1 tablespoon butter, melted

Combine flour, sugar, and beer; stir just until all ingredients are moistened. Pour into a greased loaf pan. Bake at 375° for 30-35 minutes. Brush with melted butter. Remove bread from pan and cool.

Savannah Style

Mama Jenkins' Bread

2 cups lukewarm milk
1/2 cup cornmeal
1 cake yeast
3/4 cup (or less) sugar

1/2 cup oil
1 1/4 teaspoons salt
4 or 5 cups flour

At night mix 1 cup lukewarm milk, cornmeal and yeast. Cover and put in warm place. Next morning add 1 cup lukewarm milk, sugar, oil, salt, and flour. Cover and let rise 2 hours in warm place. Let rise again 1-2 hours. Knead. Put in greased loaf pan (3). Cover with damp cloths. Let rise again 1-2 hours. Bake in 300° oven 30-45 minutes. Put in cold oven.

Remarks: Do not allow to rise in too warm a spot as it will cause air holes and drying. This is excellent cooked over the open-hearth in a small deep round spider pot. The receipt has been in the family for many generations and is considered a real treat by all, especially at holiday time.

Tullie's Receipts

Old-Fashioned Syrup Bread with Lemon Sauce

SYRUP BREAD:

2 1/2 cups all-purpose flour
1 teaspoon baking powder
1 teaspoon baking soda
1 teaspoon salt

2 cups pure sugar cane syrup
1/2 stick butter, softened
2 eggs

Preheat oven to 350°. Grease 9x13-inch pan. Sift flour. Add baking powder, baking soda, and salt, and sift again. In separate bowl, pour cane syrup. Add eggs and butter, mixing well. Add dry ingredients to creamed mixture slowly, a small amount at a time, mixing well. Pour into pan and bake 30-40 minutes. Remove from pan and cut into 2-inch squares.

LEMON SAUCE:

1/2 cup sugar
1 tablespoon cornstarch
1 cup boiling water
1 tablespoon grated lemon
 rind

2 tablespoons butter
2 tablespoons lemon juice

Combine sugar and cornstarch. Stir in water and lemon rind and cook over moderate heat until thick and clear. Remove from heat and add butter and lemon juice. Stir until smooth. Serve slightly warm over syrup bread. Yield: 24 servings.

Bear in Mind: A favorite from the plantation kitchens of Sumter County for generations, this recipe predates the War Between the States.

Unbearably Good!

 The Annual Sorghum Festival, held in Blairsville, features sorghum products as well as a working, old-fashioned cane mill, handmade wares, music, and contests.

Augusta's Best Strawberry Bread

3 cups all-purpose flour
2 cups sugar
1 teaspoon baking soda
1 teaspoon salt
1 teaspoon cinnamon
4 eggs, beaten

1 1/4 cups vegetable oil
2 (10-ounce) packages frozen
 strawberries, thawed and
 chopped
1 cup chopped pecans

Sift flour, sugar, baking soda, salt, and cinnamon into large mixing bowl. Make well in center. Combine eggs, oil, strawberries, and pecans. Add to sifted ingredients, stirring until well combined. Spoon batter into 2 greased and floured 9x5-inch loaf pans. Bake at 350° for 1 hour. Cool bread in pans 10 minutes. Remove bread from pans. Cool completely on wire racks. Yield: 2 loaves.

Second Round, Tea Time at the Masters®

Stone Ground Whole Wheat Bread

DRY MIX:

2 1/2 pounds stone-ground
 flour
2 1/2 pounds all-purpose
 flour

2 cups dry milk powder
2 teaspoons salt
5 packages yeast

WET MIX: (Should be very wet.)

1/2 cup butter
1/2 cup honey
5 cups water, warm from tap

1 pound sunflower seeds
 (optional)

Combine dry and wet mix; knead 5-10 minutes. Let set in warm place until double in size. Knead 5-10 minutes. Cut into 5 parts for large bread tins. Let rise until double and then bake 45 minutes at 375° or until brown to suit. Yield: 5 loaves.

Somethin's Cookin' in the Mountains

Bread of Barbados

Never before has banana bread tasted so good!

1/3 cup chopped blanched
  almonds
1 cup flour
3/4 cup fine graham cracker
  crumbs
2 tablespoons ground baking
  chocolate

2 teaspoons baking powder
1 teaspoon baking soda
1/2 teaspoon salt
1/3 cup butter
2/3 cup sugar
2 eggs
1 cup mashed ripe bananas

Combine almonds with flour, graham cracker crumbs, chocolate, baking powder, soda, and salt. Mix well. Cream butter with sugar until fluffy. Beat in the eggs, 1 at a time and then beat in the mashed bananas. Beat until smooth. Stir in the almond mixture. Spoon into well-greased 9x5-inch loaf pan. Bake at 350° for 1 hour or until well done. Turn out onto wire rack to cool. Cool before slicing. To serve, cut thin slices. Spread, if you wish, with soft butter or cream cheese. Yield: 12-14 servings.

Quail Country

Spicy Pineapple Zucchini Bread

3 eggs, beaten
1 cup oil
2 cups sugar
2 teaspoons vanilla
2 cups zucchini squash,
  unpeeled, shredded
1 (8 1/4-ounce) can crushed
  pineapple, well drained

3 cups plain flour
2 teaspoons soda
1 teaspoon salt
1/2 teaspoon baking powder
1 1/2 teaspoons cinnamon
3/4 teaspoon nutmeg
1 cup nuts, finely chopped
1/2 cup raisins

Beat eggs with oil, sugar, and vanilla until thick and foamy. Stir in zucchini and pineapple. Sift flour with soda, salt, baking powder, and spices. Stir nuts and raisins into flour mixture, then add to zucchini. Stir together just until blended. Divide evenly between 2 greased and floured 9x5-inch loaf pans. Bake at 350° until done, about 1 hour. Yield: 2 loaves.

Potlucks & Petticoats

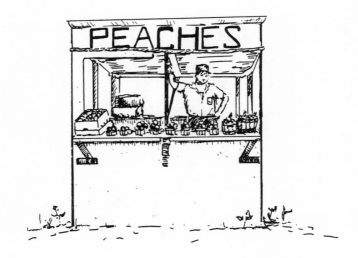

Vineboro Crescent Rolls

ROLLS:

1 1/2 cups milk
1 cup (2 sticks) butter
1/2 cup sugar
1 teaspoon salt
3 eggs

1 package active dry yeast
2 teaspoons sugar
5-5 1/2 cups flour
Butter, at room temperature

Scald milk. Add butter, 1/2 cup sugar, and salt. Blend and cool. Add eggs, 1 at a time, beating well after each. Add yeast and 2 teaspoons sugar, following package directions. Add the flour to make a firm batter. Beat well. Set aside in warm place until double in bulk.

Punch down and place covered in the refrigerator overnight. Next day, divide into 3 parts. Roll into a round, as for pie crust, and spread with softened butter. Cut each round into 16 wedges, and begin to roll from the wide to the pointed end. Bend to form a crescent. Set aside to rise on a greased cookie sheet or pan for about 2 hours. Preheat oven to 375°. Bake for about 15 minutes, or until golden brown. Frost while still hot with Glaze. Yield: 48.

GLAZE:

1 cup confectioners' sugar
6 tablespoons milk

1/8 teaspoon almond extract,
or to taste

Place confectioners' sugar in a small bowl. Slowly stir in milk and extract to make a glaze of spreading consistency.

Georgia Entertains

Professional baseball legend Ty Cobb, nicknamed the "Georgia Peach," was born in Banks County. He was purchased by the Detroit Tigers in 1905 from Augusta of the South Atlantic League for $500.

Effie's Dinner Rolls

2 packages active dry yeast
1/2 cup warm water
3/4 cup vegetable oil
2 cups cold water
2 eggs, beaten
3/4 cup sugar

2 teaspoons salt
8 cups sifted all-purpose
 flour
1/4 cup butter
Flour (as needed for rolling
 dough)

Dissolve yeast in 1/2 cup warm water. Pour yeast mixture, vegetable oil, cold water, beaten eggs, sugar, and salt in large bowl of electric mixer; beat well. Gradually add flour, beating after each addition. When dough becomes too stiff to be mixed with electric mixer, beat last additions of flour in by hand; mix well. (Dough will be very sticky.) Transfer to bowl with tight-fitting lid. Cover; refrigerate overnight.

Flour hands well. Pinch off half of dough. Return remaining dough to refrigerator. Melt butter. Sift about 3/4 cup flour onto board. Flour hands again. Place dough on floured board; work in just enough flour to make it possible to roll out dough. Roll dough to 1/4-inch thickness; cut with 2-inch biscuit cutter. Slightly stretch each round of dough from center. Dip half of each round in melted butter; fold top half of dough over buttered half. Place on ungreased, heavy baking sheet 2 inches apart. Allow to rise for 2 hours.

Preheat oven to 475°. Bake for 6-8 minutes. Watch carefully. (*Note:* Remainder of dough can be refrigerated for up to 1 week.) Yield: 8 dozen (entire recipe).

Guess Who's Coming to Dinner

Stone Mountain, 16 miles east of Atlanta, is the largest exposed granite mountain in the world. A popular feature there is the Memorial Carving, which is the largest high-relief sculpture in the world.

Brittle Bread

2 3/4 cups flour
1/4 cup sugar
3/4 teaspoon salt
1/2 teaspoon soda

1/2 cup butter
8 ounces plain yogurt (not
   the lowfat kind)

Mix flour, sugar, salt, and soda. Cut butter into dry mixture, add yogurt and mix. When you have a soft dough, break off small pieces (about the size of a marble) and roll very thin on a floured surface. (This is the secret.) Sprinkle with salt. Bake at 400° for 5-8 minutes on ungreased cookie sheet. Turn off heat and allow to crisp in oven.

Macon Sets a Fine Table

Crisp Corn Bread

1 cup flour
1 tablespoon baking powder
1/4 teaspoon baking soda
1 teaspoon salt
1 cup stone-ground white
  cornmeal

1 egg
1 1/2 cups buttermilk
4 tablespoons butter, melted

Preheat oven to 425°. In medium-sized mixing bowl, stir together flour, baking powder, baking soda, and salt. Stir in cornmeal. In small bowl, beat egg until foamy. Add buttermilk. Mix well. Stir egg-buttermilk mixture into dry ingredients. Beat with spoon until smooth. Stir in butter. Turn batter into buttered, 9x9x1 3/4-inch, square pan. Bake about 25 minutes, or until sides shrink away from pan and top is light brown. Serve with softened butter. This bread is only about an inch high.

Note: For those who don't like dense, thick corn bread, this is a treat. Serves 6.

Cooking in the New South

Baby Broccoli Muffins

1 (10-ounce) package frozen
  chopped broccoli
1 (7 1/2-ounce) box corn
  muffin mix

4 eggs, beaten
1 stick margarine, melted
3/4 cup cottage cheese
1 large onion, chopped

Preheat oven to 425°. Grease miniature muffin tins. Cook broccoli according to package directions. Drain well. Mix corn muffin mix, eggs, melted margarine, cottage cheese, onion, and drained broccoli until blended. Put in miniature muffin tins and bake 10-12 minutes. Yield: About 5-6 dozen muffins.

Bear Flair: Dollop with sour cream and a tiny fresh broccoli floweret. Marvelous. These freeze very nicely.

Unbearably Good!

Mexican Corn Brunch Bread

Like eating cake. Even good served cold at a picnic.

1 cup butter
1 cup sugar
4 eggs
1 (4-ounce) can green chilies,
  seeded and chopped
1 (1-pound) can cream-style
  corn
1/2 cup shredded Monterey
Jack cheese

1/2 cup shredded Cheddar
  cheese
1 cup flour
1 cup yellow cornmeal
4 teaspoons baking powder
1/4 teaspoon salt

Preheat oven to 350°. Cream butter and sugar. Add eggs 1 at a time, mixing well. Add chilies, corn, and cheeses; mix well. Sift together flour, cornmeal, baking powder and salt. Add to corn mixture. Pour into greased and floured 9x13-inch pan. Put in oven and reduce heat to 300°. Bake 1 hour. Serve warm. Serves 12.

The Historic Roswell Cook Book

Sour Cream Corn Bread

4 eggs	2 cups self-rising cornmeal
1 pint sour cream	1 small can cream corn
1 cup Wesson oil	1/2 teaspoon salt

Using hand beater, beat eggs. Add sour cream, then oil and beat well. Add cornmeal with spoon as well as corn and salt. Bake in oven at 400° for 30-35 minutes in 9x13-inch Pyrex baking dish sprayed with Pam. Serves 12. Recipe may be cut in half and freezes very well.

Atlanta's Pet Recipes

Frozen Cheese Sandwich

4 ounces cream cheese, room temperature	1 teaspoon dry sherry wine
	1/2 teaspoon lemon pepper
2 ounces sharp Cheddar cheese, grated, room temperature	1/2 teaspoon dry minced garlic
	1/4 teaspoon mustard powder
1 ounce butter, room temperature	8 slices bread
	1/2 cup chopped walnuts or pecans
1 tablespoon sour cream	

Mix all ingredients together except bread and nuts. Spread cheese mixture evenly on 4 slices of bread, reserving 1 tablespoon of mix. Place the other 4 slices on top to make sandwiches and cut them in half diagonally. Spread the cut edge of each sandwich with reserved cheese mixture and dip into chopped nuts. Wrap halves individually and store in an airtight container in the freezer.

Note: Take 1 of these sandwiches with you in the morning to work and by lunchtime, it is perfectly thawed and ready to eat. They are also great for picnics. For a toasted cheese sandwich, spread the outside of the frozen sandwich lightly with butter and put under broiler while still frozen. Toast on each side.

You Are The Boss in the Kitchen!

Overnight Strawberry Jam

3 cups sugar   3 cups strawberries

Add sugar to strawberries and let set overnight. Next morning, boil for 20 minutes, then let the mixture set all day and seal cold. Never cook more than 3 cups at a time. This is delicious. The berries stay whole, and jam is a nice color.

Golden Isles Cuisine

Strawberry Fig Preserves

3 cups peeled mashed figs   2 packages strawberry Jello
3 cups sugar

Mix well, cook for 10 minutes. Pour mixture into jars and seal.

Flatlanders Cook Book

Green and Red Pepper Jelly

1/2 cup hot red peppers,   1 medium onion, quartered
  seeded and coarsely chopped   1 1/2 cups vinegar
1/2 cup hot green peppers,   5 1/2 cups sugar
  seeded and coarsely chopped   1 bottle liquid pectin

Finely process peppers, onion, and vinegar in food processor. Put mixture and sugar in 6-quart pot. Boil 1 minute. Remove from heat. Add pectin. Stir and skim foam for 5 minutes. Ladle into hot, sterilized jars. Shake to keep peppers mixed. Cool.

Many southerners keep pepper sauce on their tables and put a dash of it on everything they eat. Pepper jelly is piquant but more refined, and is often seen, green or red-colored, on top of cream cheese spread on crackers. It is also excellent with country ham.

Betty Talmadge's Lovejoy Plantation Cookbook

Soups

The Great American Scream Machine at Six Flags Over Georgia is one of the largest, highest, and fastest wooden roller coasters. Atlanta.

Peanut Soup à la Crème

1/4 cup butter
3 tablespoons flour
2 1/2 quarts chicken stock
2 cups smooth peanut butter

2 cups light cream
Chopped peanuts for garnish
Chopped watercress for
  garnish

Melt the butter in a large, heavy saucepan and stir in the flour, mixing well. Gradually add the chicken stock. (Fresh chicken stock is best. To prepare, boil a fat hen with two medium onions, 2 stalks of celery, a grated carrot, and poultry seasoning.) Bring the mixture to a boil, stirring constantly. Reduce heat and add peanut butter. Stir until very smooth. Blend in the cream. Do not boil. Spoon the soup into small bowls and top with chopped peanuts and chopped watercress. Serves 10-12.

Recipes from The Olde Pink House

Root Soup!

1 large or 2 small carrots,
  peeled
1 medium turnip or parsnip,
  peeled
1 medium yellow or white
  onion, peeled
1 medium boiling potato,
  peeled
1 clove garlic, crushed
4 tablespoons butter

2 cups chicken stock, or 1
  (13 3/4-ounce) can chicken
  broth plus water to make 2
  cups
2 tablespoons vodka
Salt
Freshly ground pepper
Whipped cream or yogurt,
  optional

Slice vegetables thin. Melt butter in skillet. Add the vegetables and sauté until onions are translucent, about 10 minutes. Do not brown. Meanwhile, heat chicken stock in large saucepan. Add vegetables to stock, cover, and simmer until vegetables are soft, about 15 minutes. Remove from heat, add vodka, and purée in food processor or food mill. Taste for seasonings; add salt and pepper

CONTINUED

CONTINUED

as needed. Pour into soup bowls. Top with a blob of lightly salted whipped cream or yogurt and sprinkle with ginger if desired.

Note: May be made in advance and reheated. Do try this recipe—despite the unglamorous name, it is absolutely delicious! Serves 4.

The Pirates' House Cook Book

Sour Cream Potato Soup

1/4 cup butter
1 medium onion, chopped
4 cups water
3 pounds potatoes, peeled
 and diced
1 stalk celery, chopped

1 tablespoon salt
1/4 teaspoon pepper
2 tablespoons chopped fresh
 parsley
1 (8-ounce) carton sour
 cream

Melt butter in large pot. Add onion and sauté. Add water and bring to a boil. Add everything else except sour cream. Reduce heat and simmer for 15 minutes. Remove from heat. Stir in sour cream. Return to heat and heat through but do not boil. Serve immediately. Serves 8-10.

Country Cupboard Cookbook

Goulash Soup

This recipe is the best treasure I brought home from Germany.

1 to 1 1/2 pounds beef
  chuck, cut into bite-size
  pieces
1/2 stick margarine, melted
4 medium onions, chopped
2 cloves garlic, minced
3 tablespoons flour
4 tablespoons paprika

1 (10 1/2-ounce) can tomato
  purée
2 quarts beef bouillon
1 (10-ounce) can beef
  consommé
2-3 potatoes, cubed
Salt and pepper, to taste

Brown beef well in margarine. Sauté onions and garlic. Add flour, paprika, tomato purée, bouillon, consommé, and potatoes. Add salt and pepper. Simmer for 3 hours. Serve with hot French bread and a salad.
Easy. Do ahead. Serves 10-12.

Culinary Classics

Roasted Pepper and Tomato Soup
A unique and tasty blend of flavors.

4 red bell peppers
2 cups peeled, chopped, and
  seeded tomatoes or 1
  (35-ounce) can tomatoes,
  drained
3 tablespoons olive oil
2 cloves garlic, minced
3 cups chicken broth

1/2 teaspoon salt
1/4 teaspoon freshly ground
  pepper
1 1/2 tablespoons chopped
  fresh basil or 1 1/2
  teaspoons dried whole basil
2 tablespoons red wine
  vinegar

Cut peppers into quarters; remove stems and seeds. Place on foil-lined baking sheet; broil until skins are charred, about 10 minutes. Cover with plastic wrap; let stand 10 minutes. Peel off skins and discard. Combine peppers and tomatoes. Purée in blender in small batches. Heat olive oil in medium saucepan. Add garlic; sauté about 30 seconds. Add tomato-pepper mixture and chicken broth.

CONTINUED

CONTINUED

Simmer 10-15 minutes, stirring occasionally, until slightly thickened. Remove from heat; stir in salt and pepper. Let cool to room temperature. Before serving, blend in basil and vinegar. Must prepare ahead. Serves 4-6.

Peachtree Bouquet

Instant Borscht

Easy, fun soup—gorgeous color.

1 medium onion, chopped	1 cup condensed beef broth
1 cup canned sliced beets	1 cup beet juice from can
Thin peel from 1/2 lemon	3 tablespoons sour cream
3/4 teaspoon salt	2 1/2 tablespoons lemon
Pepper to taste	juice
2 tablespoons sugar	

With metal blade in place, chop onions, add beets, lemon peel, salt, pepper, and sugar. Turn on and add all other liqui ingredients. Blend until smooth. Serve chilled with a dollop of sour cream on top. Can also be done in a blender. Very easy. Do ahead. Serves 4.

Culinary Classics

Southern Corn Chowder
(Microwave)

1/2 cup chopped salt pork
  (may substitute 4 slices
  bacon)
1 medium onion, chopped
1/2 cup sliced celery
1/2 cup green pepper, diced
2 cups milk
1/4 cup flour

2 potatoes, microwaved and
  diced
1 teaspoon salt
1 bay leaf
1/2 cup light cream
2-3 cups fresh corn, cut
  from cob

Microwave salt pork 2-3 minutes on HIGH. Add onion, celery, and pepper. Microwave 2-3 minutes. Mix flour with small amount of the milk and add to above mixture along with the diced potatoes. Add remaining milk, salt, and bay leaf, and heat on HIGH until thickened. Add cream and corn. Microwave again on HIGH 4-6 minutes.

Simply Scrumptious Microwaving

Spinach Soup

6 cups fresh spinach
3 tablespoons butter
1 small onion, chopped
1 cup parsley sprigs
1/4 teaspoon nutmeg
3 tablespoons flour
2 cups chicken stock,
  divided

1 cup half-and-half
1 egg yolk
Salt and pepper to taste
Chopped parsley or chives
  for garnish

Wash and drain spinach; tear to make 6 cups. Saute onion in melted butter until limp. Add spinach, parsley and nutmeg and cook for a few minutes. Stir in flour and cook for 1 minute, stirring. Add 1/2 cup chicken stock, bring to a boil, and boil 1 minute, stirring. Pour spinach mixture into a blender and blend to a semi-smooth consistency. Return mixture to pan and add remaining stock and half-and-half. Simmer 2-3 minutes. Separate egg yolk into bowl and whisk about 1/2 cup soup into yolk; return to pan. Stir and heat until soup thickens slightly. Do not boil. Season with salt and pepper to taste. Chill at least 2 hours or overnight. Garnish each serving with chopped parsley or chives. Yield: 4-6 servings.

Feast and Fellowship

Cream of Asparagus Soup

1 small bunch green onions
2 medium onions, sliced
1 stick butter, unsalted
1 1/2 pounds fresh asparagus
  or 2 (10-ounce) packages
  frozen
1 cup water
Salt and pepper to taste

1 tablespoon sugar
4 tablespoons all-purpose
  flour
2 cups chicken stock
3 cups milk
1/2 teaspoon white pepper
2 teaspoons salt
Sour cream to garnish

Wash and slice green onions, including green tops. In 4 1/2-quart saucepan, sauté green onions and other onions in butter. Simmer 30 minutes covered. Cut tips from asparagus 1 inch long. Cook tips in 1 cup water 5 minutes with salt, pepper and sugar; set aside for garnish. Add asparagus stalks to onions and cook a few minutes longer. Stir flour into vegetables until smooth. Add stock, milk, white pepper, and salt. Simmer 2-3 hours, stirring occasionally. Cool. Put in blender and purée. When ready to serve, add 1 dollop of sour cream to each bowl and garnish with drained asparagus tips. Yield: 6-8 servings.

Bear in Mind: You may add some sherry to soup when cool.

Unbearably Good!

Cream of Carrot Soup

2 stalks celery, finely
  chopped
1 medium onion, finely
  chopped
1/4 pound butter
3/4 pound carrots, coarsely
  chopped
5 1/2 cups water
7 chicken bouillon cubes
1 1/4 pounds potatoes,
  peeled and diced

1 1/2 cups milk
1/2 cup flour
1/3 teaspoon white pepper
1/8 teaspoon freshly ground
  nutmeg
1-3 tablespoons lemon juice
Chopped parsley, optional
Chives, optional
Scallions, optional
Paprika, optional

In a soup pot, sauté celery and onions in butter until onions are almost transparent. In a separate pot, cook carrots in water with bouillon until about 3/4 done. Add potatoes to carrots and continue cooking until both are done. Drain and reserve liquor. Purée vegetables, using a small amount of reserved liquor, if needed. Add flour to onion-celery-butter mixture. Blend well into butter and cook several minutes being careful not to let brown.

Add vegetable liquor and milk to flour and cook over high heat with constant whisking or stirring until a medium-thin white sauce forms. Immediately reduce heat and add purée, white pepper and nutmeg. Simmer for 10-15 minutes with occasional stirring to prevent sticking or scorching. Add lemon juice to taste and serve hot. Garnish bowls as desired with parsley, chives, scallions, paprika, or your own variation. Refrigerating overnight and reheating to serve even improves flavor, which becomes more like Cheddar than carrots. Yield: 8 servings.

Feast and Fellowship

Savannah Crab Stew

1 quart milk
4 tablespoons flour
1 teaspoon salt
1/4 teaspoon white pepper
1 tablespoon butter
1 tablespoon Worcestershire
  sauce

1 tablespoon lemon juice
1/4 cup sherry
1/2 pound crabmeat
Dash Tabasco sauce

Combine flour, salt, and pepper. Add mixture to milk. Add butter and stir until smooth. Cook over low heat until slightly thickened. Add remaining ingredients and serve at once.

Crab Chatter

Shrimp Bisque

1 pound shrimp, boiled and
  peeled
4 tablespoons butter
4-5 tablespoons flour
1 quart milk
2 teaspoons salt

3 teaspoons lemon juice
1/2 teaspoon Tabasco
Dash white pepper
Sherry
Lemon slices

Grind shrimp in blender or food processor. Combine butter and flour in saucepan. Add milk and salt and stir until thickened. Add lemon juice, Tabasco, and pepper. Add shrimp and sherry (approximately 2 tablespoons per serving). Serve hot with lemon slice floating on top. Serves 6-8.

Savannah Style

Margaret Mitchell, author of *Gone With the Wind*, was born in Atlanta. Her book sold over one million copies in its first six months, and is still one of the best-selling books of all times. It has been translated into 36 languages. In 1985, the Georgia legislature named Margaret Mitchell its "most famous citizen."

Fisherman's Stew

The traditional Marseilles bouillabaisse is made with fish that are found only in the Mediterranean Sea. Abbey bouillabaisse, flavored strongly with saffron, garlic, and fennel, substitutes the fresh fish available to us: red snapper, sea bass, shrimp, salmon, sole, mussels, clams, and Maine lobster. The base of the soup can be made ahead of time, and the fish added at the last minute so that it will not be overcooked.

2 cups fish stock
1 cup chicken stock
1/4 cup each diced celery, carrots, onions, and white part of leek
1/4 cup olive oil
1 tablespoon butter
3 scallions, chopped
1/2 cup diced peeled tomatoes
1/4 cup tomato paste
1/2 cup dry white wine
1 teaspoon green peppercorns, in brine
4 cloves garlic, minced
Saffron
2 teaspoons chopped fresh parsley
1 sprig of thyme

Bay leaves, 4-5 fresh or 3 dried
1/2 teaspoon fennel
Touch of absinthe or anisette or Pernod
Salt
Freshly ground white pepper
Approximately 4 pounds assorted fish: snapper, sole, turbot, lobster tails (in shell), scampi, crayfish (in shell), oysters, sea bass scallops, clams, mullet, etc., cut into 1/2-ounce pieces
16 slices French bread, buttered, srinkled with fresh minced or powdered garlic and toasted.

Sauté celery, carrots, onions, and leek in half of the olive oil and the tablespoon of butter for 5-8 minutes over medium heat. Add scallions and tomatoes, then tomato paste. Braise for 3-4 minutes while stirring. Add fish stock, beef or chicken stock, and white wine. Blend in green peppercorns, garlic, saffron, herbs, and absinthe; season with salt and pepper. Simmer for 10-15 minutes.

While soup is simmering, pour the remaining olive oil into a large skillet and sauté all the fish except for oysters, mussels, and clams for a few minutes. Place all the sauteed fish into the fish soup. Add oysters, clams and mussels and simmer for 3-4 minutes. Divide all seafood

CONTINUED

CONTINUED

into individual serving dishes. Pour soup over the fish, sprinkle with chopped parsley, and top each with 2 garlic croutons.

The Abbey Cookbook

Oyster Bisque

1 pint oysters, including juice	1 bay leaf
2 cups chicken broth	4 cups thick White Sauce
1 rib of celery, coarsely chopped	1 teaspoon thyme
1 small onion, sliced	Salt
	Pepper

Drain oysters. Save juice. Remove hard parts of oysters. Chop remainder and reserve. Simmer hard parts of oysters with juice, chicken broth, celery, onions, and bay leaf. When vegetables are tender, strain. Add strained broth to White Sauce, thyme, and oysters. Taste. Season with salt and pepper. Simmer just until hot. Soup will curdle if it boils. Dish up and sprinkle with topping.

WHITE SAUCE:

3 tablespoons melted fat, butter, or oleo	1 cup milk
3 tablespoons flour	1/2 teaspoon salt

Melt fat in heavy saucepan. Slowly add flour. Do not brown. Add milk and salt. Stir constantly until thick.

BREAD CRUMB TOPPING:

3 slices crisp toast	1/4 cup chopped parsley
2 tablespoons butter, melted	

Crush toast. Pour melted butter over crumbs. Toss with parsley. Sprinkle 1/4 cup on each serving. Makes 6 1-cup servings.

Tea Room Notes: The crisp, buttery crumbs really distinguished this Oyster Bisque from other restaurants' oyster soups. Don't serve it without them.

The Frances Virginia Tea Room Cookbook

Seafood Gumbo

1 six-pack cold beer or bottle of white wine "for the cook"
1 cup flour
1/2 cup olive oil
1/2 cup cooking oil
1/2 pound bacon, diced
1 pound okra, sliced
10 stalks celery, chopped
4 large onions, chopped
1 green pepper, chopped
2 cloves garlic, chopped
1/2 cup chopped parsley
1 quart chicken stock
4 cups Chablis
2 quarts water
1/2 cup Worcestershire sauce

Louisiana Hot Sauce, to taste
1 (6-ounce) can tomato paste
1 (6-ounce) can tomato sauce
2 tablespoons salt
2 bay leaves
1/4 teaspoon thyme
1/4 teaspoon rosemary
1/4 teaspoon cayenne
2 cups chopped cooked chicken
2 pounds cooked crabmeat
4 pounds raw shrimp
2 pints oysters
1 teaspoon molasses
1 tablespoon lemon juice
Cooked rice

Preheat oven to 400°. Make a roux by mixing flour, olive oil, and cooking oil in oven-proof glass container. Bake for about 2 hours. Stir roux every 15 minutes. The roux should look like chocolate brownies when done. While this is cooking, have a cold beer or glass of wine. Dice bacon and fry in a heavy iron pot. Remove bacon, and fry in a heavy iron pot. Leave grease in pot, cook okra in bacon grease until slime is gone. Help yourself to beer or wine. This takes a long time.

When roux is done, add to bacon grease and okra. Add celery, onions, pepper, garlic, and parsley. Cook 45 minutes at low heat, stirring constantly. Add little more oil, and chicken stock may be added if mixture is difficult to work. Add chicken stock, wine, water, Worcestershire, hot sauce, tomato paste, tomato sauce, salt, bay leaves, thyme, rosemary, and cayenne. Simmer for 2 1/2 hours. Enjoy beer or wine. The hard part is over! Peel shrimp at this time. Be careful—do not let gumbo stick.

Add chicken, crabmeat, and shrimp about 30 minutes before serving. Add oysters and molasses during last 10 minutes. Add lemon juice and taste. It will be good if you did it right. Serve in soup bowl with about 1/4 cooked

CONTINUED

CONTINUED

rice and 3/4 gumbo. Serve at once with French bread toasted with garlic butter. Gumbo is better after it is frozen or refrigerated. Make more than you need and enjoy it another day. Yield: 10-12 servings.

Quail Country

Crab Bisque Thirty-Seventh

Elizabeth of 37th is one of Savannah's most popular restaurants, and its owner/chef, Elizabeth Terry, is one of the nation's most publicized cooks. She was one of Food and Wine's 25 "Hot New Chefs," and has been featured in *Town and Country* and *Time*, among other magazines. Elizabeth creates all the recipes herself, and does much of the actual cooking while her husband, Michael, is chief host, wine steward, and worrier. They make a great team. Here is one of the restaurant's specialties.

6 tablespoons butter
1 cup minced green onion
1/2 cup minced celery
1 tablespoon minced carrot
6 tablespoons flour
2 1/2 cups milk
2 1/2 cups chicken broth,
  preferably homemade

1/4 teaspoon nutmeg
1/4 teaspoon white pepper
1/8 teaspoon cayenne pepper
1 cup cream
1/4 cup good sherry
1 pound claw crabmeat,
  picked over

Melt butter over low heat in saucepan. Mince green onion, celery and carrot in food processor. Add to butter and cover. Sweat until tender, about 5 minutes. Whisk in flour and cook for 2 minutes to remove starchy taste. Whisk in milk and broth. Bring to a boil, whisking occasionally. Add seasonings, cream, sherry, and crab. Serve immediately. Serves 12.

Savannah Collection

Creamy-Rich Seafood Chowder

1 1/2 pounds raw, chopped
  shrimp
1 pint chicken stock
1 pound crabmeat
1/2 cup heavy cream
1 quart milk

White pepper
1/4-1/2 teaspoon thyme (to
  taste)
1/2 stick butter
Salt to taste

Simmer raw, chopped shrimp in the chicken stock till pink. Add the remainder of the ingredients and heat till hot, but be very careful not to let boil, as it will curdle. Serve right away or allow to stand up to 45 minutes or an hour, but don't leave heat on.

    This makes a delightful main dish with crusty French bread and tossed salad or served in mugs as an appetizer before dinner with company. Add a good cold California chablis wine and put anchovies on top of the salad and you have a festive and almost instant company meal. Serves 4-6.

Frederica Fare

Clam Chowder

1 dozen Cherrystone clams,
  shucked and chopped (save
  juice)
1/2 cup chopped bacon
1/4 cup chopped onion
1 cup diced potatoes

1/2 teaspoon salt
Dash of pepper
1 cup clam liquor
2 cups milk
Chopped parsley

Shuck and drain clams. Save juice. Fry bacon until partially cooked. Add onion and cook until tender. Add potatoes, seasonings, clams, and liquor. Supplement with bottled clam juice if needed for measurement. Cook over medium heat until tender. Add milk, and heat slowly while stirring constantly. Garnish with parsley. Serves 4-6.

Vincent Russo's Seafood Cookbook

Salads

The Governor's Mansion. Atlanta.

Peaches and Cream Salad

1 regular package peach
 Jello
1 cup boiling water
3/4 cup cold water
3 cups peaches, sliced
1 small banana, sliced
1 envelope unflavored
 gelatin

3 tablespoons cold water
1/2 cup half-and-half cream
1 (8-ounce) package cream
 cheese, softened
1 cup whipping cream
1/2 cup plus 2 tablespoons
 sugar
1 cup peaches, puréed

Dissolve peach gelatin in boiling water; stir until dissolved. Add 3/4 cup cold water and mix well. Chill until the consistency of an unbeaten egg white. Stir in sliced peaches and banana. Pour into a lightly oiled 8-cup mold. Chill until set. Soften gelatin in 3 tablespoons cold water. Scald half-and-half cream and stir into gelatin mixture. Beat cream cheese until smooth. Add whipping cream, sugar, and puréed peaches; mix well. Add to gelatin mixture and stir well. Pour over peach and banana layer. Chill at least 8 hours, or until firm. Yield: 10-12 servings.

Potlucks & Petticoats

Layered Fruit Salad

Fresh fruit is best—can use canned fruit or mix fresh and canned fruits.

3 soft pears
2 packages strawberries
1 pineapple (chunk
 pineapple, if canned)

4 peaches, sliced
1 pint blueberries
4 bananas, sliced

Dip pears, bananas and peaches in pineapple juice or sprinkle Fruit Fresh over fruit. Layer in glass bowl. Cover with following dressing:

DRESSING:

1 package instant vanilla
 pudding
1 1/4 cups milk

4 tablespoons frozen
 concentrate orange juice
1 cup Cool Whip

Mix all ingredients together. Pour over layered fruits.

Foresters' Favorite Foods

Wine-Cherry Mold

1 (1-pound 13-ounce) can
  bing cherries
3/4 cup hot water
1 package black cherry
  gelatin

1/2 cup sherry
1/2 cup chopped walnuts (or
  pecans)
1 cup sour cream
Nutmeg

Drain cherries, reserving juice. Add hot water to the gelatin and stir until dissolved. Add sherry and 3/4 cup of the cherry juice. Stir well. Chill until partially set.

Stir in cherries and nuts. Pour into a 1 1/2-quart mold. Chill until firm. Unmold and serve with sour cream sprinkled lightly with nutmeg.

Cherries Galore

Congealed Coca-Cola Cranberry Salad

A Georgia Thanksgiving classic.

1 (16-ounce) can whole
  cranberry sauce
1 (3-ounce) package orange
  gelatin
1 cup boiling water
1 envelope gelatin, softened
  in 1/2 cup cold water
1 (20-ounce) can crushed
  pineapple, undrained

1 tablespoon lemon juice
1 tablespoon grated orange
  rind
1 cup pecans or walnuts,
  chopped
6 ounces Coca-Cola Classic

Dissolve orange gelatin in boiling water; add cranberry sauce and blend well. Add plain gelatin. Add remaining ingredients and stir just to blend. Spray an 8-cup mold with nonstick cooking spray. Pour mixture into mold. Chill. When mixture begins to gel, stir to distribute nuts evenly. Continue to chill until firm. Yield: 8 servings.

Georgia On My Menu

 Coca-Cola was first invented in Georgia in 1886.

Cranberry Salad

1 large package black cherry
  gelatin
1 cup hot water
2 (3-ounce) packages cream
  cheese
3/4 cup mayonnaise

1/2 pint whipping cream
1 large can crushed
  pineapple
1 large can cranberry sauce
1 cup chopped nuts

Mix black cherry gelatin with cup of hot water. Blend the cream cheese and mayonnaise. Add the whipped cream, pineapple, and cranberry sauce (which is cut in small pieces). Add chopped nuts, gelatin and mix well. Freeze. Thaw before serving.

Country Cupboard Cookbook

Orange Soufflé Gelatin Salad

2 (3-ounce) packages orange
  Jello
2 cups boiling water
1 cup reserved pineapple and
  orange juices, mixed
1 pint orange sherbet

1 (9-ounce) can crushed
  pineapple, reserve juice
1 (11-ounce) can mandarin
  oranges, reserve juice
1/2 cup chopped nuts
  (optional)

Mix together Jello and boiling water to dissolve, then add drained juices. Allow to partially set. Fold in sherbet, crushed pineapple, oranges, and nuts. Pour into 9x13-inch glass tray. Refrigerate until firm. Serve on lettuce leaf with dollop of sour cream.

Traditionally Wesleyan

Valentine Salad

1 1/2 tablespoons unflavored
  gelatin
1/4 cup cold water
2 cups crushed pineapple
1/2 cup sugar
2 tablespoons maraschino
  cherry juice

2 (3-ounce) packages cream
  cheese
12 maraschino cherries,
  chopped
1/2 pint whipping cream

Soften gelatin with 1/4 cup of water. Heat pineapple with sugar and add gelatin and cherry juice. Cool. Soften and mash cream cheese and add finely chopped cherries. Add pineapple to cream cheese, mixing a small amount in at a time. Whip until slightly thickened. Whip cream and blend into pineapple mixture. Pour into mold and chill.

Boarding House Reach

Mandarin Orange Salad

2 packages orange gelatin
1 1/2 cups boiling water
1 pint orange sherbet
1 (11-ounce) can mandarin
  oranges, drained

1 (#2) can crushed
  pineapple, drained

Dissolve gelatin in boiling water. Add sherbet and stir until melted. Add fruit and pour into mold. Chill. Serves 12-15.

Country Cupboard Cookbook

V-8 and Cottage Cheese Aspic

2 envelopes plain gelatin
1 1/2 cups V-8 juice,
  (12-ounce can)
1 tablespoon lemon juice
3/4 cup cottage cheese
1/2 cup mayonnaise

1 cup finely diced celery
1/2 cup finely diced green
  pepper
1 small onion, minced
Salt to taste
1 drop red food color

Soak gelatin in 1/2 cup of the V-8 juice. Heat remaining 1 cup juice with lemon juice. Dissolve gelatin in hot juice. Chill. Beat cottage cheese with mayonnaise until smooth. Add vegetables and V-8 mixture. Taste and season with salt. Add 1 drop red food color for pink color. Pour into molds. Chill. Makes 7-8 1/2-cup servings.

The Frances Virginia Tea Room Cookbook

Quick Aspic Salad

1 (15-ounce) can stewed
  tomatoes
1 (3-ounce) box strawberry
Jello

2-3 tablespoons tarragon
  vinegar

Heat tomatoes in small saucepan. Add dry Jello and vinegar, stir to make sure Jello has dissolved. Pour into dish and refrigerate. Be sure and get stewed tomatoes, not just regular canned ones.

The Bachelor's Cookbook

Asparagus Vinaigrette

Favorite warm weather vegetable dish. Perfect for patio lunch or supper and very pretty!

1 pound fresh asparagus
Bibb lettuce
1 hard-cooked egg, chopped
  fine

3 slices cooked bacon,
  crumbled

Boil or steam asparagus until done, but crisp (about 10 minutes). Cool and arrange on bed of Bibb lettuce. Sprinkle with egg and bacon. Just before serving, pour Vinaigrette Dressing over all.

CONTINUED

CONTINUED

VINAIGRETTE DRESSING:

1/2 cup olive oil or Wesson oil
3 tablespoons vinegar
1 teaspoon salt
1/2 teaspoon freshly ground pepper
Dash cayenne pepper
1/4 teaspoon paprika
1 tablespoon pimiento, chopped fine

1 tablespoon cucumber pickle, chopped fine
3/4 tablespoon chopped green pepper
1/2 teaspoon chopped parsley
1/2 tablespoon chopped olives

Combine oil, vinegar, salt, pepper, cayenne, and paprika. Heat thoroughly. Add chopped pimiento, pickle, green pepper, parsley, and olives. Serves 4.

The Historic Roswell Cook Book

Stuffed Onion Salad

4-6 large Vidalia onions
1 (8-ounce) package cream cheese

2 tablespoons deviled ham
1 teaspoon salt
Few grains pepper

Peel onions. With apple corer, remove centers of onions for use in other dishes. Beat cream cheese until soft and creamy. Blend in deviled ham and remaining ingredients. Fill center of onions with mixture and chill several hours or until cheese centers are firm. To serve, slice onions and serve on lettuce leaves. Serves 6-8.

The Original Vidalia Onion Cookbook

 Vidalia onions are so good, they are bought in quantity during their season. Two popular storing methods are: hang in the legs of pantyhose with a knot tied between each onion; set on window screens or air conditioner filters, being sure they don't touch.

A Tomato Well Stuffed

2 cups canned artichoke
  hearts, chopped
1/2 cup chopped celery
1/2 cup chopped green onions
  and tops

1 cup Hellman's mayonnaise
8 tomatoes
1 1/2 cups cooked shrimp,
  shelled and deveined
12 slices of bacon, cooked

Combine artichoke hearts with celery, green onions, and mayonnaise. Just before serving, add shrimp to stuffing. Peel and scoop out 8 tomatoes; stuff with mixture. Place on lettuce. Sprinkle with crumbled bacon on top. Filling is better if made ahead. Yield: 8 servings.

Quail Country

Italian Tomatoes and Peppers

Colorful—tender green peppers in a seasoned tomato sauce.

1/2 cup onions, coarsely
  chopped
2 cloves garlic, minced
2 tablespoons olive oil or
  vegetable oil
1 (1-pound) can Italian plum
  tomatoes

2 teaspoons sugar
1 1/2 teaspoons salt
1/4 teaspoon pepper
1/2 teaspoon dried oregano
  leaves
5 green peppers, 3/4 to
  1-inch strips

In a large skillet, sauté onion and garlic in oil until soft. Break up tomatoes and add (undrained) to onion mixture; add seasonings. Simmer, uncovered, 20 minutes or until sauce thickens slightly. In the meantime, simmer green peppers, uncovered, in about 1 1/2 quarts water for 10-15 minutes. Drain well and add to tomato sauce, continue to simmer (uncovered) until peppers are tender. Serves 4-6. *Note:* Basil may be substituted for oregano.

Variation: Add sliced cooked Italian sweet sausage to Italian Tomatoes and Peppers and serve over thick slices of French bread.

Lasting Impressions

Shanghai Salad

1 large head crisp lettuce, shredded
2 (16-ounce) cans bean sprouts, drained well
2 green peppers, coarsely chopped

2 (5-ounce) cans water chestnuts, thinly sliced
Shanghai Dressing
1/2 cup toasted almonds, chopped

Place first 4 ingredients in very large bowl. Right before serving, pour dressing over all and toss well. Sprinkle almonds over top. Yield: 12-15 servings.

SHANGHAI DRESSING:

2/3 cup mayonnaise
1 teaspoon prepared mustard
1/2 teaspoon Tabasco sauce
2 teaspoons chili powder
1 clove garlic, crushed
2 teaspoons grated onion
5 tablespoons tarragon vinegar

1 1/2 teaspoons dried marjoram
1/2 teaspoon dried thyme
1/4 teaspoon coarsely ground pepper
1 teaspoon salt
2 teaspoons soy sauce

Blend all ingredients in bowl. Transfer to jar with tight-fitting lid. Cover and shake vigorously. Refrigerate over-night. Yield: 1 cup.

Guess Who's Coming to Dinner

Gourmet Chinese Salad

1 (10 1/2-ounce) package
  frozen English peas, cooked
  and drained
1 (5-ounce) package yellow
  rice, cooked according to
  package directions
2 1/2 pounds cooked, peeled
  shrimp

1 1/2 cups diced celery
1/2 cup chopped onion
1/3 pound fresh mushrooms,
  sliced
1 (14-ounce) can artichoke
  hearts, drained and sliced
Soy Almond Dressing
8-10 cherry tomatoes

Combine peas, rice, shrimp, celery, onion, mushrooms, and artichokes in large bowl. Add Soy Almond Dressing; toss to coat. Cover; chill 5 hours or overnight. Garnish with cherry tomatoes.

SOY ALMOND DRESSING:

1/2 cup salad oil
3 tablespoons cider vinegar
2 tablespoons soy sauce
2 teaspoons curry powder
1 teaspoon sugar

1/2 teaspoon celery seed
1/2 teaspoon salt
1/2 teaspoon monosodium
  glutamate
1/4 cup sliced almonds

Combine all ingredients, mixing well. Must do ahead. Serves 10-12.

Perennials

Augusta's Favorite Salad

1/2 cup salad oil
1/4 cup red wine vinegar
1 teaspoon monosodium
  glutamate
1 teaspoon seasoned salt
1/2 teaspoon oregano leaves
1 tomato, chopped

2 teaspoons green onion tops
  or chives
2 teaspoons fresh chopped
  parsley
1 medium head lettuce, torn
  or chopped in small pieces
Croutons, optional

Mix all ingredients, except lettuce. Add chopped lettuce and toss. Toss with croutons or toasted pita bread chips. Yield: 6 servings.

The Market Place

Avocado and Ripe Olive Salad

1 avocado
Ripe olive, sliced
Mayonnaise

Chili sauce
Lettuce leaf, to serve

Buy ripe but firm avocado. Cut in half. With a teaspoon, scoop out the meat in small pieces, leaving the shell whole and still firm. Mix avocado meat with 1/2 cup sliced ripe olives. Marinate for 1 hour with a dressing made of 1/2 mayonnaise and 1/2 chili sauce. Catsup or cocktail sauce could be substituted, but the chili sauce is better. Serve on lettuce leaf right in the shell.

From Mother with Love

Curried Avocado Salad

24 (1/4-inch thick) slices
  cut from small ripe
  avocadoes

24 (1/4-inch thick) slices
  ripe tomato
1/2 cup Curry Dressing

Arrange the avocado and tomato slices on 6 salad plates. Top each portion with 2 teaspoons Curry Dressing. Serve immediately. (*Note:* If you can't serve immediately, be sure to brush the avocado slices with a little lemon juice, to prevent their darkening. Serves 6.

Cal. per serving 69 - Pro. .83gm. - Carb. 5gm. - Fat 5gm. - Sod. 3mg.

CURRY DRESSING:

1 cup low-fat cottage cheese   Curry powder to taste

Season the cottage cheese to taste with your favorite brand of curry powder. Purée until very smooth in a food processor or blender. This will take about 1 1/2 minutes in the processor—somewhat less time will be needed in the blender. Serves 24.

Cal. per serving 6.8 - Pro. 1.16gm. - Carb. .25gm - Fat 0gm. - Sod. 21.5mg.

Southwind Cuisine

Salad with Brie Dressing

A nice salad for entertaining. Easy but elegant.

SALAD:

1 medium head curly endive
1 medium head iceberg
  lettuce

1 medium head romaine
  lettuce
Garlic croutons

Wash and drain lettuce. Tear into bite-sized pieces.

DRESSING:

10 ounces Brie cheese
1/2 cup olive oil
4 teaspoons minced green
  onion
1 large garlic clove, minced
1/2 cup sherry wine vinegar

2 tablespoons fresh lemon
  juice
1 1/2 tablespoons Dijon
  mustard
Freshly ground pepper

Remove rind from Brie. Cut cheese into small pieces and allow it to soften to room temperature. Heat oil in skillet over low heat for almost 10 minutes. Add onion and garlic and sauté about 5 minutes or until tender. Blend in vinegar, lemon juice, and mustard. Add cheese and stir until smooth. Season to taste with pepper. Toss warm dressing with lettuce and croutons. Serve immediately. Serves 10.

Temptations

Stuffed Lettuce

1 (3-ounce) package cream
 cheese
2 tablespoons Roquefort
 cheese, crumbled
2 tablespoons grated carrots
1 tablespoon minced green
 pepper

2 tablespoons chopped tomato
1 teaspoon onion juice
1/2 teaspoon salt
1 head lettuce

Blend all ingredients except lettuce. Hollow out center of lettuce head and fill with the cream cheese mixture. Wrap securely in waxed paper or plastic wrap. Refrigerate until ready to serve. Cut in wedges or slices as desired. Serve with your favorite dressing.

Golden Isles Cuisine

Wilted Lettuce

Guests will ask for your recipe.

3-4 slices bacon, crumbled
Grease from bacon
1 egg, beaten
3 tablespoons sugar
1 teaspoon salt

Pepper, to taste
3 tablespoons vinegar
1/4 cup water
1 head lettuce

Fry bacon crisp; break into small pieces, leaving it in bacon grease. Beat egg. Add sugar, salt, pepper, vinegar and water. Pour this mixture into bacon and bacon grease. Keep heat low and stir constantly until slightly thickened. Pour over lettuce, torn into bite-size pieces. Serve immediately. Easy. Prepare same day. Serves 8.

Culinary Classics

 At 71 stories, the Peachtree Center Plaza in Atlanta is the tallest hotel building in the United States.

Make Ahead Lettuce Salad

1 head lettuce, shredded
1/2 cup celery, chopped
1/4 cup green pepper, chopped
1/2 cup onion, chopped
2 cups fresh chopped spinach
1 (10-ounce) package frozen peas (cooked slightly and cooled)

1 pint Hellmann's mayonnaise
2 tablespoons sugar
1 cup Parmesan cheese
1/2 cup crumbled bacon

Grease 9x13-inch pan. Arrange first 6 ingredients in order given. Do not stir. Spread mayonnaise over all evenly. Add next 3 ingredients in order. Cover tightly and refrigerate 24 hours. Cut in squares. Serves 16.

The Stuffed Griffin

Greek Salad

Greek cook Pauline Georges is a good friend always willing to share a recipe. When I asked about the secret of her delicious Greek salads, she said it in 2 words: lemon juice. She promptly sent me a recipe for a basic Greek salad and salad dressing. I serve it often, and each time, I appreciate the delicate blend of herbs and lemon all over again.

1 small head lettuce (Romaine preferred), washed and chopped
2 green onions, chopped in 1-inch pieces
2 stalks celery, chopped
1 cucumber, chopped

1 fresh tomato, chopped
1 green pepper, cut in strips
Feta cheese, crumbled
Calamata olives (large Greek olives)

Mix salad ingredients, except feta and olives. Pour dressing over salad. Toss to coat. Top each salad serving with feta cheese and olive.

CONTINUED

CONTINUED

GREEK SALAD DRESSING:

1/2 cup olive oil
1/4 cup vegetable oil
1/3 cup fresh lemon juice
  (about 3 lemons)
1 teaspoon salt
1/4 teaspoon freshly ground
  black pepper

1 clove garlic, minced or
  pressed
3/4 teaspoon dried oregano
1/4 teaspoon sugar

Place in jar. Shake well. Store in refrigerator. Allow to come to room temperature before using. Makes 1 cup. Note: Double or triple for large groups.

Savannah Collection

Julia Ann's Beau Rivage Salad

1 head lettuce
3/4 cup Swiss cheese
1 cup ham
2 cups apple
1 cup chopped walnuts
Green onion (small amount,
  chopped)

1/2 cup juice of lemon
1 cup salad oil (or olive
  oil)
Salt and pepper

Break up lettuce; cut small julienne strips of cheese, ham, and apple. Add walnuts and green onion. Make a dressing of 1 part lemon juice and 2 parts salad oil or olive oil, seasoned with salt and pepper. Toss ingredients together and serve immediately. Use your own judgment as to amount of ingredients. Served with bread sticks or French bread, it is enough for a luncheon.

Feast and Fellowship

Spinach Salad Roswell

From the Public House restaurant in Roswell, Georgia.

1/2 cup soy sauce
1 ounce fresh lemon juice
1/2-3/4 teaspoon fresh
  ground black pepper
1 1/2 teaspoons sugar
1/8 medium onion
1 1/2 teaspoons sesame seeds

1 cup peanut oil
Fresh spinach
Water chestnuts
Mushrooms
Bean sprouts (fresh taste
  best)

Mix soy sauce, lemon juice, black pepper, sugar, onion and sesame seeds in blender until onion is pulverized. Slowly add peanut oil and blend a few more seconds until thoroughly mixed. (If dressing is made ahead, let it come to room temperature and shake very well before using). Tear desired amount of spinach which has been washed well and spun dry. Add sliced water chestnuts, sliced mushrooms, and bean sprouts. Refrigerate until crisp. (Refrigerate salad plates). To serve: Toss salad with dressing and serve immediately. Makes 12 servings.

Encore

Spinach Strawberry Salad

An unlikely pair that is a real winner!

1 pound leaf spinach

1 pint strawberries, sliced

Tear well-washed and dried spinach into bite-size pieces. Combine spinach and strawberries; add dressing, toss and serve.

LIZ'S DRESSING:

1/2 cup sugar
1 teaspoon dry mustard
1 teaspoon salt
1/2 cup celery seed

3 tablespoons onion, grated
1 cup salad oil
1/3 cup wine vinegar

Blend dry ingredients, add grated onion. Beat oil and vinegar together and add. Chill for several hours. Before tossing with salad, beat with whisk or fork until well blended. Dressing keeps well for several weeks. Serves 8.

Lasting Impressions

Mandarin Spinach Salad with Poppy Seed Dressing

1/3-1/2 cup white wine
  vinegar
4 teaspoons sugar
2/3 teaspoon dry mustard
2/3 teaspoon salt
2 teaspoons fresh lemon
  juice
2/3 cup vegetable oil
1 tablespoon poppy seeds

1 pound fresh spinach
1 large can mandarin
  oranges, drained
1/4 pound bacon, cooked and
  crumbled
1 large avocado
1/4-1/2 medium red onion,
  sliced

Mix vinegar, sugar, mustard, salt, lemon juice, vegetable oil, and poppy seeds in food processor. Assemble remaining ingredients and pour dressing over and serve.

The Holiday Hostess

Amaretto Chicken Salad

SALAD:

2 cups cubed, cooked chicken
1/4 cup mayonnaise
1 (8 1/4-ounce) can crushed
  pineapple, drained
1 tablespoon amaretto

1 teaspoon salt
2 tablespoons toasted
  slivered almonds
1/2 cup chopped celery

DRESSING:

2 tablespoons amaretto

1/2 cup mayonnaise

Combine all salad ingredients. Chill overnight. Combine amaretto and mayonnaise for dressing, cover and chill overnight. To serve, place salad on a bed of lettuce leaves or in hollowed-out pineapple boats. Top with dressing and garnish with additional almond slices. Yield: 4-6 servings.

The Market Place

Hot Chicken Salad
(Microwave)

4 tablespoons melted
  butter/margarine
2-3 chicken breasts, boned
  and cut into bite-size
  pieces
1 (10 3/4-ounce) can cream
  of chicken soup
1 tablespoon Worcestershire
  sauce
2 tablespoons finely minced
  onion

1 cup diced celery
3 diced, hard-cooked eggs
1/3 cup pecans, chopped
1/2 cup mayonnaise
3/4 teaspoon salt
3/4 teaspoon curry powder
1/2 cup toasted buttered
  bread crumbs
Paprika

In a 2-quart utility dish melt butter/margarine 1-1 1/2 minutes on Full Power or until melted. Stir chicken into butter/margarine and cook 6-7 minutes on Full Power, stirring and turning chicken after 3 minutes. Allow to carry-over cook 5-6 minutes then drain away accumulated liquid. Combine all other ingredients together except for bread crumbs and paprika. Stir the sauce and chicken pieces together in utility dish. Spread out evenly. Cook 4-5 minutes on Full Power or until very hot. Before last minute of cooking, sprinkle bread crumbs on top of casserole and sprinkle lightly with paprika. Serves 4.

The Dapper Zapper

Chicken-Cranberry Salad

1 envelope unflavored
  gelatin
1/4 cup cold water
1 can whole cranberry sauce

1 (9-ounce) can (1-cup)
  crushed pineapple
1 tablespoon lemon juice

Soften gelatin in cold water. Dissolve over hot water. Add cranberry sauce, crushed pineapple, and lemon juice and pour into mold and chill until firm.

CONTINUED

CONTINUED

1 cup mayonnaise
1/2 cup water
3 tablespoons lemon juice
3/4 teaspoon salt
2 cups diced chicken

1/2 cup diced celery
2 tablespoons chopped parsley
1 tablespoons soy sauce

Blend mayonnaise, water, lemon juice, and salt. Add chicken, celery, parsley and soy sauce. Pour over first layer and chill until firm. Serve in squares topped with mayonnaise.

The Holiday Hostess

Shrimp Lutece

6 heads Bibb lettuce (1 small head per serving)
16 ounces canned artichoke hearts, drained and halved
2 avocados, sliced

2 pounds large, raw shrimp in shell, cooked and peeled
4 hard-cooked eggs, quartered

Wash and dry lettuce; gently separate leaves. Combine with other ingredients and toss lightly.

DRESSING:

3/4 teaspoon salt
White pepper, to taste
1/2 teaspoon prepared mustard
1/2 clove garlic, crushed
1/4 cup tarragon vinegar

1 egg yolk
1 cup oil
1/2 teaspoon sugar
1 tablespoon Worcestershire sauce
1/4 cup chili sauce

Make a paste of salt, pepper, mustard, garlic, and small amount of vinegar. Blend in egg yolk until smooth. Start adding oil very slowly until dressing is consistency of mayonnaise. (May use blender or rotary beater.) Continue adding oil alternately with remaining vinegar. Beat in suagr and Worcestershire sauce; fold in chili sauce and chill thoroughly. Serves 6

Savannah Style

Baked Seafood Salad

1 small green pepper,
  chopped
1 small onion, chopped
1 cup celery, chopped
1 pound crabmeat
1 pound raw shrimp, peeled
  and deveined

1 cup mayonnaise
1/2 teaspoon salt
Pepper
1 teaspoon Worcestershire
  sauce
1 cup bread crumbs, buttered

Cook shrimp. Mix all ingredients in casserole; sprinkle buttered bread crumbs on top. (Grated cheese may also be added to crumb topping.) Bake 30 minutes at 350°. Do not overbake. Serves 6.

Savannah Style

Shrimp and Pasta Salad
Great hot weather dish.

3 cups water
1 pound fresh shrimp, peeled
  and deveined
1/3 (16-ounce) package
  spiral pasta
1/2 cup diced celery
1/2 cup sliced ripe olives
1/2 cup sliced fresh
  mushrooms
1/2 cup sliced water
  chestnuts

3/4 cup mayonnaise
2 tablespoons sugar,
  optional
1 tablespoon vinegar
1 tablespoon lemon juice, or
  more to taste
1/2 teaspoon salt
1/8 teaspoon pepper

Bring water to a boil; add shrimp and return to a boil. Reduce heat and simmer 3-5 minutes. Drain well; rinse with cold water. Chill. Cook pasta according to package directions and drain. Rinse with cold water. Combine pasta, shrimp, celery, olives, mushrooms, and water chestnuts. Combine mayonnaise, sugar, vinegar, lemon juice, salt, and pepper. Pour over pasta mixture and toss until coated. Cover and chill Yield: 4-6 servings.

Bear in Mind: For a more colorful dish you may use multicolored spiral pasta.

Unbearably Good!

Shrimp Mold

Delicious as a main salad or as an hors d'oeuvre.

1 1/2 tablespoons plain
  gelatin
1/4 cup cold water
1 can tomato soup
1 (8-ounce) package cream
  cheese
1 1/2 cups cooked shrimp,
  chopped
1 cup mayonnaise

1 tablespoon lemon juice
3/4 cup finely chopped
  celery
1/2 cup finely chopped onion
1/3 cup finely chopped
  olives
Salt
Red pepper-dash

Soften gelatin in cold water. Heat soup and add softened gelatin and cream cheese. Stir until smooth. When cool, add remaining ingredients. Pour into 4-cup mold. Chill overnight. Yield: 4 cups.

Cooking with Tradition

Crab Shrimp Salad

2 pounds shrimp
Garlic salt
Lemon squeeze
1 teaspoon vinegar
Mayonnaise

1 pound claw crabmeat
3 stalks celery
Ripe or stuffed olives
2 or 3 hard-boiled eggs
Salt to taste

The day before: Boil shrimp. Peel and clean. Sprinkle generously with garlic salt. ("I use lots of it," says Mildred.) Squeeze a bit of lemon over top. Coat with vinegar and a little mayonnaise, about 1 heaping table-spoon. Refrigerate overnight.

The next day: Add crabmeat, chopped celery, sliced ripe or stuffed olives, and hard-boiled eggs, chopped. Salt to taste. Then add just enough mayonnaise to hold the salad together nicely. Serve in lettuce cups.

Crab Chatter

Avocado Stuffed with Crabmeat

2 heads Boston lettuce
4 ripe avocados
1 1/2 pounds fresh lump
  crabmeat
8 strawberries
8 slices cantaloupe
8 small clusters of seedless
  grapes
16 orange segments, free of
  membrane
8 slices lime
8 slices lemon
16 slices kiwi fruit
8 sprigs fresh dill

This colorful and delectable dish is a constant favorite at the Abbey. Fresh lump crabmeat is served in an avocado bed with Curry Cream Mayonnaise providing a delightful contrast. If fresh crabmeat is not available, frozen king crab or lobster or shrimp might be substituted by the home cook.

Wash lettuce well and pat dry; arrange the leaves on individual serving plates. Split avocados in half lengthwise, remove pit, and peel. Slice each half into 4-5 lengthwise pieces and set these closely together in the center of each plate on top of the lettuce leaves, retaining the half avocado shape. Divide the lump crabmeat into 8 servings (3 ounces each) and place into center of each avocado "half." Surround the avocado with fresh fruit and top crabmeat with Curry Cream Mayonnaise, garnishing with fresh dill.

The Abbey Cookbook

Seaside Crab and Avocado Salad

2 cups crabmeat, flaked
2 avocados, peeled and diced
1 1/2 teaspoons lime juice
2 hard-cooked eggs, chopped
2 tablespoons onion, minced
1 tablespoon capers
1/2 cup celery, chopped
1/2 teaspoon salt
Dash of pepper
1/2 cup mayonnaise
1 clove garlic, pressed
3 tablespoons chili sauce
Lettuce leaves

Combine crabmeat and avocados in a bowl and sprinkle with lime juice. Add eggs, onion, capers, celery, salt, and pepper Blend mayonnaise, garlic and chili sauce. Pour over salad and toss lightly. Serve on lettuce leaves. Yields 6 servings.

Educated Taste

Rice Salad

1 1/2 cups Minute rice
1 package frozen LeSeuer
  Peas in butter sauce
3/4 cup mayonnaise
1/3 cup Durkee's sauce

3/4 teaspoon curry powder
1/2 teaspoon dry mustard
1 cup diced celery
1 tablespoon grated onion

Cook Minute rice as directed. Cook peas as directed and drain. Add all other ingredients to rice and peas while still warm. Toss lightly and chill several hours or overnight. Serves 6-8. Good with cold turkey or ham.

Atlanta's Pet Recipes

Fiesta Pasta Salad

DRESSING:

1/2 cup red wine vinegar
1/2 cup sour cream

1/2 cup mayonnaise

Combine all ingredients for Dressing. Blend well.

SALAD:

1 (12-ounce) package twist
  or shell macaroni
1/2 cup chopped green pepper
1/4 cup chopped celery
1/4 cup chopped onion
1/2 cup sliced fresh
  mushrooms
1 cup chopped fresh
  broccoli, cooked

2 hard-cooked eggs, chopped
1 cup grated Cheddar cheese
Salt and pepper to taste
2 cups chopped, cooked
  shrimp, chicken, or ham,
  optional
Grated Parmesan cheese
Cherry tomatoes and pitted
  black olives to garnish

Cook pasta according to package directions. Drain. Rinse with cool water. Drain again. Pour Dressing over warm pasta. Add green pepper, celery, onion, mushrooms, broccoli, eggs, cheese, salt, and pepper. Toss. Stir in shrimp, chicken, or ham, if desired. Chill. Serve on a bed of lettuce. Sprinkle with Parmesan cheese and garnish with tomatoes and olives. Yield: 10-12 servings.

Second Round, Tea-Time at the Masters®

Layered Potato Salad "Bernice"

6 cups water	7-8 medium unpeeled potatoes
1 teaspoon salt	

Bring salted water to boil. Add potatoes. Cook covered until tender. Do not overcook. Peel potatoes.

DRESSING:

1 1/2 cups mayonnaise	1 tablespoon lemon juice
1 cup sour cream	1 teaspoon salt
2 tablespoons prepared horseradish	

Mix well; set aside.

IN SEPARATE BOWL PREPARE:

1 cup onions, cut fine	1 cup parsley, stems
1 cup celery, cut fine	included, cut fine

Mix well; set aside. In a 2-quart bowl, layer as follows: Spread 1/3 of dressing in bottom of bowl. Slice 1/3 of the potatoes on top of dressing (potatoes should be warm, but not hot or completely cooled). Then spread 1/3 of the onion, celery, parsley mixture. Repeat twice, ending with the onion mixture. Let sit 1 hour in refrigerator, then cover with Saran Wrap and serve the next day. This salad needs 12-36 hours in the refrigerator. Makes 8 servings.

You Are The Boss in the Kitchen!

My Favorite Potato Salad

8 cups unpeeled red-skinned
  potatoes, boiled and chunked
  (about 3 pounds)
1 medium onion, chopped
2 cloves garlic, minced
2 tablespoons olive oil
2 tablespoons white wine
  vinegar
Salt, to taste
Pepper, to taste

Dash red pepper
1/2 cup parsley, chopped
1/4 cup chives, chopped
1/2 cup homemade Lemon
  Mayonnaise (page 109)
1/2 cup plain, low-fat
  yogurt
Black olives, sliced, as
  garnish

Cut still-warm potatoes into chunks. Place in mixing bowl with onion and garlic. Season with olive oil, vinegar, salt, pepper, and red pepper. Toss to coat. Cover. Refrigerate until chilled. Mix in parsley and chives. Mix together mayonnaise and yogurt. Add to potato mixture. Toss to coat. Adjust seasonings. Place sliced olives on top as a garnish.

Note: Two secrets to a good potato salad are waxy potatoes, seasoned while still warm, and a homemade mayonnaise. Unlike some potato salads, this recipe is not sweet. I believe cole slaw should be sweet, not potato salad. This recipe was inspired by those lovely potato salads you find made with all sorts of homemade mayonnaises in the markets of Paris. Serves 8.

Cooking in the New South

Kathy's Freezer Slaw

1 large head cabbage
1 green pepper
1 or 2 carrots
1 tablespoon salt
2 cups sugar

1/2 cup vinegar
1 teaspoon mustard seed
1 cup water
1 teaspoon celery seed

Grate cabbage, pepper, and carrots. Sprinkle with salt, mix and let stand 1 hour. Squeeze water out of vegetables and drain. Boil remaining ingredients and cool. After cooled, pour over cabbage mixture. Mix and pack in square container and freeze, until ready to serve.

Ramblin' Chefs From Georgia Tech

Corn Bread Salad

1 (8 1/2-ounce) package Jiffy corn bread mix	1 egg 1/3 cup milk

Combine and stir well. Put in 8-inch greased pan. Bake at 400° 15-20 minutes. Cool and crumble and set aside.

4 medium tomatoes, peeled and chopped	1/2 cup sweet pickles, chopped
1 green pepper, chopped	9 slices bacon, cooked and crumbled
1 medium onion, chopped	

Toss gently. Mix and set aside.

1 1/4 cup mayonnaise	1/3 cup pickle juice

Mix and set aside.

Layer 1/2 crumb mixture, 1/2 tomato mixture, 1/2 mayonnaise mixture. Repeat. Let set at least 2 hours. Keep refirgerated.

Windsor Academy Cookbook

Curry Cream Mayonnaise

A strong cold curry sauce that is delicious served with a stuffed avocado or cold seafood. Tomato catsup adds a little sweetness, Worcestershire sauce and lemon give a stronger flavor, and cream makes it especially smooth. Use only imported Madras curry powder for the best results.

3/4 cup mayonnaise	Salt to taste
1/4 cup créme fraiche	Freshly ground white pepper to taste
2-3 teaspoons Madras curry powder	Touch Worcestershire sauce
3 tablespoons tomato catsup	2 tablespoons fine-chopped parsley
1/3 cup heavy cream	
Juice from 1-2 lemons	

Place mayonnaise into a bowl and add all the other ingredients. Mix with a wire whip until sauce is smooth. Refrigerate until needed.

The Abbey Cookbook

Lemon Mayonnaise

2 egg yolks
2 tablespoons lemon juice,
  freshly squeezed
1 heaping teaspoon dry
  mustard

Dash cayenne pepper
Dash salt
1 cup vegetable oil or olive
  oil

In electric blender or food processor, blend all ingredients, except oil. With machine still running slowly, add oil in steady stream just until the mixture thickens, about a minute.

Note: Easy to make. This is delicious in potato salads or spread on ham sandwiches with sliced ripe tomatoes. Makes 1 1/4 cups.

Cooking in the New South

Parmesan Cream Dressing

Perfect for the non-vinegar salad dressing lover.

2 egg yolks
1/2 cup white wine vinegar
1/2 teaspoon dry mustard
1/2 teaspoon basil, crushed
1/2 teaspoon oregano,
  crushed

1/2 teaspoon thyme, crushed
1 teaspoon salt
1/2 teaspoon white pepper
2 cups sour cream
1/2 cup Parmesan cheese
1/2 pound Provolone cheese

Beat together egg yolks, vinegar, mustard and seasonings until thick. Carefully fold in sour cream and Parmesan cheese. Chill. While the dressing is in the refrigerator, I marinate 1/2 pound piece of Provolone cheese in the dressing.

To serve: use a mixture of many different greens. Julienne the Provolone cheese and top with bell pepper rings. Easy. Do ahead. Stores well. Yields 3 cups.

Culinary Classics

Pink House Sherry Cream Dressing

2 cups mayonnaise
1 cup sour cream
1/2 cup dry sherry
1 tablespoon dried tarragon,
 finely crushed

1 teaspoon garlic powder
1/4 teaspoon Tabasco
Few drops of red food
 coloring or beet juice

Combine the mayonnaise, sour cream, sherry, tarragon, garlic powder and Tabasco in a mixing bowl and blend thoroughly. Add a few drops of red food coloring or beet juice, if desired, to give the dressing a slightly pink color. If the dressing is too thick, thin with a little milk.

Chill well in the refrigerator before spooning onto salad greens. Makes about 3 cups.

Recipes from The Olde Pink House

Northwest Georgia and six neighboring states are visible from Lookout Mountain, which sits on the Georgia-Tennessee line.

Vegetables

Hikers enjoy a breath of fresh mountain air and a scenic view from atop
Mt. Yonah. Northeast Georgia.

Cauliflower and Cheese

1/2 head of fresh
 cauliflower
2 cups water
1/2 teaspoon salt

4 tablespoons mayonnaise
1 teaspoon prepared mustard
1/2 cup grated or shredded
 cheese

Turn oven on to 375° to preheat. Remove outer green leaves from cauliflower and wash under running water. In a saucepan on top of the stove, bring water to a boil, add salt and cauliflower, cover, reduce heat and slowly boil for 15 minutes. Carefully remove cauliflower to a baking dish (use a flat spatula to keep it from breaking up). Mix mayonnaise, mustard, and cheese together and spread over the cauliflower. Place in preheated oven for 10 minutes. This can be prepared in advance. You can cook cauliflower—remove to baking dish, spread with cheese mixture and then set aside. Just before serving slide into your heated oven for 10-15 minutes—makes it a good dish for company since you can prepare it ahead of time.

The Bachelor's Cookbook

Brussels Sprouts and Artichokes

1 (10-ounce) package frozen
 brussels sprouts
1/2 cup water
1 (14-ounce) can artichoke
 hearts, drained

2/3 cup mayonnaise
1/2 teaspoon celery salt
1/4 cup margarine
2 teaspoons lemon juice
1/4 cup sliced almonds

Cook brussels sprouts in 1/2 cup water just until tender; drain. Arrange brussels sprouts and artichokes in a greased 1-quart casserole. Combine remaining ingredients and spoon over vegetables. Bake, uncovered, at 425° for 8-10 minutes. Serves 6.

Fancy Foods & Flowers

Zucchini Cobbler

1/2 cup butter or margarine
4 cups zucchini, peeled and
  sliced
Juice of 1 lemon
1/4 teaspoon nutmeg
1/4 teaspoon cinnamon

1/4 teaspoon allspice
1 cup sugar
1 cup Bisquick baking mix or
  self-rising flour
1 cup milk

Melt butter in a 9x13-inch pan; spread zucchini evenly over butter. Sprinkle with lemon juice, nutmeg, cinnamon and all-spice. Combine sugar, Bisquick and milk; blend well. Pour over zucchini. Do not stir. Bake at 350° for 30-40 minutes until golden brown. Yield: 12-16 servings.

Potlucks & Petticoats

Zucchini, Corn, and Peppers

2 tablespoons peanut oil
3 cups zucchini, thinly
  sliced crosswise
3 cups whole kernel corn,
  fresh cut or frozen
1 cup sweet red pepper,
  seeded and chopped

1 cup chopped onion
3 cloves pressed garlic
1 tablespoon dried coriander
  (or 3 tablespoons fresh
  cilantro)
3-6 tablespoons water

Heat oil in wok or heavy skillet for 1 minute at medium-high heat. Stir-fry zucchini for 2 minutes, then move to another dish. Add remaining ingredients to wok or skillet. Cover tightly, lower heat, and steam for 12-15 minutes or until vegetables are tender-crisp. Add a little more water if necessary to keep from burning. Return zucchini to mixture and heat through before serving. Cooking time: 15-20 minutes. Serves 6.

Cal.-142 Pro.-4g Fat-6g Carb.-24g Fib.-4g Sod.-4mg Chol.-0mg

Adventures in Healthful Cooking

Eggplant with Fresh Tomatoes and Cheese

SAUCE:

2 cups chopped onions
2-3 cloves garlic, pressed
1/4 cup olive oil
3 teaspoons salt
1 tablespoon sugar
1 teaspoon oregano
1 tablespoon basil

1/2 teaspoon anise seed
8 large ripe tomatoes,
 peeled, seeded, and chopped
3/4 cup chicken stock
1/4 cup white wine
2 tablespoons parsley,
 chopped

Sauté onions and garlic in oil. Add seasonings, liquid and tomatoes. Simmer 25-30 minutes. Add chopped parsley and simmer 5 more minutes.

EGGPLANT:

2 medium eggplants, or 1
 large eggplant
2 eggs, well beaten
1 cup Progresso bread crumbs
1/2 cup olive oil

1 heaping cup Parmesan
 cheese (grated)
1/2 pound mozzarella cheese,
 grated or sliced

Peel and slice eggplant. Dip in salted ice water; pat dry, salt, and let drain 15-20 minutes. Dip in beaten eggs, then bread crumbs, and brown in hot oil. Layer eggplant, sauce, and cheese—repeating layers. Dot with butter. Bake 30 minutes in a 350° oven. May make ahead, refrigerate, and bake before serving.

Little Bit Different!

Squash-Tomato-Asparagus Sauté

4 yellow squash, sliced
1/4-1/2 pound fresh
 asparagus, sliced on
 diagonal with tough ends
 removed
2-3 tomatoes, cut into
 wedges

2-3 tablespoons butter
Herbs to taste (any
 combination of dill, basil,
 tarragon, and oregano)
Morton Nature's Seasons

CONTINUED

CONTINUED

Blanch squash and asparagus. Sauté squash, asparagus, and tomatoes in butter with herbs and Nature's Seasons. Serve when vegetables are bright and fork tender. Yield: 6 servings. Very colorful! Broccoli florets can be substituted for fresh asparagus.

Second Round, Tea-Time at the Masters®

Oriental Marinated Vegetables

2 cups fresh snow peas, trimmed
1 (8-ounce) can sliced water chestnuts, drained
1 (8-ounce) can sliced bamboo shoots, drained
1/2 cup sliced fresh mushrooms
1/2 cup chopped scallions
1/2 cup red pepper, diced
1/2 cup Southwind Vinaigrette
2 tablespoons low-sodium soy sauce
1 teaspoon freshly grated ginger root

Blanch snow peas in boiling water. Drain well. Combine snow peas, water chestnuts, bamboo shoots, mushrooms, onions, and red pepper in a medium bowl; set aside. Combine soy sauce with vinaigrette. Whisk in ginger root. Pour over vegetables; toss lightly. Chill 2 hours. Toss lightly before serving. Serves 10.

Cal. per serving 63 - Pro. 2.7gm. - Carb. 8.9gm. - Fat 1 .8gm. - Sod. 48 mg.

SOUTHWIND VINAIGRETTE:

2 tablespoons safflower oil
2 tablespoons red wine vinegar
2 tablespoons Perrier
1 1/2 tablespoons lime juice
1 tablespoon Dijon mustard
2 tablespoons scallions, minced
White pepper, to taste

In small mixing bowl whisk together all ingredients, refrigerate overnight. Makes 3/4 cup.

Cal. per serving 17 - Pro. 1.25gm. - Carb. .5gm. Fat 1gm. - Sod. 9g.

Southwind Cuisine

Cossock's Delight

1 pound small mushrooms
2 tablespoons butter
2 tablespoons olive oil
1 large clove garlic, minced
1 small onion, grated
1/2 teaspoon - 1 tablespoon
  soy sauce, to taste

1/2 teaspoon Worcestershire
1/8 teaspoon ground mustard
1/8 teaspoon paprika
1/8 teaspoon seasoned salt
Salt and pepper to taste
1 tablespoon flour
1 cup sour cream

Wash mushrooms, separating stems and caps; reserve stems for later use. Heat butter and oil in medium saucepan. Add mushroom caps, garlic, onion, soy sauce, Worcestershire, mustard, paprika, salt, and pepper. Cook, stirring, 1-2 minutes, heat over high heat. Cover, reduce heat and simmer 5 minutes, stirring occasionally. Meanwhile, blend flour and sour cream until smooth; add to mushroom mixture. (If mushrooms have released a great deal of liquid, some liquid should be poured off before adding sour cream.) Heat thoroughly; do not boil. (For a different presentation, use to fill 4-6 baked patty shells; or use as chafing dish appetizer with crackers.) Serves 4.

Perennials

Mushroom Magnifique

12 large mushrooms
2 tablepoons softened butter
1/2 cup finely chopped
  pecans
1 1/2 tablespoons chopped
  parsley

1/2 clove garlic, minced
  (optional)
1/4 teaspoon salt
1/8 teaspoon thyme
1/2 cup heavy cream

Remove stems from mushrooms; chop finely enough to make 1/2 cup. Salt caps lightly. Mix stems, butter, nuts and next 4 ingredients. Heat caps with filling and place in shallow baking pan. Pour cream over all. Bake in 350° oven 20 minutes, basting once or twice with cream. Rich and good! Serves 6-8, depending on size of mushrooms.

Atlanta Natives' Favorite Recipes

Connoisseur's Casserole

1 (12-ounce) can white shoe
  peg corn, drained
1 (16-ounce) can French-cut
  string beans, drained
1/2 cup celery, chopped
1/2 cup onion, chopped
1 (2-ounce) jar pimientos,
  chopped

1/2 cup sour cream
1/2 cup sharp Cheddar
  cheese, grated
1 (10 3/4-ounce) can cream
  of celery soup
1/2 teaspoon salt
1/2 teaspoon pepper

TOPPING:

1 cup Ritz cracker crumbs
1/2 stick butter, melted

1/2 cup slivered almonds

Mix all ingredients except topping. Place in 1 1/2-quart casserole. Sprinkle topping over casserole. Bake at 350° for 45 minutes. Serves 8. May be frozen. Delicious! Give it a try.

Tea-Time at the Masters®

Scalloped Okra and Corn

Fresh, frozen or canned okra—whatever you have available.

1 (14 1/2-ounce) can cut
  okra, drained
4 tablespoons butter,
  divided
1 (15-ounce) can corn,
  drained

2 tablespoons flour
1 cup milk
1/2 pound sharp Cheddar
  cheese
1 cup dry bread crumbs

Stir-fry okra in 2 tablespoons butter for 10 minutes. Place in baking dish alternating layers with drained corn. Make a white sauce by melting remaining butter in a saucepan over low heat and blending in flour. Milk should be added all at once, cooking quickly and stirring constantly. Cheese is stirred in until blended. Pour this mixture over vegetables, and cover with crumbs topped with dots of butter. Bake at 350° for approximately 45 minutes until the casserole is heated through and the crumbs are brown. Yield: 6-8 servings.

Georgia On My Menu

Old-Time Fried Okra
Truly southern.

1/2 cup plain flour	1 quart okra, sliced
1/2 cup cornmeal	crosswise, 1/4-inch or less
1/2 teaspoon salt	1 egg, beaten
1/8 teaspoon pepper	1 cup shortening

Combine flour, cornmeal, salt and pepper; mix well.   In separate bowl, stir beaten egg into okra. Dredge in flour mixture. Heat shortening in large skillet until hot. Add okra and fry until brown and crisp.   Remove from pan and drain well on paper

Encore

Broccoli and Tomato Casserole

From Dr. Ann Smith of Georgia College, this recipe is often used in this cook's catering service.   She always has requests for this recipe.

3 tablespoons butter	1 tablespoon onion or lemon
2 tablespoons flour	juice
1 1/4 cups milk	1 1/2 pounds frozen broccoli
1 teaspoon salt	4 ripe tomatoes
1 cup grated cheese	1/2 pound bacon
(Cheddar)	

Make a cheese sauce of butter, flour, milk, salt, cheese and juice. Place broccoli, which has been cooked until tender, in bottom of casserole. Cover with sauce. Cut tomatoes in halves and place on top of sauce and broccoli. Place bacon on top. Bake until bacon is crisp.

Good Cookin'

The Greek word "Georgia" means agriculture.

Broccoli Casserole

2 packages frozen broccoli,
  thawed
1 can water chestnuts
1 jar Cheez Whiz

1 cup Minute rice
1 can celery soup
Grated cheese for topping

Mix first 5 ingredients together. Top with grated cheese.
Cook in 350° oven for 30 minutes.

Flatlanders Cook Book

Broccoli Puff

1 (10-ounce) package frozen
  broccoli
1 can cream of mushroom soup
1/2 cup grated sharp cheese
1/4 cup milk

1/4 cup mayonnaise
1 beaten egg
1/4 cup dry bread crumbs
1 tablespoon margarine

Cook broccoli according to package directions, omitting
salt. Drain well and place in a 1 1/2-quart baking dish.
Stir together soup and cheese. Gradually add milk, mayonnaise, and egg to soup mixture stirring until well
blended. Pour over broccoli and sprinkle with mixture of
bread crumbs and margarine. Bake at 350° for 45 minutes.

Head Table Cooks

Oriental Broccoli
(Microwave)

2 (10-ounce) packages
  frozen, chopped broccoli
1 stick butter/margarine
1 package dry onion soup mix
1 (8-ounce) can water
  chestnuts, drained and
  sliced

1 (8-ounce) can bamboo
  shoots, drained
3/4 cup Parmesan cheese

Cook broccoli in pierced packages on Full Power for 5-7 minutes. Do not defrost before cooking. Drain broccoli in a collander. Melt butter/margarine in a 2 1/2-quart glass dish for 45 seconds-1 minute on Full Power. Evenly stir in broccoli. Add onion soup mix, water chestnuts, bamboo shoots and Parmesan cheese. Stir until all ingredients are mixed together evenly. Cover tightly with plastic wrap, allowing a corner open for steam to escape. Cook 5 minutes on Full Power. Let stand 5 minutes before serving. Serves 4-6.

The Dapper Zapper

Spinach Pie Superb

1 (10-ounce) package frozen
  chopped spinach
1 (3-ounce) package cream
  cheese, softened
1 cup shredded sharp Cheddar
  cheese
5 eggs, slightly beaten
1/2 teaspoon salt
1/4 cup chopped green onion or
  1 tablespoon dehydrated onion

1/4 cup chopped parsley or 1
  1/2 teaspoon dehydrated
  parsley
1 unbaked (9-inch) pastry
  shell
1 tomato, thinly sliced
1/4 cup grated Parmesan
  cheese

Cook spinach according to directions on package. Drain well and squeeze to remove excess water; set aside. Combine cream cheese, Cheddar cheese, eggs, salt, onion, and parsley. Beat lightly with a fork. Stir in spinach and pour into pie shell. Arrange tomato slices on top and sprinkle with Parmesan cheese. Bake at 450° for 35 minutes or until set (depending on if oven gets too hot).

Windsor Academy Cookbook

Spinach Eléganté

2 tablespoons butter
1 shallot, finely chopped
1/8 to 1/4 teaspoon ground
  nutmeg
2 tablespoons flour

1 cup milk
1 1/2 pounds fresh spinach
  or 2 (10-ounce) packages
  frozen, chopped
1 teaspoon Pernod, optional

When using fresh spinach, make sure that there is about 1 1/2 pounds after trimming. After thoroughly washing and rinsing the spinach in lukewarm water a couple of times, place it in a saucepan, cover and place over high heat until it steams. Cover and cook over lower heat 3-5 minutes. The water clinging to the leaves will be sufficient. When it cools enough, chop the spinach and it's ready to use for this recipe.

Melt the butter and when it stops foaming, add the shallot, cooking until transparent. Add the nutmeg after this and then the flour. Stir. Add the milk slowly and stir constantly until it thickens. Add the spinach, stirring, and let it gently heat. Bless it with a splash of Pernod and serve. Yield: 4 servings.

Feast and Fellowship

Spinach Madeline
(Microwave)

This spinach dish would be nice used as a filling for tomatoes or whole onions (especially Vidalias).

2 (10-ounce) packages frozen
  chopped spinach
4 tablespoons
  butter/margarine
2 tablespoons flour
2 tablespoons chopped onion
1/2 cup evaporated milk
1/2 cup vegetable liquor
1/2 teaspoon pepper

3/4 teaspoon celery salt
3/4 teaspoon garlic salt
1 teaspoon Worcestershire
  sauce
6 ounces jalapeño or
  Monterey Jack cheese
1/2 cup toasted buttered
  bread crumbs

Cook frozen spinach in pierced packages for 5-7 minutes on Full Power. Press spinach in a collander to remove moisture, but reserve liquid (vegetable liquor). In large glass measuring cup, melt butter/margarine for 45 seconds on Full Power. Gradually stir in flour, then add onion and cook 2 minutes on 80% power. Add milk and vegetable liquor slowly, stirring until lumps are gone. Cook on Full Power for 3-4 minutes, stirring after 2 minutes, until sauce thickens. Add seasonings and cheese, stirring rapidly until cheese melts. Stir in drained spinach. Pour into small (6-inch square is nice) glass casserole. Top with buttered toasted bread crumbs, if desired, then reheat on Full Power for 2-3 minutes or until bubbly. Serves 4.

"There's a cute story about this recipe. A friend of mine who grew up 'in the North' was going to use this recipe for entertaining. She called one night and said she had been to two liquor stores to find 'vegetable liquor' and it was not available. Of course, 'Down South' we just call it 'pot likker,' but vegetable liquor is the same thing—any juice that remains after cooking a vegetable. My friend will never live this down!"

The Dapper Zapper

Spinach Ricotta Tart

1 (9 or 10-inch) pie shell
2 packages chopped spinach,
  cooked and drained
1 chopped onion
3 tablespoons margarine
1/2 teaspoon salt

1/4 teaspoon nutmeg
1 (15-ounce) carton ricotta
  cheese
1 cup cream
1/2 cup Parmesan cheese
3 eggs, beaten

Combine all ingredients in pie shell, sprinkle with more Parmesan cheese. Bake 350° 50 minutes or until set. Yield: 6 servings.

Cooking with Tradition

Asparagus in Sour Cream

2 pounds fresh asparagus
3 green onions and tops,
  chopped
1/2 teaspoon seasoned salt
1/4 teaspoon pepper
1 (8-ounce) carton sour
  cream

1/3 cup dry vermouth
1/3 cup grated Parmesan
  cheese
Seasoned bread crumbs

Snap off ends of asparagus and cook for 5 minutes in boiling water. Drain well. Blend remaining ingredients, except bread crumbs. Mix with cooked asparagus. Place in baking dish; sprinkle bread crumbs on top and bake at 400° for 15 minutes. Serves 4-6.

Little Bit Different!

Stuffed Carrots

12 medium carrots, scraped
1/2 cup cooked regular rice
1/2 cup dry bread crumbs
1/3 cup shredded Cheddar
 cheese
1/2 teaspoon salt
1/8 teaspoon pepper

1 teaspoon finely chopped
 onion
1 teaspoon finely chopped
 green pepper
1 tablespoon butter, melted
Chopped parsley (fresh)

Cut carrots 3 inches from tops; reserve smaller ends for another use. Cook carrots in small amount of water 20 minutes or until tender but firm. Let cool. Scoop out center of each carrot. Combine rice and next 7 ingredients. Toss to mix. Stuff carrots with mixture. Place in 13x9x2-inch baking dish. Cover and chill up to 24 hours. Remove from refrigerator; let stand 30 minutes. Bake uncovered at 350° for 15 minutes or until carrots are hot. Sprinkle with fresh chopped parsley. Garnish with carrot curl and parsley sprigs if desired.

Foresters' Favorite Foods

Callaway Gardens' Carrot Soufflé

3 pounds carrots (cooked and
  mashed)
1/3 cup butter
2 tablespoons flour
1 pinch salt
1/3 cup milk

2 eggs
Sugar to taste
Vanilla to taste
1/2 teaspoon cinnamon
1 pinch nutmeg

Blend mashed carrots, butter, salt, milk, sugar, cinnamon, and nutmeg. Add flour and blend until smooth. Fold in beaten eggs. Pour this mixture into a buttered baking dish. Place dish in oven. Bake at 350° for 30-40 minutes, or until browned evenly.

Country Cookin'

Cool Carrots

2 packages carrots, sliced
1 cup tomato soup, undiluted
1/2 cup cooking oil
3/4 cup vinegar
1 cup sugar

1 teaspoon dry mustard
1 teaspoon Worcestershire
Salt, pepper, garlic powder
  to taste

Cook carrots until tender. Make marinade sauce by combining other ingredients. Marinate carrots overnight. Can refrigerate a long time. Sauce can be used for barbecued chicken or other chilled vegetables.

Atlanta Natives' Favorite Recipes

Atlanta's Hartsfield International Airport is the largest in the world.

Carrot Mold with French Peas

A rich and delicious way to serve carrots. The cake-like texture of the mold eliminates the need to serve bread.

CARROT MOLD:

1 1/2 sticks butter, softened
1/2 cup brown sugar, firmly packed
2 eggs, separated
1 1/2 cups finely grated raw carrots (approximately 1/2 pound)

1 tablespoon cold water
1 tablespoon lemon juice
1 cup plain flour
1/2 teaspoon baking soda
1 teaspoon baking powder
1/2 teaspoon salt
Bread crumbs

Preheat oven to 350°. In mixer, cream butter and brown sugar. Add egg yolks and beat until thick. Add carrots, water, lemon juice, flour, soda, baking powder, and salt. Mix thoroughly.* Beat egg whites until stiff peaks form and fold into carrot mixture. Generously oil 1 1/2-quart ring mold and dust with bread crumbs. Turn mixture into mold. Bake for 45 minutes or until firm. Turn onto serving dish. Fill with French Peas.

*May be prepared ahead to this point.

FRENCH PEAS:

3 tablespoons butter
1/4 cup lettuce, finely chopped
1 box frozen green peas (top quality)
1/4 cup minced shallots or green onions

1 large sprig parsley
2 teaspoons sugar
1/2 teaspoon salt
Dash of white pepper

Melt butter in saucepan. Place lettuce on top of butter. Add remaining ingredients. Simmer covered 5-7 minutes, stirring occasionally until peas are tender. Remove parsley. Serves 4.

Puttin' on the Peachtree

Green Peas Atlanta
(Microwave)

1 (10-ounce) package frozen green peas	12 small fresh pearl onions (1 package of frozen pearl onions or 1 medium, finely chopped white onion will do if pearls are out of season)
3 tablespoons butter/margarine	
2 cups coarsely shredded lettuce	
1 tablespoon sugar	4 strips bacon, cooked and crumbled

Melt butter/margarine for 45 seconds on Full Power in glass measuring cup. Place lettuce, sugar, onions and peas in a 2-quart casserole. Cook bacon on bacon grill covered with a paper towel, for 3-4 minutes on Full Power or until crisp. Allow to cool, then crumble. Sprinkle over other ingredients in casserole. Pour melted butter/margarine over casserole, then toss ingredients until mixed evenly. Cover with plastic wrap and cook for 6-7 minutes on Full Power, stirring after 3 minutes. Serves 4-6.

The Dapper Zapper

Green Pea Casserole

2 (6-ounce) cans sliced
mushrooms (reserve juice)
2 sticks butter
1/2 teaspoon MSG
Dashes of Tabasco,
Worcestershire
4 medium onions, chopped
2 stalks celery, chopped

1 tablespoon flour
2 (10-ounce) packages frozen
early green peas, thawed
2 (8 1/2-ounce) cans water
chestnuts, thinly sliced
Salt and pepper to taste
4 ounces herb stuffing mix

Sauté mushrooms in 1/2 stick butter with MSG, Tabasco and Worcestershire. Set aside. In the same skillet, melt 1 1/2 sticks butter. Add onions and celery. Sauté until soft. Add mushroom juice and flour. Stir a few minutes. Add all ingredients except stuffing mix and season with salt and pepper. Pour into greased 2-quart casserole and cover with stuffing. Bake at 325° for 30 minutes. Serves 10-12.

Tea-Time at the Masters®

Crockpot Baked Beans

2 (12-ounce) cans pork and
beans
1/3 cup dehydrated onion
flakes
1/2 cup catsup

1/2 cup brown sugar
1 teaspoon cinnamon
1/2 teaspoon allspice
1/4 teaspoon ground cloves

Combine all the ingredients in a crockpot and mix well. Cook on high until bubbling hot. Then reduce heat to low and cook 3-6 hours, stirring occasionally.

Educated Taste

Atlantan Ted Turner's Cable News Network brings international news to the world from its CNN studios at the Omni. Public tours are conducted daily. Turner's yacht *Courageous* earned him the 1977 America's Cup.

Company French Bean Casserole

Freezes well!

2 packages French string
  beans, thawed
1 can water chestnuts,
  sliced
1 can bean sprouts, rinsed
  and drained
2 (4-ounce) cans sliced
  mushrooms, drained

1 medium chopped onion
4 tablespoons butter
4 tablespoons flour
2 cans cold milk
Grated American cheese
1 can French fried onion
  rings, crumbled

Place 1 package thawed beans evenly in a buttered casserole. Cover with combined chestnuts, bean sprouts, onions, and mushrooms. Spread second package of beans on top. Make cream sauce of butter, flour and milk. Add grated cheese to sauce and when slightly thickened, pour over vegetables. Bake at 350° for 40 minutes. Sprinkle French-fried onions on top and bake 10 more minutes.

Frederica Fare

Vidalia Soufflé
A great alternative to quiche.

6 ounces stale or day-old
  French or Italian loaf (cut
  into chunks)
1/2 cup butter or margarine
3 large sweet onions, cut
  into thin slices

1 tablespoon fresh thyme or
  1/2 teaspoon dried thyme
1 cup Swiss cheese, grated
1 pint light cream
3 eggs, beaten
Salt and pepper, to taste

Preheat oven to 350°. Place bread chunks in a 1 1/2-quart soufflé dish. Melt butter in a large skillet. Cook the onions until slightly limp, or translucent. Pour butter and onions over the bread. Scatter thyme and cheese over the top. Blend cream into eggs until mixture is light and frothy. Add salt and pepper if desired. Pour over mixture in soufflé dish. Press down to make sure bread is thoroughly soaked. Bake 45 minutes or until knife inserted in center comes out clean. Serve with a salad. Add ham or bacon for a different flavor, or more onions, if you like! Yield: 6-8 servings.

Georgia On My Menu

Onion Pie

1 pie crust, unbaked
3 tablespoons butter
3 medium onions, sliced
2 eggs
1/2 cup half-and-half

1 cup Cheddar cheese
2 tablespoons sour cream
4 strips bacon, fried and
    drained

Make sure to prick pie crust with a fork. Sauté onions in butter. Place in pie crust. Mix other ingredients together, excluding hot bacon, and place over onions. Cook at 350° for 30-35 minutes. Top with crumbled bacon and serve with cold fruit.

The Original Vidalia Onion Cookbook

Baked Onions

4 medium onions
1 tablespoon Worcestershire
    sauce
1 tablespoon butter
1/4 teaspoon salt

Dash of pepper
Dash of garlic salt, if
    desired
1 teaspoon cream cheese

Wash and clean onions; slit 4 times in top 1/8-1/4 inch. Add other ingredients and cook until tender in 350° oven 20-30 minutes. The ingredients in the above-mentioned recipe are to be added individually to each of the 4 medium onions.

The Original Vidalia Onion Cookbook

The Yellow Granex Type F Hybrid onion is also grown in other parts of the country. But when combined with the South Georgia climate and Vidalia area soil, the result is the wonderfully mild and succulent "sweet Vidalia onion."

Tomato Cheese Casserole

This recipe comes from Skip Caray, voice of the Atlanta Braves.

1/4 cup butter	1/2 teaspoon crumbled fresh
2 large onions, sliced	or dried whole basil
1 (6-ounce) package plain	1/2 teaspoon salt
croutons	3 cups grated Danish Havarti
6 large tomatoes, sliced	cheese

In skillet, heat butter; sauté onion for 5 minutes. Add croutons; sauté 3 minutes. In greased 3-quart casserole dish, layer half of crouton-onion mixture and half of tomato slices; sprinkle with 1/4 teaspoon basil, 1/4 teaspoon salt, and half of cheese. Repeat layers, ending with cheese. Bake at 350° for 40 minutes. Serves 6-8.

Peachtree Bouquet

Tomato Pie

12 slices bacon	1 (9-inch) deep-dish pastry
3 large tomatoes, seeded,	shell, baked
sliced (enough to fill	8 green onions, chopped
shell)	

Fry bacon; drain and crumble. Arrange tomato slices in pastry shell, place chopped onions and crumbled bacon on top. Add Topping. Bake at 350° for 30 minutes. Yield: 6 servings.

TOPPING:

1 1/2 cups grated extra	1 1/2 cups Hellman's
sharp Cheddar cheese	mayonnaise

Mix cheese and mayonnaise together. Spread topping evenly over top of pie. Yield: 3 cups.

Quail Country

Tomato Quiche

Bake pie crust in a quiche pan or large pie tin for 10 minutes at 400-425°.

3 good-sized tomatoes,
  peeled, seeded and chopped
1 medium onion, finely
  chopped
3 tablespoons butter
1 teaspoon salt

1/4 teaspoon thyme
1/2 pound natural Swiss
  cheese, diced
3 eggs, well beaten
1 cup half-and-half

Combine first 5 ingredients in a saucepan, and cook over medium heat until it is reduced by half. Place cheese on crust. Pour tomato mixture over the cheese. Mix eggs and cream, and pour over the tomato mixture. Bake for 10 minutes at 425°, then reduce to 375° for 35 minutes or until set. Let quiche rest for a few minutes before cutting. Serves 6-8.

Little Bit Different!

Broccoli Quiche

1 head fresh broccoli
4 ounces American cheese
4 ounces Swiss cheese
4 large eggs
1/4 teaspoon salt

1/4 teaspoon pepper
1/8 teaspoon nutmeg
1 pint half-and-half
1 teaspoon poupon mustard
1 pre-baked pastry shell

Cut flowerets from broccoli and steam till barely tender. Place broken pieces of American cheese on bottom of pastry shell, then broccoli, then Swiss cheese. Whip eggs, seasonings, mustard, and half-and-half and pour over broccoli and cheese. Bake at 350° till golden brown and set in middle, approximately 45 minutes. Serve warm with a homemade muffin and fresh fruit for a wonderful meal. From The Calico Cafe.

Somethin's Cookin' in the Mountains

Sweet Potato and Apple Bake

2 pounds sweet potatoes
1 1/2 pounds cooking apples
2/3 cup brown sugar
6 tablespoons butter or
  margarine

1/2 cup apple cider or juice
3 tablespoons maple syrup
1 tablespoon lemon juice
1 teaspoon cinnamon
1/2 teaspoon ginger

Cook potatoes in boiling water. Cool and peel. Cut into quarters. Core and peel apples; cut into thin slices. Place quartered sweet potatoes and apples in greased 2-quart casserole. Boil brown sugar, butter, cider, syrup, lemon juice, cinnamon, and ginger. Pour over sweet potatoes and apples. Bake at 350° for 25-30 minutes. Yield: 8 servings.

Potlucks & Petticoats

LaPrade's Sweet Potato Soufflé

3 tablespoons butter or
  margarine
3 cups fresh sweet potatoes,
  mashed
1 cup sugar

1/2 teaspoon salt
1/2 cup sweet milk
1 tablespoon orange
  flavoring
2 eggs

Melt the butter and mix with potatoes. Add sugar, salt, milk, and flavoring. Beat eggs and fold into potato mixture. Pour into greased baking dish; cover with Topping.

TOPPING:

1 cup brown sugar
1/3 cup flour
3 tablespoons butter or
  margarine, melted

1 cup pecan halves

Mix sugar and flour, sprinkle on soufflé; pour butter over top. Cover with pecan halves and bake at 350° for 35 minutes. From LaPrade's.

Somethin's Cookin' in the Mountains

Sweet Potato-Apricot Bake

3 sweet potatoes, peeled and
  sliced
3/4 cup brown sugar
1 1/2 tablespoons cornstarch
1/4 teaspoon salt
1/8 teaspoon cinnamon

1 teaspoon grated orange
  rind
2 tablespoons butter
1 (16-ounce) can apricot
  halves
1/2 cup pecan halves

Place sweet potatoes in greased baking dish. Combine next 5 ingredients in saucepan. Drain apricots, reserving liquid. Add enough water to apricot liquid to make 1 cup. Gradually stir into dry mixture. Cook until smooth and thickened. Add butter. Stir until it melts. Add apricot halves and pecans. Pour over sweet potatoes and bake at 375° for 50-55 minutes.

Educated Taste

Potatoes Roquefort

6 baking potatoes
1/2 cup Roquefort or bleu
  cheese
Heavy cream
Salt, to taste

Black pepper, freshly
  ground, to taste
1/3 cup dry bread crumbs
1 clove garlic, mashed
3 tablespoons butter, melted

Bake scrubbed potatoes in 350° oven 1 hour, or until easily pierced. Slice off tops. Scoop out pulp. Reserve shells. Mash potato pulp or press through ricer. Beat in cheese. Gradually beat in cream, until potato mixture is light and fluffy. Season with salt and pepper. Spoon potato mixture into reserved shells, heaping filling high. In bowl, mix bread crumbs, garlic, and butter. Sprinkle mixture over potatoes. Bake in 350° oven 20-25 minutes, or until brown and crusty.

Note: Can be prepared ahead and then baked.

Cooking in the New South

Gourmet Potatoes
(Microwave)

A good "do ahead" dish that needs warming only at last minute.

6 medium-sized potatoes
8 ounces shredded Cheddar
  cheese
1/2 cup butter
1 cup sour cream
1 teaspoon salt

1/2 teaspoon pepper
  (white preferred)
1/2 cup chopped green onion
  (tops included)
Paprika

Cook unpeeled potatoes for 18-20 minutes on HIGH. Cool slightly and slice. Melt 1/2 cup butter and add cheese, stirring to blend. Add sour cream, salt, pepper, and onions. Pour into 8x12-inch glass baking dish and cook uncovered for 6-8 minutes on HIGH. Saves 1 hour over conventional cooking. Serves 6-8.

Simply Scrumptious Microwaving

Potato Balls

Mix mashed potatoes with the yelk (yolk) of an egg; roll them into balls; flour them, or egg and bread-crumb them; and fry them in clean drippings, or brown them in a Dutch oven. The Cook's Oracle and Housekeeper's Manual (circa 1831).

Remarks: Use 1 yolk to 3 small potatoes. It may be preferable to flour them. Fry in a pan of hot oil until brown all over.

Tullie's Receipts

Peachtree Potato Balls

Men love these!

2 1/2 pounds baking
  potatoes, unpeeled, no
  substitutions
2 tablespoons butter,
  softened
2 egg yolks, beaten
1 1/2 teaspoons salt
1/2 teaspoon freshly ground
  pepper
1/8 teaspoon ground nutmeg

2 eggs
1 tablespoon water
1 tablespoon vegetable oil
1/2 cup fresh bread crumbs
1 tablespoon poppy seeds
1/2 cup all-purpose flour
1/2 cup coarsely ground
  almonds
Vegetable oil for deep
  frying

Cook potatoes in boiling water until soft, about 45 minutes. Peel potatoes when cool enough to handle. Force through ricer or sieve into large bowl. Beat in butter, egg yolks, salt, pepper, and nutmeg. Roll into 1-inch balls. Recipe can be prepared to this point, covered, and refrigerated; let stand at room temperature for 30 minutes before frying. In large bowl, beat eggs with water and oil. In medium bowl, combine bread crumbs and poppy seeds. Roll balls lightly in flour. Dip in egg mixture. Roll half the balls in bread crumb mixture and the other half in ground almonds. Let stand on waxed paper 10 minutes. Heat oil in deep fryer to 375°. Fry almond-coated balls 45 seconds, crumb coated balls 30 seconds; drain on paper towels. Potato balls can be kept warm in a 200° oven for up to 30 minutes. This is a different potato dish to serve with a meat entrée. Yield: 60 potato balls.

Peachtree Bouquet

Parmesan Potatoes

1/2 cup oil
1 teaspoon salt
1/2 teaspoon pepper

2 tablespoons Parmesan
  cheese
1/2 teaspoon garlic powder

Wash well and cut unpeeled potatoes into wedges lengthwise. Arrange in pan. Mix above ingredients and pour over potatoes. Bake at 375° for 45 minutes.

Ramblin' Chefs From Georgia Tech

Crusty Baked Potatoes

4 tablespoons butter	1 teaspoon salt
4 medium baking potatoes	1 teaspoon paprika
1 cup fine dry bread crumbs	

Preheat oven to 350°. Melt butter in saucepan. Wash and peel potatoes; pat dry. Mix bread crumbs, salt, and paprika together. Roll potatoes in butter; coat evenly with bread crumb mixture. Place potatoes in buttered 2-quart casserole. Cover and bake for 45-50 minutes. Remove cover; turn potatoes. Bake another 15-20 minutes, until potatoes are tender. Serve with butter and sour cream, if desired. Yield: 4 servings.

Guess Who's Coming to Dinner

Juanita's Macaroni and Cheese
(Microwave)

Like Grandmother used to make, and perhaps still does! Children love it.

1 cup macaroni, uncooked	1/2 cup milk
1/2 pound sharp cheese,	1/2 teaspoon salt
shredded	1/2 teaspoon black pepper
3 eggs	1/4 cup butter
1 (5.3-ounce) can evaporated	
milk or half-and-half	

Cook macaroni conventionally while preparing other ingredients. Shred cheese and blend eggs with milk, salt, and pepper. Layer macaroni in 9-inch casserole dish, alternating with cheese. Pour milk and egg mixture on top. Dot with butter. Microwave on HIGH for 5 minutes. Stir. Cook on 70% power 10-12 minutes, stirring once.

This dish is better if made the day before serving. The macaroni may absorb the milk. If the macaroni dish appears dry upon removing from refrigerator, add 1/4 cup milk before cooking. This dish can be browned conventionally, if desired.

Simply Scrumptious Microwaving

Red Rice

4 strips bacon (fried crisp)
2 medium onions
2 medium bell peppers
1 can tomatoes
1 cup tomato sauce or catsup

1/2 teaspoon Tabasco sauce
2 cups rice (cooked)
Salt and pepper to taste
1 teaspoon Parmesan cheese

Fry bacon, remove, and place on paper towel. Brown onion and bell pepper in drippings. Add tomatoes, sauce, Tabasco, rice, seasoning, and crumbled bacon. Pour in greased casserole, sprinkle top with Parmesan cheese, and bake at 325° for 30 minutes or until rice is dry enough to separate.

For shrimp rice, and other meat casseroles, add 1 pound of cooked deveined shrimp to red rice recipe or 1 cup cooked sausage, pork or ham.

Famous Recipes from Mrs. Wilkes' Boarding House

Savannah Red Rice

1/4 pound bacon
1/2 cup onion, chopped
1/2 cup celery, chopped
1/4 cup green pepper, seeded
 and chopped
2 cups rice, uncooked

2 (16-ounce) cans tomatoes,
 puréed
3 teaspoons salt
1/4 teaspoon pepper
1 teaspoon sugar
1/8 teaspoon Tabasco

In a large frying pan, fry bacon until crisp; remove from pan. Crumble and reserve. Sauté onions, celery, and green pepper in bacon grease until tender. Add rice, tomatoes, crumbled bacon, and seasonings. Cook on top of the stove for 10 minutes. Pour into large, greased casserole dish, cover tightly and bake at 350° for 1 hour. Serves 8.

Savannah Style

Nutted Rice Torta

3/4 cup long-grained rice, cooked
1 (10-ounce) package frozen chopped spinach, cooked
5 eggs
1 (15-ounce) carton ricotta cheese
1 cup grated Parmesan cheese
1 teaspoon salt
1/8 teaspoon pepper
2 tablespoons olive oil
1/4 cup bread crumbs
1/3 cup sliced almonds

After cooking spinach, drain well (press out as much water as possible). In a large bowl beat eggs slightly; reserve 3 tablespoons of the beaten egg. Add rice, spinach, ricotta, Parmesan, salt, and pepper to beaten egg. Stir well. Brush bottom and sides of a 13x9x2-inch baking pan with olive oil; sprinkle with bread crumbs. Spoon in egg, rice, spinach mix, leveling top. Brush top with reserved beaten egg; sprinkle with almonds. Bake at 350° for 30 minutes or until firm. Cut into 1 1/2-inch squares. Transfer to warm platter. Baked torta can be refrigerated for up to 4 day; reheat at 350° for 15 minutes.

Feast and Fellowship

Oven Rice

1 stalk celery
1 small onion
1/2 green pepper
1 carrot
1 1/2 cups uncooked rice
2 1/2 cups chicken broth
1 1/2 tablespoons butter
1/2 teaspoon salt
1/8 teaspoon garlic powder
Dash ground red pepper

Finely chop all vegetables. Combine all ingredients in a 2-quart deep baking dish, stirring well. Cover and bake at 350° for 1 hour. Serves 6.

Educated Taste

Summer Pasta

4 fresh tomatoes, peeled,
  seeded, and chopped
1 pound mozzarella cheese,
  diced
1/4 cup fresh minced basil
  or 2 tablespoons dry basil

1-2 cloves garlic, crushed
1 cup olive oil
Salt and pepper to taste
1 pound spaghetti, cooked
Grated Parmesan cheese

Combine all ingredients except the spaghetti. Let stand at room temperature. Toss with 1 pound hot cooked spaghetti. Serve immediately with grated Parmesan cheese. Serves 4-6.

Puttin' on the Peachtree

Fettucine Primavera

A modern updated recipe—wonderful with shrimp scampi.

1 cup broccoli florets
1 cup zucchini squash,
  sliced
1/2 cup green pepper, diced
1/2 cup onion, chopped
1/2 teaspoon dried basil
  leaves
3/4 cup margarine (1 1/2
  sticks)

2 fresh tomatoes, peeled and
  cut into wedges
1/2 cup mushrooms, sliced
1 teaspoon salt
1 (12-ounce) package
  fettucine noodles
Parmesan cheese, grated

In skillet, over medium-high heat, sauté broccoli, zucchini, green pepper, onion, and basil in margarine until tender. Stir in tomatoes, mushrooms, and salt and simmer 5-10 minutes. In the meantime, cook fettucine as directed on label; drain. Toss vegetable mixture with hot fettucine. Sprinkle with Parmesan cheese. Serves 5.

Note: Use diet margarine to cut calories.

Lasting Impressions

Ambrosia

1 fresh coconut or canned
  grated coconut
8 oranges
2 pounds Malaga or Tokay
  grapes

Pulp from 4 grapefruits
Sugar
8 grapefruit baskets, to
  serve

Open a fresh coconut by hitting hard with a hammer. Put halves into a hot oven a few minutes to loosen meat from shell. Cut off brown skin and grate the meat. (Or you can use canned coconut.) Peel 8 oranges (1 per person) and remove membrane, discarding core and seeds. Slice pulp lengthwise. Cut into halves 2 pounds Malaga or Tokay grapes and remove seeds. Mix with orange slices and grapefruit and blend in the grated coconut. Sprinkle with sugar and fill grapefruit baskets.

To make grapefruit baskets, cut 4 grapefruits in half, scoop out pulp, and discard seeds and membrane. (Use pulp for Ambrosia). Make your cups look festive by sticking (with toothpick) a sprig of holly or mistletoe on either side. Flute edges of cup with knife. Makes 8 baskets.

From Mother with Love

Spiced Peaches

4 cups sugar
2 cups cider vinegar
1 cup water
1 tablespoon whole allspice

1 tablespoon whole cloves
4 (3-inch) sticks cinnamon
4 pounds (16 medium) peaches

Mix sugar, vinegar, and water in 5-quart pan. Tie allspice and cloves in cheesecloth. Put this and cinnamon into mixture. Cover and boil 5 minutes. Peel peaches; drop into boiling syrup a few at a time. Simmer until tender, about 5 minutes. Pack in sterile jars. Cover with syrup. Seal. Yield: 2 quarts.

A Taste of Georgia

Apple-Cheese Casserole

1 can unsweetened apples
3/4 cup sugar
3/4 cup self-rising flour

8 ounces sharp Cheddar
cheese, grated
1 stick butter

Place apples with juice in dish. Mix sugar, flour, cheese, and butter that has been chopped in small pieces. Pour over apples and bake 30-35 minutes at 350°.

Traditionally Wesleyan

Ye Olde Coffee Shop's Pineapple Delight

2 (14-ounce) cans chunk
pineapple
6 tablespoons flour
1 cup sugar

2 cups grated sharp Cheddar
cheese
Ritz crackers
1 stick margarine

Drain the pineapple. Stir together the flour and sugar, then stir in the pineapple chunks and grated cheese. Put mixture into a casserole and crumble Ritz crackers over the top. Melt the margarine and drizzle it over the crumbs. Bake at 375° for 25-30 minutes. This hot fruit makes a perfect accompaniment to baked ham or other baked meat. Serves 8.

Georgia's Historic Restaurants

Pineapple Soufflé

Terrific with ham or pork.

4 slices white bread, crust
trimmed
2 teaspoons flour
Pinch of salt
1/2 cup sugar

3 eggs, beaten
1 (14-ounce) can crushed
pineapple
1 stick margarine

Break up bread into a greased 1 1/2-quart casserole. Add flour, salt, sugar, eggs, and pineapple. Mix well. Dot with margarine and bake at 350° for 45 minutes. Easy. Do ahead. Serves 6.

Culinary Classics

Meats

The Double Barreled Cannon, invented in 1863, is the only one of its kind in the world. The cannon failed to fulfill its mission of simultaneously firing two balls connected by a chain. Athens.

Frenchy Pecan Stuffed Meat Roll

1 1/2 pounds ground beef
1 1/2 teaspoons salt
1/2 teaspoon pepper
2 tablespoons grated onion

1/4 cup crumbled fried bacon
1 egg, slightly beaten
1 tablespoon milk

PECAN STUFFING:

1/4 cup French salad
  dressing
2 cups soft bread crumbs
1/2 cup chopped pecans
1/2 cup finely chopped
  celery

1/4 cup milk
2 tablespoons diced green
  pepper
1/2 teaspoon salt
1/4 teaspoon paprika

Combine all ingredients (except stuffing and French dressing). Mix thoroughly. Press mixture into a rectangle 1/2-inch thick on waxed paper or foil. Combine all stuffing ingredients except salad dressing. Mix together thoroughly and spoon evenly over meat. Roll up jelly-roll style. Place seam down in greased 8 1/2 x 4 1/2 x 2 1/2-inch loaf pan. Brush top with half of dressing once during baking. Bake in a 350° oven for 1 to 1 1/4 hours. Brush top of loaf with remaining half of French dressing. Serves 6.

Golden Isles Cuisine

Ionia's Meatloaf

1 1/2 pounds ground beef
1/2 cup bread crumbs
1/3 cup finely chopped
  celery
1/3 cup finely chopped onion
1/3 cup finely chopped bell
  pepper

1 egg
1 tablespoon tomato paste
1/3 cup catsup
3-4 tablespoons evaporated
  milk
1/2 teaspoon salt
Black pepper

Preheat oven to 350°. Combine all ingredients with hands and shape into a loaf. Place in a baking dish and top with Franklin's Sauce. Bake for 1 hour. "Pull from the oven and amaze your friends!!!" Serves 4-6.

CONTINUED

CONTINUED

FRANKLIN'S SAUCE:

2/3 cup catsup
1/3 cup firmly packed dark
  brown sugar

Mix together until sugar is dissolved and pour over meat-loaf.

The Pirates' House Cook Book

Rolled Meat Loaf
(Microwave)

1 (2 1/2-ounce) jar sliced
  mushrooms
1 1/2 pounds lean ground
  beef or chuck
1/2 cup dry bread crumbs
1 egg
2 teaspoons salt
1 1/2 teaspoons
  Worcestershire sauce

3 tablespoons onion, minced
1/3 teaspoon pepper
1 cup sharp grated Cheddar
  cheese
1/2 cup catsup or tomato
  sauce

In mixing bowl combine all ingredients except cheese and catsup. Mix until evenly combined. On a sheet of foil spread mixture in a 9x12-inch rectangle or until meat is about 1/2-inch thick. Sprinkle cheese over meat. Using foil, roll meat up in a roll, so that cheese is on inside of meat loaf.

Place in a 1 1/2-quart shallow baking dish. Spread top with tomato sauce or catsup. (It's best to cook on a bacon grill or meat rack.) Cook, uncovered, for 12-14 minutes on Full Power, rotating dish once during cooking time. Allow to stand 10 minutes before serving. Serves 4-6.

The Dapper Zapper

Meat Loaf

2 eggs	2 tablespoons soy sauce
2 pounds ground chuck	2 1/2 teaspoons salt
2 cups cornflakes (crushed)	1 tablespoon mustard
3/4 cup minced onion	1/4 cup milk
1/4 cup minced green pepper	1 can mushroom soup

Preheat oven to 400°. With fork, beat eggs slightly. Lightly mix in meat, crumbs, onions, and pepper. Combine with other ingredients. The secret is to mix well but lightly. Do not pack. In baking dish shape meat into oval loaf. Bake for 50 minutes at 350° or until done.

Famous Recipes from Mrs. Wilkes' Boarding House

Pizza Burger

1 pound ground meat	1/4 to 1/2 cup pizza sauce
1/2-1 teaspoon salt	4 slices mozzarella cheese

Combine the meat, salt and 1/2 of the pizza sauce. Mold into 4 patties and fry over medium heat for 5-6 minutes on each side. Just before burgers are done, top each with a spoonful of pizza sauce and a slice of cheese. Continue cooking until cheese melts.

Look Mom, I Can Cook

Extra Special Burgers

Hamburgers don't have to be ordinary. Dress them up with one of these stuffings or, for a group, make all 3 and let guests choose their favorite.

1 pound ground beef	3/4 cup grated Cheddar
1/4 teaspoon salt	cheese
1/4 teaspoon garlic salt	6 slices bacon, fried,
1/8 teaspoon pepper	drained, and crumbled
1 tablespoon soy sauce	1 tablespoon dried parsley
1 (2 1/2-ounce) jar mushroom	
stems and pieces, drained	

CONTINUED

CONTINUED

Thoroughly combine ground beef, salt, garlic salt, pepper, and soy sauce. Divide mixture into 8 equal patties (patties should be thin). Combine remaining ingredients; divide evenly atop 4 patties. Place another patty on top of each; seal edges (may be refrigerated at this point until ready to cook). Cook on grill or under broiler to desired doneness.

Variations: Reuben Burger—Combine 1 cup shredded Swiss cheese and 6 tablespoons well-drained sauerkraut. Use as burger stuffing instead of mushroom mixture.

Bleu Cheese Burgers—Combine 1/2 cup crumbled bleu cheese, 1/4 cup sour cream, and 1/4 cup drained sweet pickle cubes. Use as burger stuffing instead of mushroom mixture. Serves 4.

Perennials

Mezetti
(Microwave)

An all-time favorite! Try it and be prepared to have many more requests for this dish.

1 pound ground beef
1/4 cup green pepper, chopped
1 medium onion, finely chopped
1/4 cup celery, chopped
2 garlic cloves, minced
1 (8-ounce) package fine egg noodles
1-3 teaspoons chili powder (season to taste)

1/2 teaspoon paprika
1/2 teaspoon salt
1 (10-ounce) can tomato soup
1 (10-ounce) can mushroom soup
1 (4-ounce) can mushroom pieces, drained
1 cup water
3/4 cup Cheddar cheese, shredded

Place ground beef, green pepper, onion, celery, and garlic in water-soaked clay pot. Cover with water-soaked lid. Cook on HIGH for 6 minutes. Drain off excess liquid. Sprinkle noodles on meat mixture. Stir together in a bowl, chili powder, paprika, salt, tomato soup, mushroom soup, mushrooms, and water. Pour mixture over meat and noodles. Re-cover and microwave on HIGH for 10 minutes and on 50% power for 15-18 minutes or until noodles are cooked. Sprinkle cheese on top and cover. Let stand 5 minutes. Serves 6-8.

Simply Scrumptious Microwaving

Marie's Birds

1 (12-ounce) box large (jumbo) shells
1 pound ground pork
1 pound ground veal
1/2 pound ground beef
1 (8-ounce) package cream cheese

1 (10-ounce) package frozen spinach, chopped and cooked
1 egg, beaten
1/2 cup bread crumbs
Parmesan cheese
1 recipe of basic Sauce

CONTINUED

CONTINUED

Cook shells according to package directions. Mix well in a large bowl the pork, veal, ground beef, and cream cheese. Add spinach and mix; add egg and bread crumbs. Should be similar to the consistency of meat loaf. Put shells in colander and run cool water over them. In a large baking dish, 9x13-inch, put 2 large ladles of sauce to cover the bottom. Stuff each shell with meat mixture, making sure not to use too much. Place them seam side down in pan. When pan is full, ladle sauce over all and sprinkle lightly with Parmesan cheese. Bake at 350° for about 25 minutes. Serve with sauce and Parmesan cheese on the table.

Note: Leftover stuffing makes excellent stuffed green peppers.

SAUCE:

1 tablespoon olive oil
2 cloves garlic, minced
1 large onion, chopped
1 pound lean ground beef
2 (1-pound) cans tomatoes, cut up
1/4 teaspoon thyme
1/2 teaspoon oregano
2 tablespoons sweet basil
1/4 cup dry parsley flakes
2 cups seasoned vegetable juice
Salt and pepper to taste

Cover bottom of pan with olive oil, add garlic, and cook until oil bubbles. Add onion and cook until translucent. Add ground beef and brown. Add tomatoes, (drain off juice and put tomatoes in blender before adding to pan). Add vegetable juice and spices. Bring mixture to a boil and then cook or simmer for 2 1/2 hours.

Note: This is an excellent basic sauce for all Italian cooking. It freezes well.

Feast and Fellowship

Beer Chili

A hearty dish men love!

1 pound ground beef
Salt and pepper, to taste
1 (8-ounce) can tomato sauce
1 (6-ounce) can tomato paste
1 1/2 tablespoons chili
  powder

1 can beer
1 (8-ounce) package
  spaghetti
1 (15-ounce) can kidney
  beans

Brown meat. Add salt, pepper, tomato sauce, tomato paste, chili powder, and beer. Simmer. The longer it simmers, the better. Add more chili powder if desired. Boil spaghetti and drain. Add kidney beans and spaghetti to chili mixture just before serving. Easy. Do ahead. Serves 6.

Culinary Classics

My Spaghetti

1 (#2) can tomatoes
1 can water
1 bell pepper, chopped
1 onion, chopped
Several stalks of celery,
  chopped
1 garlic button, chopped
  Butter
1/2-1 pound round steak,
  ground

1 tablespoon chili powder
1 box spaghetti
Salt
2 tablespoons cornstarch
1/2 cup water
Chopped onions
Grated Parmesan cheese

Put tomatoes and water on to heat in large boiler. Chop bell pepper, onion, celery, and garlic, and put into tomatoes. Brown in butter in skillet ground round steak. Add to tomatoes with chili powder and let simmer a long, long time, until sauce is thick and dark. Add more water if it cooks down too thick.

CONTINUED

CONTINUED

Thirty minutes before supper, drop spaghetti into boiling water, salted, and cook until tender. Drain and pile on platter. Bind sauce with cornstarch rubbed smooth in water. When thick, pour over spaghetti on platter. Sprinkle chopped onions over this and add a heavy coating of grated Parmesan cheese. If this sauce is made the day before, it is better, but if made early in the morning, it is very good. The trick is to let it cook until it gets dark red and pulpy before serving. Serves 4-6.

From Mother with Love

Onion and Potato Casserole

2 pounds lean ground beef
2 tablespoons salt
4 tablespoons fat
6 large white potatoes

6 large Vidalia onions,
  sliced
2 cans condensed mushroom
  soup

Season meat and brown in hot fat. Peel and slice potatoes, thinly. Make alternate layers of potatoes, onions, and meat. Pour mushroom soup on top and bake at 350° for 45 minutes.

The Original Vidalia Onion Cookbook

Mother's Stuffed Cabbage Rolls

3 pounds ground chuck
2 teaspoons salt
3/4 teaspoon pepper
2 teaspoons celery salt
1/2 cup catsup
2 eggs
1/2 cup crushed unsalted
   crackers

2 heads (2-pound size) green
   cabbage
6 quarts boiling water
3 cups chopped onion
2 bottles chili sauce (2
   cups)
1 (12-ounce) jar grape jelly

In large bowl, combine chuck, salt, pepper, celery salt, catsup, eggs, and crushed crackers. Mix with hands just until mixture is well combined. Cut out and discard hard center core of cabbage. Place cabbage in large kettle. Pour boiling water over it; let stand until leaves are flexible and can be removed easily from the head—about 5 minutes. (If necessary, return cabbage to hot water to soften inner leaves.)

Preheat oven to 375°. Using a 1/4 cup measure, scoop up a scant 1/4 cup meat mixture. With hands, form into rolls 3 inches long and 1 inch wide, making about 28 rolls in all. Place each meat roll on a drained cabbage leaf; fold top of leaf over meat, then fold sides, and roll up into an oblong. Continue rolling remaining meat rolls and cabbage leaves. In bottom of lightly greased 12 x 11 1/2 x 2 1/4-inch roasting pan, spread chopped onion evenly. Arrange cabbage rolls in neat rows on top of onion.

In 2-quart saucepan, combine chili sauce and grape jelly with 1/4 cup water; heat over medium heat, stirring to melt jelly. Pour over cabbage rolls. Cover pan tightly with foil. Bake 2 hours. Remove foil; brush rolls with sauce; bake uncovered, 40 minutes longer, or until sauce is thick and syrupy and cabbage rolls are glazed. Serve with sauce spooned over rolls. Makes 28 cabbage rolls, 14 servings.

Atlanta's Pet Recipes

Corned Beef and Cabbage
Maiteoil Shaillte le Cabaiste

Since the Irish are famous for their corned beef and cabbage, this could not be considered an Irish cookbook without including this much loved recipe which is as popular today as it was many long years ago. Corned beef is a piece of meat which varies a great deal in quality with the grade of the meat, the cut, and the method of curing. The salt petre in the curing liquid gives the meat a red colour.

4 pounds corned beef
6 potatoes
6 carrots
6 small whole onions

1 small turnip cut in small
  pieces
1 head of cabbage
Pepper to taste

Put meat in a pot and cover with cold water, heat to boiling point, skim, and reduce the heat. Simmer for about 3 hours or until tender. One hour before cooking is completed add the potatoes, carrots, onions, and turnip. Half an hour later add the cabbage cut in wedges. Serve the corned beef on a platter surrounded by the vegetables.

Cooklore and Recipes of Ireland

Deviled Short Ribs

4 pounds beef short ribs,
 lean
4 teaspoons brown sugar
1 1/2 teaspoons salt
1 teaspoon dry mustard
1/2 teaspoon ground ginger
1/8 teaspoon pepper

3/4 cup catsup
1/4 cup soy sauce
2 tablespoons lemon juice
1 cup water
1 bay leaf
1 onion, sliced
Flour (optional)

In a large skillet with a lid, brown short ribs on all sides. Pour off drippings. Cover tightly, and cook slowly for 1 1/2 hours, adding a little water if desired. Combine all remaining ingredients except flour, and add to ribs. Cover and simmer 1 hour longer, or until meat is tender, adding more liquid if necessary. Before serving, discard bay leaf and thicken gravy with a little flour if desired. This is also good cooked in a crockpot, and is even better reheated the next day.

Georgia Entertains

Ten-Minute Beef Stroganoff
(Microwave)

1 pound round steak
3 tablespoons butter
1 (3-ounce) can mushroom
 slices with liquid (or 2/3
 cup fresh mushrooms
 sautéed in 2 tablespoons
 butter)

1 envelope dry onion soup
 mix
1 cup dairy sour cream
2 tablespoons catsup
1/4 teaspoon garlic powder
2 tablespoons flour

Trim fat from meat. Cut meat diagonally across the grain in very thin strips. (It is easier to cut thinly if meat is slightly frozen first.) Melt butter for 45-60 seconds on HIGH. Add meat and cook for 3 minutes on HIGH. Add 2/3 cup water and mushrooms. Stir in soup mix and heat to boiling. Mix sour cream with flour, stirring to blend. Add hot mixture. Add catsup and garlic powder. Cook on 70% power until mixture thickens. Do not overcook or meat will be tough. Serve over rice or noodles. Serves 4-5.

Simply Scrumptious Microwaving

Pineapple Shortribs

4 pounds beef shortribs
1-2 teaspoons salt
1/4 teaspoon garlic powder
3 cups Johnny Harris
  barbecue sauce
  or your favorite
2 (13-ounce) cans pineapple
  tidbits (packed in own
  juice)

2 tablespoons liquid smoke
1/4 cup brown sugar (packed)
1 teaspoon lemon pepper or
  juice of 1/2 lemon plus
  cracked pepper

Have butcher cut the ribs in serving pieces. Brown on all sides, placing fat-side-down first, so no additional fat need be used. When ribs are browned, drain off and discard any fat in pan. Sprinkle meat with salt and garlic powder. Add water to barely cover, and heat to boiling. Cover and simmer 1 1/2 hours, just until meat is tender. Drain meat saving broth. Place ribs in shallow roasting pan. Combine remaining ingredients and pour over meat. Bake in moderate oven (350°) 1 1/2 hours, basting frequently. If sauce becomes too thick, add some of the broth. Makes 6-8 servings. Leftover broth may be used to cook vegetable soup.

Little Bit Different!

Chinese Pepper Steak
Delicious!

2 pounds round steak, 1 1/2
  inches thick
1/4 cup vegetable oil
1/2 teaspoon garlic salt
3 medium green peppers,
  seeded and thinly sliced

2 large onions, thinly
  sliced
1/4 cup soy sauce
1 (8-ounce) can tomato sauce
1/4 teaspoon sugar

Trim all fat from steak. Slice into 1/8-inch-thick slices. Heat oil in large skillet. Sprinkle meat with garlic salt and add meat slices to oil. Cook rapidly for 1 minute or until meat is light brown, stirring once or twice. Remove meat with slotted spoon. Add green peppers and onions to remaining oil in pan. Cook 2 minutes, stirring often. Add soy sauce, tomato sauce, and sugar. Simmer 3-4 minutes. Return meat. Cook 1 minute or until heated. Serve over rice. Yield: 6 servings.

A Taste of Georgia

Cold Stuffed Tenderloin
Elegant summer entrée!

1 stalk celery, chopped
1 carrot, chopped
1 medium onion, chopped
2 tablespoons butter
Whole beef tenderloin
2 tablespoons butter
Freshly ground pepper
1/2 pound bacon, cut into
  1/4-inch cubes

1 tablespoons olive oil
2 or more cloves garlic,
  pressed
1 cup sour cream
1 1/2 tablespoons reserved
  pan juice
1 tablespoon grated onion
1 tablespoon chopped chives
White pepper

Preheat oven to 450°. Combine celery, carrot, onion, and 2 tablespoons butter. Sauté in bottom of roasting pan until soft. Leave this in pan. Remove fat membrane from meat and place meat on roasting pan with ends tucked under. Rub with 2 tablespoons butter and sprinkle with freshly ground pepper. Roast until desired doneness is reached with meat thermometer. Reserve 1 1/2 tablespoons of strained pan juice. Cool meat completely in refrigerator.

CONTINUED

CONTINUED

Fry bacon in oil with garlic until crisp. Drain. Combine sour cream, reserved pan juice, onion, and chives. Add bacon, salt, and white pepper to taste. About 2 hours before serving, remove a wedge the length of the tenderloin from top of tenderloin. Wedge should be 2 inches wide and 1 inch deep. Fill cavity with sour cream mixture and trim meat from wedge into 3/4-inch squares. Reassemble in a checkerboard pattern on top of tenderloin. Keep refrigerated until 20 minutes before serving. Slice 1 1/2 inches thick. Serves 8-12.

Temptations

Tenderloin Florentine

5 pounds tenderloin of beef
4 pounds fresh spinach,
 cooked about 5 minutes
2 onions, chopped
1 tablespoon finely minced
 garlic

4 cups cooked rice
3 cups Parmesan cheese
2 tablespoons fresh basil
Fresh ground pepper

Stir last 7 ingredients together, mixing well. Stuff inside butterfly fillet of tenderloin and secure with string or sew seam together. Rub entire tenderloin with butter and place seam-side-down on grill (on low, if gas). Bake for 30-45 minutes.

Note: Boneless turkey breast may be substituted. Cook for 3-4 hours in 350° oven.

The Holiday Hostess

Six Flags over Georgia, a 331-acre theme park near Atlanta, offers visitors over 100 rides, shows, and attractions.

After Opera Special

1/2 pound beef, chopped in
  small cubes (any tender cut)
2 tablespoons butter
1 (16-ounce) can artichoke
  hearts, thinly sliced
1 pint sour cream

1/2 cup dry white wine
1 tablespoon grated Parmesan
  cheese
English muffins or toast
  points
Paprika to garnish

Brown beef in butter. Stir in artichoke hearts, sour cream, white wine, and Parmesan cheese. Cook until well blended and heated thoroughly. Serve on English muffins or toast points. Sprinkle with paprika. Yield: 4 servings.

Bear in Mind: Good as a late night supper or appetizer.

Unbearably Good!

Beef Fillets in Flaky Pastry

1 tablespoon butter
6 small beef fillets (3 or 4
  ounces each) cut 1-inch and
  trimmed of fat - (I have the
  butcher cut them from the
  small ends of fillets)
10 tablespoons madeira or
  sherry

1 1/2 pounds mushrooms,
  minced
1 (10-ounce) package frozen
  patty shells, thawed
Salt
Bearnaise Cream Sauce

Melt butter in wide frying pan over highest heat, and sear steaks on each side just to give brown color. Pour in 2 tablespoons of the wine; transfer steaks to another container and chill thoroughly. To frying pan add the remaining wine and the mushrooms, and cook over medium heat, stirring, until all the liquid has evaporated. Chill mixture. Roll out the thawed pastry, 1 at a time on a lightly floured board to make a circle about 8 inches in diameter. (It doesn't matter which side of the pastry is up.)

CONTINUED

CONTINUED

Divide mushroom mixture into 6 parts. Now take 1 of the 6 parts and divide it in half. Put one of those halves in the center of a rolled-out pastry. Set 1 of the cold steaks on top, salt lightly, and put the remaining half of mushrooms on top of the steak. Fold pastry over steak to enclose, and place folded-side-down on a rimmed baking sheet. Repeat to wrap each steak. Cover steaks and refrigerate overnight. DO NOT remove from the refrigerator until the minute you plan to put the steaks into the oven (very important).

Bake in 475° oven for a total of 13 minutes. For the first 10 minutes put the baking sheet on the lowest rack in the oven, then move it to the highest rack for the last 3 minutes. Serve at once, passing the Bearnaise Cream Sauce to spoon over each steak. Meat should be medium rare at the most. The idea is to brown the pastry as quickly as possible without overcooking the meat.

BEARNAISE CREAM SAUCE:

4 tablespoons minced onion	1/2 pound fresh mushrooms,
2 tablespoons wine vinegar	sliced
1/2-1 teaspoon tarragon	1 cup whipping cream
8 tablespoons butter	4 egg yolks

In a small saucepan, combine onion, wine vinegar, and tarragon. Boil over medium heat, stirring until liquid is evaporated. Add butter and mushrooms. Cook until mushrooms are lightly browned. Pour in whipping cream; bring to boiling. Stir in some of the hot mixture into egg yolks, then return to saucepan and cook briefly, stirring until thickened slightly. Sauce can be reheated if warmed gently, stirring over hot (not simmering) water. Can be made ahead and frozen, if desired.

Little Bit Different!

Beef Tips in Wine

Perfect "Open Hearth" recipe! Try it some cold winter Saturday in a black iron pot swung from a cooking crane in an open fireplace. A very successful recipe.

4 pounds sirloin tip, or eye
  of round, cubed
1 teaspoon salt
1 teaspoon coarse-grind
  black pepper
1/2 cup flour
1 clove garlic, crushed
3 medium onions, sliced thin
2 (4-ounce) cans sliced
  mushrooms, drained

1 cup chopped celery hearts
  with tops
1 teaspoon Worcestershire
  sauce
2 teaspoons tomato paste
1 (10-ounce) can beef broth
3 tablespoons flour
1/4 cup dry red wine
Buttered noodles

Toss beef cubes with salt, pepper, and 1/2 cup flour until thoroughly coated. Place in bottom of large slow cooker or iron pot. Add garlic, onions, mushrooms and celery. Stir Worcestershire and tomato paste into beef broth. Pour over meat and vegetables; mix together well. Cover and cook slowly 5-6 hours in fireplace, or 7-12 hours in slow cooker on low setting.

One hour before serving, turn cooker to high, or move pot to hotter place over fire. Make smooth paste of 3 tablespoons flour and wine. Stir into meat and vegetables; cook only until thickened. If using iron pot, empty immediately into covered soup tureen, as wine should not stand in iron. Serve over hot buttered noodles. Serves 8-10.

The Historic Roswell Cook Book

Gold was first discovered in the United States in the Georgia mountains near Dahlonega in 1828. A U.S. mint was established there and before it became inactive, processed millions of dollars worth of gold coins. Would-be prospectors can still pan and hunt for gold there and keep what they find.

Veal Parmigiana

Olive or salad oil
3 garlic cloves, finely
  minced
1 onion, minced
1 (16-ounce) can tomatoes
1 1/4 teaspoon salt
1/4 teaspoon pepper
1 (8-ounce) can tomato sauce
1/4 teaspoon thyme
1 egg

1/4 cup packaged dried bread
  crumbs
1/2 cup grated Parmesan
  cheese, divided
1 pound thin veal cutlets
  cut into 8 pieces—about
  4 1/2 by 2 inches
1/2 pound mozzarella or
  Muenster cheese

About 1 hour before serving sauté onion and garlic in 3 tablespoons of oil until golden. Add tomatoes, salt and pepper. Break tomatoes apart with spoon and simmer uncovered 10 minutes. Add tomato sauce and thyme and simmer uncovered 20 minutes more. Beat egg well with fork. Combine bread crumbs and 1/4 cup of the Parmesan cheese. Dip each piece of veal into egg, then into crumb mixture, and cook in 1 tablespoon of hot oil.

Sauté a few pieces at a time until golden brown on both sides. Arrange slices in 12x8x2-inch baking dish. Place thinly sliced mozzarella on top of veal pieces and spoon tomato mixture over. Sprinkle with 1/4 cup Parmesan. Bake, uncovered in a preheated 350° oven for 30 minutes or until fork tender. Yield: 4 generous servings.

Boarding House Reach

Greek Lamb with Egg-Lemon Sauce
Delicious and different.

2 pounds boneless lean lamb,
  cut into 1-inch cubes
3 tablespoons olive oil
2 large onions, thinly
  sliced, chopped fine
1 teaspoon salt
1/4 teaspoon pepper
1 clove garlic, minced

1/4 teaspoon dried dill weed
1 teaspoon fresh parsley,
  minced
1/2 cup water
1 package frozen artichoke
  hearts
4 egg yolks
1/4 cup fresh lemon juice

In heavy kettle brown lamb on all sides in 1/2 the olive oil; remove and set aside. Add remaining oil to kettle and sauté onions. Return meat to kettle. Add salt, pepper, garlic, dill weed, parsley, and water. Cover and simmer 50 minutes or until lamb is tender. Add artichokes and cook 10 minutes or until hearts are tender. Meanwhile, beat egg yolks until light and fluffy and slowly beat in lemon juice. Gradually beat in 2 tablespoons of the liquid cooking with the lamb. Gradually stir egg sauce into finished lamb dish, remove from heat. Cover and let stand 5 minutes before serving. Serve with rice. Yield: 6 servings.

Cooking with Tradition

Lamb Shanks in Red Wine

3 slices bacon
4 lamb shanks
Flour
Salt
Pepper
1 (1-pound) can tomatoes
1 cup chopped celery
1/2 cup chopped parsley
2 medium-sized onions,
  chopped

1 clove garlic, chopped
1 teaspoon Worcestershire
  sauce
1 tablespoon grated
  horseradish
1 cup dry red wine
1/2 pound fresh mushrooms

CONTINUED

CONTINUED

Render 3 slices of bacon, diced, and remove bacon. Coat 4 lamb shanks thickly with seasoned flour. Brown slowly in bacon fat, turning until nicely browned. Use a deep iron kettle, Dutch oven. When shanks are browned, add tomatoes, bacon bits, celery, parsley, onions, garlic, Worcestershire sauce, horseradish, and wine (Burgundy is preferred). Cover and simmer for 2 hours. Add mushrooms, separating stems from tops and, if large, halve or quarter them. Cook for 1/2 to 3/4 hour longer. If gravy has not thickened, just before serving, add flour paste (flour and small amount of water). Yield: 4 servings.

Quail Country

Pork Loin with Red Plum Sauce

5-8 pound pork loin
Garlic salt
Onion salt
2 tablespoons butter
3/4 cup chopped onion
1 cup red plum preserves
1/2 cup brown sugar, packed

2/3 cup water
2 tablespoons lemon juice
1/3 cup chili sauce
1/4 cup soy sauce
2 teaspoons prepared mustard
3 drops Tabasco

Prepeat oven to 325°. Sprinkle pork generously with garlic and onion salts; place fat-side-up in roasting pan. Roast at 325°, 25 minutes per pound. If you prefer, place roast on rack and add water to roasting pan. Melt butter, add onion, and cook until tender. Add remaining ingredients, simmer 15 minutes. Pour fat off pork; pour about half the sauce over meat. Cook about 20-30 minutes longer, basting often. Serve extra sauce on side. Yield: 4-6 servings.

Quail Country

Marinated Pork

Great for dinner at Chastain Park!

3 pounds pork tenderloin
2/3 cup soy sauce
2/3 cup brown sugar
2 tablespoons cornstarch
3 cloves minced garlic

2 tablespoons vinegar
2 teaspoons ground ginger
1/3 cup finely chopped
  candied or crystallized
  ginger

Trim tenderloins, place in a large enameled or glass baking dish. Combine all ingredients and pour over meat. Marinate 6-8 hours or overnight. Remove from marinade, boil marinade, and simmer 3-5 minutes. Bake meat in a preheated 350° oven, 30-45 minutes. Remove meat from pan and let cool. Slice meat into 1/4-inch slices and arrange in a small baking dish. Pour marinade over and refrigerate 4-6 hours before servng. Wine suggestion: Zeller Schwarze Katz. Yield: 6-8 servings.

Georgia On My Menu

Apple Brandy Pork Chops

4 tablespoons vegetable oil
4 loin chops, 1-inch thick
1/4 teaspoon pepper
1/4 teaspoon ground cinnamon
1 pound fresh mushrooms,
  sliced

4 medium onions, quartered
1/2 cup apple brandy or
  unfiltered apple juice
1/2 cup cream
Minced parsley

In a heavy skillet, heat oil over medium heat; add chops and brown both sides. Add pepper, cinnamon, mushrooms, and onions. Cook 15 minutes, turning chops occasionally. Remove chops, onions, and mushrooms to platter; keep warm. Add brandy (or juice) to skillet; scrape meat bits from bottom. Gradually add cream to pan; cook until slightly thickened. Pour sauce over pork and vegetables. Sprinkle with parsley. Yield: 4 servings.

The Market Place

Pork Chops, En Casserole

6 pork chops, cut 1/2-inch
  thick
1/2 cup flour
Salt and pepper
2 tablespoons fat
1 can mushrooms, drained

1 bay leaf
2 tablespoons lemon juice
1 tablespoon Worcestershire
1/2 cup water
1 teaspoon paprika

Flour pork chops and sprinkle with salt and pepper; brown lightly in 2 tablespoons fat which has been pre-heated in skillet. Place pork chops in casserole. Add remaining ingredients to the drippings in skillet, stirring to remove crusty bits from bottom of pan. Pour over chops. Cover and bake 1 hour at 350°.

Foresters' Favorite Foods

Atlanta Baked Ham

1 (7-pound) half or whole
  ham
2 tablespoons prepared
  mustard
1/3 cup firmly packed brown
  sugar

2 tablespoons peanut butter
1 teaspoon horseradish
18 to 20 whole cloves
1/2 cup Coca-Cola

Preheat oven to 325°. Bake ham 25 minutes per pound for a half ham, or slightly less for a whole ham. Combine mustard, brown sugar, peanut butter, and horseradish, mixing well. Set aside. When about 45 minutes baking time remains, remove ham from oven. Trim off rind and fat; pour excess fat from pan. Stud top of ham with cloves, and spread with mustard sauce. Pour Coca-Cola in pan and return to oven, basting ham several times with pan juices. Easy, can prepare ahead, can freeze. Preparation time 20 minutes. Serves 8-10.

Atlanta Cooknotes

Glazed Ham Loaf

1 cup bread crumbs	1 1/2 pounds ground fresh
1 cup milk	pork
1 pound ground smoked ham	2 egg, slightly beaten

Soak bread crumbs in milk for 15-20 minutes. Mix ham and pork together and combine with eggs, milk, and bread crumbs. Mix well. Shape into a loaf and place in pan. Bake at 325° for 1 1/2 hours.

SAUCE FOR GLAZING:

1 cup brown sugar	2 tablespoons mustard
1/2 cup vinegar	

Mix together and heat, basting loaf about every 15 minutes while it is cooking. Place pineapple slices on top of loaf after 30 minutes of cooking and cook another hour.

Head Table Cooks

Ham Pie—Mrs. Campbell

Equal quantities of light bread crumbs and cold ham fat and lean, 3 eggs, 3 spoonfuls of butter, some pepper, and enough sweet milk to make a batter. Bake in a deep dish. From handwritten receipt book (circa 1860).

1 cup chopped (very fine) ham	3 eggs
1/2 cup bread crumbs (or more)	1 teaspoon onion
1/4 cup milk	1 teaspoon dry mustard (optional)

Mix ham and bread crumbs and 1/4 cup milk. Beat eggs with a fork. Add milk and then all other ingredients.

Bake in a 1 1/2-quart casserole at 350° for 45 minutes. A teaspoon of onion and dry mustard will spice up this receipt a little. This is a very good brunch dish.

Tullie's Receipts

French Toasted Ham Sandwiches

12 slices firm textured
  white or rye bread
Mustard
6 thin slices cooked ham
6 thin slices Swiss cheese
6 slices chicken

2 eggs, slightly beaten
1/2 cup milk
1/2 teaspoon salt
Dash black pepper
3-4 tablespoons butter

Spread each slice of bread with mustard. Make 6 sandwiches, using 1 slice of ham, cheese, and chicken in each. Combine eggs, milk, salt, and pepper in a shallow dish. Dip each sandwich in egg mixture, turning to coat on both sides. Brown sandwiches in butter over low heat.
   Serves 6.

Little Bit Different!

German Sauerkraut Steamed In Beer
(With frankfurters in a bun)

8 slices bacon, cubed
1 large onion, sliced
2 (16-ounce) cans
  sauerkraut, drain only 1 can
7 ounces beer

8 cloves
5 bay leaves
1/2 teaspoon cracked pepper
1 pound frankfurters
10 buns

Spray pot with Pam. Sauté bacon until crispy. Take out bacon and sauté onion in bacon grease until transparent. Add sauerkraut, beer, and spices and bring to boil. Turn heat down, cover and simmer 1 hour. Add bacon, place frankfurters on top and heat about 5 minutes. Meantime, heat your bread.
   Note: In Germany, the sauerkraut is put in the bun first, then add the frankfurter and mustard on top and serve it with a glass of cold beer.

You Are The Boss in the Kitchen!

Flavored Butters for Meats

GREEN PEPPERCORN BUTTER:

1 1/2 tablespoons green
  peppercorns, drained (found
  in gourmet shops)
1 stick soft butter
1/8 cup dry white wine

1/2 tablespoon tarragon
Juice of 1/4 lemon or to
  taste
1/8 teaspoon salt or to
  taste

Blend all ingredients by hand. Store covered in refrigerator. Serve with chicken, duck, or broiled meats.

MUSTARD BUTTER:

1 stick soft butter
1-2 tablespoons Dijon
  mustard

2 tablespoons minced fresh
  parsley or mixed herbs

Blend all ingredients by hand, blender, or food processor. Store in refrigerator. Serve with kidneys, liver, steaks, broiled fish, or use to enrich sauces or soups.

TARRAGON BUTTER:

2-3 tablespoons fresh
  tarragon (dry if fresh is
  not available)

1 stick soft butter
1 tablespoon lemon juice

Blend all ingredients by hand, blender, or food processor. Store in refrigerator. Serve with broiled meats and fish or use to enrich sauces or soups.

Puttin' on the Peachtree

Rosy Chutney

A dish as delicious as it is beautiful in color, by a noted grower of roses in Savannah.

1 (3-inch) cinnamon stick,
  broken into pieces
2 tablespoons mustard seed
10 whole cloves
1 1/2 cups plain red wine
  vinegar
2 1/4 cups sugar
2 teaspoons salt

2 cups minced, unpeeled,
  seeded tart red apples
1 cup minced, peeled onion
1 cup minced, ribbed, and
  seeded sweet bell peppers
1 cup minced celery (no
  leaves)

CONTINUED

CONTINUED

Tie spices in a cheesecloth bag. Place in a large, at least 6-quart, saucepot. Add vinegar, sugar, and salt. Bring to a rolling boil. Lower heat and simmer while preparing remaining ingredients. Remove spice bag. Add minced ingredients all at once to spice mixture. Bring to a boil, lower heat, and simmer, stirring occasionally, until thick and clear—about 30 minutes. Do not allow to scorch. Cool. Refrigerate covered. Will keep indefinitely. Yield: 1 quart.

Georgia Entertains

Squash Pickles

8 cups sliced squash
2 cups sliced onion
1 tablespoon salt (not
iodized)
1 cup diced green pepper

2 cups cider vinegar
3 1/2 cups sugar
1 teaspoon celery seeds
1 teaspoon mustard seed

Combine squash and onion. Sprinkle with salt. Let stand 1 hour. Combine green pepper, vinegar, sugar, seeds. Mix. Bring to boil. Pack in jars.

Country Cupboard Cookbook

Cranberries Amaretto

2 ounces butter
1 pound fresh cranberries
2 cups sugar

1 lemon, grated peel, and
juice

Spray pot with Pam. Melt butter. Add cranberries, sugar, and lemon juice and cook until cranberries are tender. Remove from heat.

3 tablespoons lightly heaped
orange marmalade

1/3 cup amaretto liqueur

Add lemon peel, marmalade, and liqueur to above mixture. Stir well. Keeps in refrigerator several months.

Note: Serve hot or cold with pork or turkey. Or serve as a salad on bed of lettuce, with sour cream. Great with ice cream, too!

You Are The Boss in the Kitchen!

Poultry and Game

Quail hunting in Callaway Gardens—a year-round family resort with 2,500 acres of scenic drives, walking trails, display greenhouses, golf, tennis, fishing, horseback riding, and hunting. Pine Mountain.

Proposal Chicken

1 whole chicken breast
2 teaspoons chutney
1/2 cup white rum
1/2 cup bread crumbs
Salt and pepper to taste

1 tablespoon Parmesan cheese
1 teaspoon parsley, minced
2 tablespoons butter or
   margarine

Skin and bone a whole chicken breast and divide it in half (or buy filets of chicken breast). Put each piece between 2 sheets of waxed paper, and pound it until it is flattened evenly. Put 1 teaspoon of chutney in the middle of each piece, and roll it up, tucking the edges in, until it resembles a Chinese egg roll in shape. Pinch the edges closed. Roll the chicken in rum, and then in bread crumbs that have been seasoned with salt, pepper, grated cheese, and parsley. Sauté in melted butter to brown lightly on all sides, but do not overcook. Transfer to an oven-proof 1-quart baking/serving dish, and sprinkle some of the leftover bread crumbs on top, and drizzle with some of the extra rum around the edges. Seal dish tightly with foil, and bake at 325° for 25 minutes. Remove the foil, and bake an additional 5 minutes to crisp. Goes nicely with rissole potatoes, broccoli with hollandaise sauce, and a tossed salad. Lemon parfait makes a nice dessert. Yield: 2 servings.

I call it "Proposal Chicken" because this was what I prepared for Bill the first time I cooked dinner for him when we were dating. He proposed that night!

Potlucks & Petticoats

Chicken Hmmmmmm

4 half-breasts of chicken,
  boned
4 teaspoons parsley flakes
Garlic salt to taste

1/4 cup butter or margarine,
  melted
1 cup herb stuffing mix

Sprinkle breasts with parsley and garlic salt. Roll up and secure with a toothpick. Roll in butter, then dressing mix. Place in a heavily greased baking dish. Sprinkle remaining crumbs over chicken and moisten lightly with water. Bake at 325° for 30-40 minutes.

Simple, but elegant served alone or on a slice of ham.

Tea-Time at the Masters®

Cherry Blossom Chicken

8 half chicken breasts,
  skinned
4 tablespoons butter
1 cup chopped onion
4 small garlic cloves,
  minced
5 ounces chili sauce
1 (10-ounce) jar blackberry
  preserves

3/4 cup water
1/2 cup brown sugar
1/2 cup raisins
2 tablespoons Worcestershire
  sauce
1 (17-ounce) can dark,
  sweet, pitted cherries,
  drain juice and reserve
1/2 cup sherry

Brown chicken breasts in 2 tablespoons of butter in large skillet. Remove to 3-quart casserole. Sauté onions and garlic in remaining 2 tablespoons butter until tender. Remove onions and garlic from skillet, draining off butter, and put in casserole with chicken.

Mix chili sauce, preserves, water, brown sugar, raisins, and Worcestershire. Pour over chicken. Bake at 350° for 1 hour, basting occasionally. Add cherries. (If sauce appears to be getting too thick at this point, add a little cherry juice.) Bake 30 more minutes. Add sherry. Bake 15 more minutes. Remove chicken to plate. Thicken sauce, if necessary, with cornstarch and cherry juice.

Arrange chicken attractively over bed of white rice on platter. Garnish with parsley and maraschino cherries.

Cherries Galore

Elegant Chicken

4 whole boned chicken breasts	1 (10 3/4-ounce) can cream of mushroom soup
8 slices bacon	1/2 pint sour cream (1 cup)
4 ounces chipped beef	Almond slivers

Halve chicken breasts and wrap each half in a slice of bacon. Cover the bottom of a greased 8x12-inch baking dish with chipped beef. Arrange chicken on top of this. Blend soup and sour cream, and pour over chicken breasts. Sprinkle with almond slivers. Refrigerate at this point, if desired. Bake uncovered at 275° for 3 hours.

The gravy is good over rice. If this is too salty, scald the beef with boiling water, drain well, and line the dish. Serves 6-8.

The Stuffed Griffin

Chicken Parmesan

Great for that date.

4 boned chicken breast halves	1/2 cup grated Parmesan cheese
Salt and pepper	1/2 cup cracker crumbs
1/2 stick margarine, melted	

We buy chicken breasts and cut the bones and ribs out. It is a lot cheaper and not difficult to do, but you can buy boned breasts or you can leave the bones in. Season chicken with salt and pepper. Dip into melted margarine and then into a mixture of half-and-half Parmesan and crumbs. (We use seasoned crumbs—found with stuffing mix, croutons, etc., in a grocery store; comes in a shaker like the Parmesan cheese.) If using boned breast, roll breast up; place in a baking dish seam-side-down. Bake at 350° for 35-45 minutes. We serve these on top of a plate of yellow rice. Not only looks impressive—it tastes great. You can fix them ahead of time and put in refirgerator; 45 minutes to 1 hour before serving time, place in preheated oven.

The Bachelor's Cookbook

Exotic Mandarin Chicken

3 large whole chicken
  breasts
1/3 cup flour
Salt and pepper to taste
1/4 cup cooking oil
1/2 cup sliced onion
3/4 cup diagonally sliced
  celery
1 clove of garlic
1 can cream of mushroom soup

1/4 cup chicken broth
1 (5-ounce) can sliced
  mushrooms, drained
1 (6-ounce) can water
  chestnuts, drained
1 (7-ounce) package frozen
  pea pods, thawed
1 (11-ounce) can mandarin
  oranges, drained

Cut chicken breasts in half. Coat chicken with flour; sprinkle with salt and pepper. Brown in hot oil in skillet. Remove chicken from skillet. Add the onion, celery and garlic; cook until tender. Remove garlic. Blend in soup, broth, mushrooms, water chestnuts, pea pods and mandarin oranges. Return chicken to skillet and simmer until serving time.

Boarding House Reach

Chinese Walnut Chicken

1 1/2 cups walnut halves
1 small head Chinese cabbage
  or Romaine
3 stalks celery
6 tablespoons peanut or
  salad oil
1 large onion
1 (8 1/2-ounce) can bamboo
  shoots
1 (5-ounce) can water
  chestnuts
2 pounds chicken breasts
3 tablespoons soy sauce
2 tablespoons cornstarch
Salt to taste
3/4 teaspoon sugar
1/2 cup chicken broth

Place walnuts in small saucepan. Add cold water to cover. Bring to boil for 3 minutes. Drain. Wash and drain cabbage. Cut crosswise to make 2 cups shredded. Wash celery and cut in 1 1/2-inch pieces, then julienne strips. Remove bone and skin from chicken breasts and discard bone and skin. Cut chicken into strips. In large skillet heat 3 tablespoons oil. Sauté vegetables quickly until tender-crisp. Remove from skillet and set aside. Add walnuts to skillet; sauté until browned. Remove and add to vegetables.

In small bowl combine soy sauce, cornstarch, salt, sugar, and stir. Add remaining 3 tablespoons oil to skillet. Dip pieces of chicken into soy sauce mixture, then sauté in hot oil until tender. Add chicken broth. Cook, stirring constantly until broth comes to a boil. Add sautéed vegetables and walnuts and heat until hot. Serve with steamed rice. Serves 6.

Atlanta's Pet Recipes

Moo Goo Gai Pan
(Microwave)

A tasty chicken dish with an Oriental flair.

4 chicken breasts
2 tablespoons oil
3 ounces snow peas
1/2 cup mushrooms, thinly
  sliced
2 tablespoons green onions,
  thinly sliced
1/2 cup water chestnuts
1 cup water
2 teaspoons instant chicken
  granules
2 teaspoons cornstarch
2 tablespoons soy sauce
1/2 teaspoon ground ginger
1/8 teaspoon pepper

CONTINUED

CONTINUED

Skin and bone chicken and cut into bite-size pieces. Mix chicken and oil in glass casserole. Microwave on HIGH 8-10 minutes. Let stand covered 5 minutes. Add peas, mushrooms, green onion, and water chestnuts. Microwave on HIGH 4-5 minutes. Remove from microwave.

In glass bowl place water, chicken granules, cornstarch, soy sauce, and spices. Cook on HIGH 3 minutes or until thickened. Stir every minute. Pour over chicken and stir well. Serve with rice.

Simply Scrumptious Microwaving

Beall's Chicken Sweet & Hot

1 stick butter	1 cup orange juice
1/4 cup Worcestershire sauce	1 teaspoon powdered ginger
1 clove garlic, minced	3 dashes of Tabasco sauce
1/2 cup red currant jelly	8 chicken breasts, skinned
1 tablespoon Dijon mustard	and deboned

In a small saucepan over simmering heat, combine all ingredients except chicken. Stir until jelly is melted and sauce is smooth. Cool. Pour sauce over chicken and marinate in refrigerator for 3 hours. Place chicken and marinade in a broiler pan and cook 350°, about 8 or 9 inches below the broiler unit. Bake for about 45 minutes, turning and basting periodically. Serves 8.

Georgia's Historic Restaurants

Chicken and Shrimp Supreme

Prepare and let season several hours or overnight before baking.

5 chicken breasts
1 onion, cut in half
Few celery tops
1 stick margarine
8 tablespoons flour
2 cups milk
2 cups chicken broth
2 cups grated medium sharp
  Cheddar cheese
1/2 cup dry white wine
1 (8-ounce) can mushrooms,
  drained
1 can cream of chicken soup
2 egg yolks, beaten
Salt and pepper to taste
2 pounds cooked, cleaned,
  and deveined shrimp

Place chicken in pot with onion and celery tops. Add water to cover and salt to taste. Cook until chicken is tender. Cool and remove from bones, leaving meat in fairly large pieces. Strain broth and reserve 2 cups.

Melt margarine in saucepan over low heat and blend in flour. Cook a few minutes, stirring constantly, but do not brown. Remove from heat; add milk and chicken broth, stirring until smooth. If sauce becomes lumpy, strain through a sieve. Add cheese and cook, stirring until cheese melts. Add wine and mushrooms. Blend in chicken soup. Add some of hot mixture to egg yolks and then blend into sauce. Salt and pepper to taste. Fold chicken into sauce and pour into buttered 9x13-inch casserole. Refrigerate several hours or overnight. Let come to room temperature and bake at 350° for 30-40 minutes. During last 15 minutes, add shrimp, pushing them into chicken mixture. Serves 12.

The Historic Roswell Cook Book

Chicken Breast Moran

6 chicken breast halves,
  skinned and boned
1/2 cup all-purpose flour
Salt and pepper
3/4 cup unsalted butter,
  divided
1 cup sliced fresh mushrooms
3/4 cup dry white wine or
  Marsala wine
1/2 cup chicken broth
Juice of 1/2 lemon
1/2 cup grated mozzarella
  cheese
1/4 cup grated Parmesan
  cheese

CONTINUED

CONTINUED

Pound chicken breasts to 1/8-inch thickness between 2 sheets of waxed paper. Season flour with salt and pepper. Dredge chicken in flour. Cook chicken, several pieces at a time, in 2 tablespoons butter over medium heat 6-8 minutes, turning once. Butter should be added as more chicken is cooked. Reserve drippings.

Place chicken in greased 9x13-inch baking dish. Sauté mushrooms on top of chicken. Add wine and chicken broth to pan drippings. Scrape sides and bottom of skillet and simmer 10 minutes. Add lemon juice. Pour over chicken and mushrooms. Sprinkle cheeses on top. Bake at 450° for 10-12 minutes. Serve immediately. Yield: 4 servings.

Second Round, Tea-Time at the Masters®

Sassy Stuffed Chicken

1 medium onion, finely chopped	1 tablespoon mixed fresh oregano and basil
3 tablespoons butter	Pepper to taste
1 (10-ounce) package frozen chopped spinach, thawed and squeezed dry	Powdered nutmeg
	4 whole chicken breasts, skinned, boned, and halved
1 pound ricotta cheese	Paprika
1 egg, lightly beaten	1 lemon, thinly sliced
1/4 cup parsley, chopped	Fresh spinach leaves

Sauté onion in 1 tablespoon butter over medium heat until soft, about 10 minutes. Combine with spinach, cheese, egg, parsley, oregano, basil, pepper, and nutmeg. Mix well. Pound each chicken breast lightly to flatten. Trim away excess fat. Place approximately 2 tablespoons spinach-cheese filling on each chicken breast and roll up. Fasten with string or toothpicks. Place in 1 layer in a glass baking pan. Dust with paprika and dot with remaining butter. Bake at 350° for 30-35 minutes, or until golden brown. Garnish with lemon slices and serve on spinach leaves. Yield: 4 servings.

Potlucks & Petticoats

Tarragon Chicken with Angel Hair Pasta

6 boneless chicken breast
halves
3 tablespoons butter
2 cloves garlic, minced
1 teaspoon dried whole
tarragon, crumbled
1 cup heavy cream

3/4 cup grated Parmesan
cheese
1/4 teaspoon salt
1/2 cup dry white wine
1/4 teaspoon cayenne pepper
1 pound angel hair pasta,
cooked

Lightly pound chicken between pieces of waxed paper.
Sauté in butter over medium-high heat, about 1 minute on
each side. Add garlic, tarragon, cream, Parmesan cheese,
salt, wine, and cayenne pepper. Stir until blended; cook
over medium heat until chicken is done and sauce is
slightly reduced, about 15 minutes. Serve over angel hair
pasta. Serves 6.

Peachtree Bouquet

Chicken Divan (or Chicken Florentine)

6 chicken breast halves,
cooked, boned, and shredded
2 packages frozen chopped
broccoli (if making Divan)
2 packages frozen spinach
(if making Florentine)
2 cans cream of mushroom
soup
1 cup mayonnaise
1 (8-ounce) carton sour
cream

1 cup grated sharp Cheddar
cheese
1 tablespoon lemon juice
1 teaspoon curry powder
Salt and pepper to taste
White wine to taste
1/2 cup Parmesan cheese
1/2 cup soft bread crumbs

Cook and drain broccoli (or spinach if making Florentine).
Mix together soup, mayonnaise, sour cream, grated
cheese, lemon juice, curry powder, and salt and pepper.
Spread shredded chicken in bottom of 13x9-inch casserole dish. Cover with broccoli or spinach. Pour soup
mixture to which wine has been added over top of broccoli
or spinach. Combine Parmesan cheese and bread crumbs
and spinkle over top of casserole. Bake at 350° about 30
minutes. Serves 6-8.

Note: Freezes well.

Savannah Collection

Chicken Bake

So easy.

1 chicken, cut-up or 8-10
  pieces that you like
1 envelope dry onion soup
  mix

1 (8-ounce) bottle French
  salad dressing

Turn oven on to 350° to preheat. Put chicken pieces in flat-bottom baking dish or pan. Combine salad dressing and soup mix and pour over chicken pieces. Bake in oven uncovered for 1 1/2 hours.

Look Mom, I Can Cook

Chicken Spectacular

2 cups diced cooked chicken
2 cups French green beans,
  drained
1 cup cooked white rice
1 cup cooked wild rice
1/2 cup mayonnaise
1 can condensed cream of
  celery soup, undiluted

1/2 cup sliced water
  chestnuts
2 tablespoons chopped
  pimento
2 tablespoons chopped onion
1/4 teaspoon salt
Pepper to taste

Mix all ingredients; place in casserole. Cover with paprika and a few bread crumbs, if desired. Bake about 25 minutes at 350°.

This recipe can easily take a bit more chicken along with same portions as in recipe. Mixed rice with seasonings can also be substituted for wild rice.

Atlanta Natives' Favorite Recipes

Heavenly Chicken Casserole

Filled with such goodies as almonds, mushrooms and wild rice, and it serves 10.

1 (4-ounce) box wild rice	2 cups Cheddar cheese,
1/2 cup margarine (1 stick)	shredded
1/2 cup onion, chopped	4 cups cooked chicken, cut
1/2 cup green pepper,	into cubes
chopped	1 (4-ounce) jar chopped
1/2 cup celery, chopped	pimiento, drained
2 (10 3/4-ounce) cans cream	1 (4-ounce) can sliced
of mushroom soup	mushrooms, drained
1 cup sliced almonds,	Salt, adjust to taste
toasted	

Heat oven to 350°. Cook wild rice according to package directions until partially done; drain. Melt margarine in Dutch oven; add onions, green pepper, and celery. Cook until tender; remove from heat. Add soup, almonds, 1 1/2 cups cheese, chicken, pimiento, mushrooms, and cooked wild rice. Blend well and add salt, if necessary. Pour mixture into a greased 13x9-inch baking dish. Bake for 20 minutes; sprinkle remaining 1/2 cup cheese over top. Continue to bake for an additional 10-15 minutes or until hot and bubbly. Serves 10.

Lasting Impressions

Poached Chicken

1 small chicken, quartered	2 tablespoons minced onion
1/2 orange	1/2 teaspoon thyme
1 cup each of chopped	Salt and pepper
carrots and celery	

Rub the chicken with orange and place in a large saucepan. Barely cover with water. Add the vegetables and seasonings. Cover and simmer gently until tender, should be about 40-50 minutes. Remove the chicken and vegetables from the pan and reserve the stock. Keep vegetables warm.

CONTINUED

CONTINUED

SAUCE:

4 tablespoons butter
4 tablespoons flour
4 tablespoons cream

2 1/2 cups chicken stock
Chopped parsley

Now make the sauce. Melt butter in the pan and stir in the flour, cook for a few minutes, stirring constantly. Add the chicken stock and bring to the boil, stir, reduce the heat and simmer for about 15 minutes, stirring occasionally. Remove the skin from the chicken and cut into serving pieces. Put chicken pieces in sauce and heat gently for 10 minutes. Serve on a bed of hot rice, topped with reserved vegetables. Garnish with parsley.

Cooklore and Recipes of Ireland

Brunswick Stew

2 pounds pork or chicken
 (chopped)
1/2 teaspoon black pepper
1 teaspoon hot sauce
2 tablespoons Worcestershire
 sauce

1/3 cup drippings (pork or
 bacon)
1/2 cup barbecue sauce
1 1/2 cups catsup
2 cups diced potato (cooked)
3 (#2) cans cream-style corn

Place all ingredients in saucepan, cover and heat slowly. Salt and more hot sauce may be needed according to taste preferred. Makes about 2 quarts.

Famous Recipes from Mrs. Wilkes' Boarding House

 Coastal Brunswick is known as the "Shrimp Capital of the World."

Chicken and Dumplings

2 1/2 pounds chicken, disjointed and ready to cook	1 teaspoon salt and pepper

Cover with water in saucepan, sprinkle with one teaspoon salt and pepper. Boil over medium heat for 30 minutes. Pour off broth, use for dumplings.

DUMPLINGS:

2 cups all-purpose flour	1/2 cup water
1/2 cup milk	

Mix in bowl and knead into another bowl of flour until dough is firm. Mash flat on floured surface. Let stand about 10 minutes. Roll out with rolling pin until knife blade thin. Cut into 2-inch squares. Drop into boiling broth. Cook about 10 minutes on high heat. Reduce heat to low and return chicken to pot. Pour 1 1/2 cups milk into mixture and stir. Remove from heat. Add salt and pepper if needed.

Famous Recipes from Mrs. Wilkes' Boarding House

Frances Virginia Fried Chicken

2 pounds fryer, cut up

BREADING:

2 cups flour	1 tablespoon salt
5 tablespoons potato flour	

EGG WASH:

1 egg	1/2 cup water
1/2 cup undiluted evaporated milk	

Wash and dry chicken pieces. Combine Breading ingredients. Combine Egg Wash ingredients. Dip chicken in Breading. Shake off excess. Dip in Egg Wash. Dip in Breading again. Fry in deep fat. Serves 2.

Tea Room Notes: The Tea Room secret was potato flour in the Breading. It gives a beautiful, even, golden-brown crust. Potato flour may be obtained from bakery supply stores.

The Frances Virginia Tea Room Cookbook

Glazed Chicken en Brochette

Chicken kabobs with a deliciously different flavor. They can be grilled, broiled, or microwaved with equal success.

2 whole boneless skinless chicken breasts, halved	1/4 cup soy sauce
	2 tablespoons honey
1/4 pound medium mushrooms	1/2 teaspoon ground ginger
3 green onions, cut in 2-inch pieces	1/2 teaspoon salt
	1 clove garlic, minced
1/2 cup orange marmalade	1 (8-ounce) package bacon

Cut breast half into 5 pieces; place in bowl. Add all remaining ingredients except bacon; stir to coat well. Cook bacon just until limp; drain. Cut each bacon piece in half. Wrap each chicken chunk with 1 piece of bacon. Thread onto skewers in following order: chicken, mushrooms, and onions. Repeat to fill skewers. Pour remaining marinade into saucepan. Bring to boil over high heat; boil gently 6-8 minutes until slightly thickened and reduced by half. Place skewers on grill rack over medium coals (may also be done under broiler). Grill 15 minutes or until chicken is fork tender, brushing occasionally with sauce and turning.

Micronote: Prepare chicken, vegetables, and sauce as directed. Cook bacon on HIGH 1 minute. Fill wooden skewers as directed. Pour marinade into large glass measure; cook on HIGH 3 minutes. Place skewers on microwave rack or across shallow glass baking dish. Cover loosely with waxed paper. Cook on HIGH 10-14 minutes, until bacon is crisp and chicken test, done; turn skewers and brush with sauce every 2-3 minutes. Rearrange skewers after 6 minutes. Serves 4.

Perennials

Gainesville, called the Poultry Capitol of the World, has a city ordinance (just for fun) against eating their delicious local fried chicken with a knife and fork.

Barbecued Chicken

8 (3 1/2-ounce) chicken breasts	1 tablespoon Worcestershire sauce
1 cup low-sodium light catsup	2 tablespoon diet brown sugar
1/2 teaspoon lemon rind, grated	2 teaspoons paprika
1/4 cup lemon juice	1 teaspoon prepared mustard
1/4 cup cider vinegar	1 clove garlic, minced
	1/4 teaspoon pepper

Trim excess fat from chicken. Place in a baking dish set aside. Combine remaining ingredients in a small sauce-pan and bring to a boil. Cover, reduce heat, and simmer 20 minutes. Remove from heat and cool slightly. Pour barbecue sauce over chicken. Cover and marinate over-night, refrigerated, turning chicken occasionally. Remove chicken from sauce the next day, reserving sauce. Place chicken, bone-side-down on a grill over medium coals. Grill 45 minutes to 1 hour, turning and basting with sauce every 15 minutes. Serves 8.

Cal. per serving 163 - Pro. 23.8gm. - Carb. 8.5gm. - Fat 3.8gm. - Sod. 517.8mg.

Southwind Cuisine

Chinese Barbecued Chicken
(Microwave)

1/4 cup soy sauce	1/2 teaspoon ground ginger
1 tablespoon vegetable oil	1 garlic clove, minced
3 tablespoons brown sugar	2 1/2-3 pounds chicken, skin removed
1 teaspoon dry mustard	

Mix first 6 ingredients in 2-quart micro-safe dish. Add chicken and coat with sauce mixture. Let chicken mari-nate in sauce for at least 30 minutes. Microwave on HIGH 8-10 minutes. Turn chicken over and baste with sauce. Continue to cook 13-16 minutes on 70% power or until chicken is tender.

This recipe works well to cook in microwave and then finish on grill.

Simply Scrumptious Microwaving

Ritz Cracker Dressing

3 cups crumbled corn bread
1 large box Ritz crackers,
  crumbled
1 cup finely chopped onion
1 cup chopped celery
1 cup chopped bell pepper
6 cups chicken broth, or
  broth from hen or turkey

4 eggs, beaten
1 stick butter or margarine
Salt and pepper to taste
2 chicken breasts, chopped
  (optional)

Combine all ingredients and mix well. Bake for 45 minutes in hot oven 325-350°.

Flatlanders Cook Book

Hot Chicken Sandwich

1 3/4 cups diced cooked
  chicken
1/2 cup sliced pitted ripe
  olives
1/2 cup mayonnaise
4 slices bread

Butter
3 hard-cooked eggs, sliced
1 (10 3/4-ounce) can cream
  of chicken or cream of
  celery soup
1 cup sour cream

Combine chicken, olives, and mayonnaise. Trim crusts from bread; butter both sides. Place 2 slices bread in glass baking dish; spread with chicken mixture. Add egg slices. Top with remaining bread. Blend soup and sour cream. Pour over sandwiches. Bake at 350° for 25 minutes or until top is lightly browned. Serves 2.

Perennials

Chicken Waldorf Sandwiches

2 whole cooked chicken
  breasts
1 cup chopped apple
1/4 cup chopped celery
1/4 cup chopped pecans or
  walnuts
1 tablespoon minced onion

1/4 teaspoon dill leaves,
  crushed
1/4 cup mayonnaise
15 ounces brown bread
8 thin apple wedges
8 walnut or pecan halves

Cut chicken into bite-size pieces. Combine with apple, celery, nuts, onion, dill, and mayonnaise. Combine with apple, celery, nuts, onion, dill, and mayonnaise. Spoon chicken mixture on slices and broil until bubbly. Garnish with apple wedges and nut halves. Yields 2 open-face sandwiches per serving. Delicious served with assorted cheeses and deviled eggs.

Encore

Turkey à la King

3 tablespoons butter
2 tablespoons chopped green
  pepper
2 tablespoons chopped
  pimiento
3 tablespoons flour

1 can mushroom soup
1/4 teaspoon salt
1 tablespoon sweet relish
2 cups diced, cooked turkey
2 egg yolks
Patty shells or toast

Melt butter in saucepan and add green pepper and pimiento. Cook slowly until slightly brown. Add flour and blend well. Add mushroom soup, and salt and stir until thick. Add relish and turkey and heat thoroughly. Add the well-beaten egg yolks and continue cooking for only 2 or 3 minutes more. Serve in patty shells or on toast. Yield: 4 servings.

Boarding House Reach

Turkey and Broccoli Casserole

1 package frozen broccoli	1 teaspoon curry powder
2 cups chopped cooked turkey	1/2 cup shredded cheese
1 can cream of chicken soup	1/2 cup Ritz crackers,
1/2 cup mayonnaise	crumbled
1 teaspoon lemon juice	1/4 cup margarine

Cook broccoli, drain. Arrange in buttered 1 1/2-quart baking dish. Spread turkey on top. Mix soup (undiluted), mayonnaise, lemon juice, curry powder. Spread over turkey. Sprinkle cheese, then cracker crumbs on top. Dot with margarine. Bake in preheated oven 30 minutes at 350°.

Atlanta Natives' Favorite Recipes

Fried Pheasant
A never-to-be-forgotten treat!

Pheasant	1 teaspoon paprika
Milk	1/2 teaspoon onion salt
2 cups all-purpose flour	1/4 teaspoon cayenne pepper
1 teaspoon salt	Vegetable oil
1 teaspoon black pepper	

Remove skin from pheasant. Cut into quarters. Soak in milk for at least 6 hours and then thoroughly coat with flour and seasonings. Fry in hot vegetable oil (1-inch deep) until brown on 1 side; turn only once. Total frying time should be about 20 minutes. Make brown gravy from drippings in pan. Serve over rice. Yield: 2 servings.

A Taste of Georgia

Georgia was the first state to grant full property rights to women, and the first state to extend the right to vote to 18-year olds.

Cornish Hens with Chinese Glaze

4 Cornish hens (14-ounces each)
1 teaspoon salt
1 large onion, cut into large pieces
2 stalks celery, cut into 1-inch pieces

4 medium carrots, cut into 1/2-inch pieces
2 tablespoons butter or margarine, melted

Rub hens inside and out with salt and pepper. Stuff with vegetables. Place breast-side-up on rack in shallow pan; brush with butter or margarine. Roast uncovered at 350° for 30 minutes. Remove from oven, brush with glaze. Return to oven and roast another 30 minutes, or until tender. Baste occasionally.

CHINESE GLAZE:

1/2 cup dried apricots
1 1/2 teaspoons grated orange rind
1/4 cup orange juice
1 tablespoon light corn syrup

1 tablespoon vinegar
1 1/2 teaspoons soy sauce
Dash of ground ginger

Use prepared Chinese duck sauce or make your own as follows: Cook dried apricots as directed on package; drain. Press through wire strainer or food mill. Add grated orange rind, orange juice, corn syrup, vinegar, soy sauce, and ginger. Bring to boil, stirring often. Makes 4 servings.

Encore

Quail in Cream Sauce

1/2 cup butter
2 scallions, chopped
2 cloves garlic, crushed
3/4 cup celery, chopped
8 quail
1/2 cup boiling water

1 cup vermouth (or dry white wine)
4 tablespoons flour
2 cups half-and-half
Salt and black pepper, to taste

CONTINUED

CONTINUED

In heavy skillet with tight-fitting lid, melt 1/4 cup butter. Add scallions, garlic, and celery, then birds. Sauté birds on both sides until lightly brown. Add 1/2 cup boiling water and vermouth. Cover and simmer on low for 1/2 hour.

Remove birds to platter, remove and reserve remaining liquid. Add 1/4 cup butter and flour. Stir and simmer for 5 minutes. Slowly add reserved liquid, the half-and-half, stirring constantly until thick. Season with salt and pepper. Return birds and simmer 10-15 minutes on low, turning once. Serve on bed of wild rice, pouring sauce over all. Serves 4.

Savannah Style

Quail with Cherries

8 quail
1/2 cup butter
1/2 cup warm brandy
1/2 cup melted currant jelly
1/2 cup warm port

1/2 orange rind, slivered
Juice of 1/2 lemon
1 cup pitted bing cherries
1/2 teaspoon cinnamon
1/2 teaspoon powdered cloves

Truss the legs of 8 quail close to the bodies and rub the birds with a little salt. In a large skillet, brown the quail carefully in butter over medium heat for 15-20 minutes, turning and basting them constantly. Cover the pan and roast the quail in a moderate oven, 350°, for 8-10 minutes. Remove the birds and keep them hot.

Pour any remaining butter out of the pan. Add 1/2 cup warm brandy, flame it, and deglaze the pan, scraping all the brown crustiness from the sides and bottom. Add 1/2 cup melted currant jelly, warm port, and the orange rind. Return the quail to the pan and simmer for 5-10 minutes, depending on their size. Add the lemon juice, salt, and pepper to taste.

Just before serving, add 1 cup preserved pitted bing cherries that have been heated in their own juice with the cinnamon and cloves. Add enough of the juice to make about 1 1/2 cups sauce. Serve with buttered wild rice. Serves 4.

Cherries Galore

Smothered Doves

10-12 doves	**1 onion, chopped**
Salt and pepper	**3 tablespoons flour**
6 tablespoons butter or bacon drippings	**1 can chicken broth**

Season doves with salt and pepper. Brown in butter or bacon drippings and set aside. Brown onions in butter; set aside. Add flour to butter in skillet and stir well. Slowly add chicken broth, salt, and pepper. Place birds and onions in casserole and add sauce. Cover casserole and bake 350° for 1 hour. Yield: 6 servings.

Quail Country

Lake Iamonia Pilau and Duck

4 ducks	**2-3 large stalks celery,**
Dry red wine, optional	**chopped**
4 strips bacon	**Salt and pepper to taste**
3 large onions, cut up	**2 cups rice**

Filet breasts from cleaned duck. Remove skin by placing breast skin-down on cutting board and running sharp thin knife between skin and meat while holding end of skin down. Salt and pepper breast halves, and for an added flourish, inject dry red wine at various points with hypodermic needle. Roll breast halves and wrap each with 1/2 piece of bacon. Secure with toothpicks. Refrigerate while preparing pilau. Take remainder of duck, add water to almost cover and boil. Add salt, pepper, onions, and celery. Cook until meat begins to fall from the bones (2-3 hours).

Measure out 3 cups stock, adding water if necessary. (It is better to let the stock cook down and add water rather than have too much stock and not be able to use it all.) Combine meat from carcass, onions, celery, and stock with rice. Cook until done. When rice is nearly ready take prepared duck breast and cook for 10 minutes over hot charcoal fire, turning often.

Little Bit Different!

Venison Chili

2 pounds ground venison
1 cup chopped onion
3/4 cup chopped green pepper
2 (1-pound) cans (2 cups)
 tomatoes, broken up
2 (1-pound) cans (2-cups)
 dark red kidney beans,
 drained

2 (8-ounce) cans tomato
 sauce
4-6 teaspoons chili powder
 (or to taste)
2 teaspoons salt

In Dutch oven, brown venison, onion, and green pepper until vegetables are tender. Drain. Stir in remaining ingredients. Cover and simmer for 1 1/2 hours. Makes 8 servings.

Ramblin' Chefs From Georgia Tech

Seafood

Okefenokee National Wildlife Refuge is the largest national wildlife refuge in the eastern United States. Waycross.

Emma's Baked Whole Fish with Wine

1 whole fish, such as striped bass, cod, or red snapper, cleaned
2 teaspoons salt
1 cup chopped green onion
2 tablespoons vegetable oil
1/4 cup fresh chopped parsley
1 teaspoon grated lemon peel
1/2 teaspoon marjoram, well rubbed
1/8 teaspoon freshly-ground black pepper

2 tablespoons fresh lemon juice
1/2 cup cracker crumbs
4 tablespoons butter
3/4 cup dry white table wine
1 lemon, thinly sliced
1 medium onion, thinly sliced
2 small tomatoes, cut in about 8 wedges each
Parsley sprigs
Lemon wedges for garnish

Preheat oven to 350°. Wash fish inside and out in cold running water. Dry inside and out with paper towels. Sprinkle with salt. Set aside. Sauté onions for about 2 minutes in 8-inch skillet in oil. Stir in chopped parsley, grated lemon peel, marjoram, pepper, and lemon juice. Place half of onion mixture in a baking dish large enough to hold fish without leaving much space on either side. Place fish on this, and spread with remaining onion mixture. Sprinkle with crumbs and dot with butter. Pour wine around, but not over fish. Bake for 15 minutes.

Arrange lemon and onion slices over fish and place tomato wedges at the sides. Bake 20 minutes more, or until fish flakes easily when gently tested with a fork. Serve with pan juice spooned over fish. Garnish with parsley and lemon wedges as desired. Yield: 8 servings.

Georgia Entertains

National award-winning wines can be sampled at Habersham Winery, south of Cornelia.

Pan-Fried Flounder

For years, I bought fresh fish, took it home, cooked it, and wondered where I went wrong. Only after I had watched restaurant chefs in demonstrations did I understand the philosophy of cooking fish: *Do it quickly at relatively high heat.* This recipe is an excellent example.

4 skinless, boneless flounder fillets, or other fillets	**2 tablespoons vegetable oil**
Salt and pepper to taste	**3 tablespoons butter, divided**
Flour for dredging fish	**Juice of one lemon**
	1 tablespoon fresh parsley

Wash fillets in cold water and pat dry. Salt and pepper. Dredge fillets in flour. Place oil and 2 tablespoons butter in flat, heavy-bottomed skillet and heat on medium-high until butter melts. Keeping heat at medium-high, cook fish on 1 side about 3 minutes (more or less depending on thickness of fillets), until browned and crispy. TURN FISH ONLY ONCE. When fillets are done, remove to serving platter. Lower heat under skillet. Add 1 tablespoon additional butter. When melted, add lemon juice and parsley- and allow to sizzle for a minute. Pour this over fish fillets. Serve at once. Serves 4.

Note: You can substitute 1 tablespoon drained capers for parsley.

Savannah Collection

Broiled Flounder

This cook and her husband created this dish together, from several recipes. The "puffy sauce" is also good on broiled chicken, she has found.

2-2 1/2 pounds flounder
Salt and pepper
1/2 cup mayonnaise
2 tablespoons pickle relish
2 tablespoons chopped
 parsley

1 tablespoon lemon juice
1/4 teaspoon salt
Dash cayenne pepper
1/2 cup Cheddar cheese
 (optional)
2 egg whites

Sprinkle flounder with salt and pepper. Place in shallow buttered pan and broil 6-10 minutes or until nearly cooked through. Stir together all other ingredients except egg whites which have been beaten until stiff but not dry. Then fold in egg whites and spread sauce over fish. Sprinkle with Parmesan cheese and broil 3-5 minutes longer or until sauce is puffed and lightly browned.

Good Cookin'

Easy Flounder Fillets

2 pounds flounder (or other
 fish) fillets, skinned,
 fresh or frozen
2 tablespoons grated onion
1 1/2 teaspoons salt
1/8 teaspoon pepper

2 large tomatoes, cut into
 small pieces
1/4 cup melted butter or
 margarine
1 cup shredded Swiss cheese

Thaw fillets if frozen. Place fillets in a single layer on a well-greased 6x19-inch bake-and-serve platter. Sprinkle fish with onion, salt, and pepper. Cover fillets with tomatoes. Pour butter over tomatoes. Broil about 4 inches from source of heat for 10-12 minutes or until fish flakes easily when tested with a fork. Remove from heat; sprinkle with cheese. Broil 2-3 minutes longer or until cheese melts. Yield: 6 servings.

Southern Seafood Classics

Flounder Parmesan
(Microwave)

1 pound fillet of flounder
1/2 cup sour cream
2 tablespoons grated
 Parmesan cheese
1 teaspoon lemon juice

1 tablespoon grated onion
1/2 teaspoon salt
Dash hot pepper sauce
Paprika
Chopped parsley

Cut fish into serving-size portions. Arrange fillets in baking dish with thickest portions to the outside. Mix remaining ingredients except paprika and parsley; spread mixture on fish; sprinkle with paprika. Cook uncovered on HIGH 5-7 minutes until done. Garnish with parsley. Serves 4.

Simply Scrumptious Microwaving

Microwave Fish Cordon Bleu

1 1/2 pounds thin fish
 fillets, fresh or frozen
4 slices ham
2 slices Swiss cheese
1/4 cup chopped tomato
4 teaspoons chopped green
 onions
1/2 teaspoon salt
1/2 teaspoon thyme
1/4 teaspoon white pepper

1/4 cup butter or margarine,
 melted
1/2 cup dry bread crumbs
1/4 cup Parmesan cheese
2 tablespoons chopped
 parsley
Tomato roses (optional
 garnish)
Parsley (garnish)

Thaw fish if frozen. Cut fillets into 4 serving-sized portions; cover each with plastic wrap. With a meat mallet, gently pound fillet portions until thin and approximately 6 1/2x4 inches. Top each fillet portion with 1 slice ham and 1/2 slice cheese. Add 1 tablespoon chopped tomato and 1 teaspoon green onion to each portion. Sprinkle with salt, thyme, and pepper. Roll up each fillet portion jellyroll style. In a shallow container, combine bread crumbs, Parmesan cheese, and parsley. Dip fillet in butter; coat with crumb mixture. Place fillet rolls seam-side-down in a shallow 1 1/2-quart baking dish. Cook in microwave oven, uncovered, on HIGH for 7-9 minutes, rotating dish 1/2 turn after 5 minutes. Garnish with tomato roses and parsley. Yield: 4 servings.

Southern Seafood Classics

Shrimp Stuffed Trout

1/2 cup butter
1/4 cup onion, minced
2 1/2 cups fresh mushrooms, chopped
1 pound shrimp, cooked, peeled, and deveined
1 cup fresh bread crumbs, toasted

2 teaspoons thyme
1 teaspoon salt
6 whole rainbow trout, dressed
Melted butter

In a skillet, sauté onion and mushrooms in butter until tender. Stir in shrimp, bread crumbs, thyme, and salt. Pat trout dry and season cavity with salt and pepper. Spoon about 2 tablespoons stuffing into each trout. Keep remaining stuffing warm while baking fish. Place trout on baking pan and brush with melted butter. Bake in a preheated 450° oven 20 minutes or until fish flakes easily when tested with a fork. Meanwhile, prepare Lemon Sauce.

LEMON SAUCE:

1/4 cup butter
1/4 cup flour
3/4 teaspoon salt
1 1/2 cups milk

Hot sauce
1 egg, beaten
1/3 cup fresh lemon juice

In a saucepan, melt butter. Stir in flour and salt. Gradually blend in milk and heat to boiling, stirring constantly. Boil 1 minute. Add a little hot sauce to the beaten egg and stir into mixture; continue heating until thickened. Stir in lemon juice. Serve Lemon Sauce with fish and additional stuffing. From Andy's Trout Farms.

Somethin's Cookin' in the Mountains

Party Salmon Steaks

4 fresh salmon steaks (1-inch thick)
2 lemons
Seasoning salt
8 tablespoons mayonnaise

Nutmeg
1 cup sliced fresh mushrooms (uncooked)
4 tablespoons Parmesan cheese

CONTINUED

CONTINUED

Place steaks in greased oblong pan (not touching). Squeeze juice of 1/2 lemon over each steak and sprinkle generously with seasoning salt. Spread 2 tablespoons mayonnaise over each, lightly sprinkle with nutmeg, top with mushrooms and 1 tablespoon Parmesan cheese on each. Bake at 400° for 15 minutes. Serves 4.

The Stuffed Griffin

Salmon Mousse

1/4 cup cold water
2 envelopes unflavored
  gelatin
1/2 cup boiling water
1 tablespoon lemon juice
1/2 cup Hellmann's
  mayonnaise
1 tablespoon grated onion
1/2 teaspoon paprika
1/2 teaspoon Tabasco sauce

1 teaspoon salt
2 (7 3/4-ounce) cans salmon,
  drained and finely chopped
3/4-1 cup heavy cream,
  whipped
Garnish: capers, lemon
  wedges and Sour Cream-Dill
  Sauce

Soften gelatin in cold water. Add boiling water, stir until dissolved. Cool. Add lemon juice, mayonnaise, onion, paprika, Tabasco, salt. Mix well. Chill until slightly thickened. Add salmon, mix well. Fold in whipped cream. Pour into well-oiled 1 1/2-quart fish mold. Chill until firm. Garnish with capers and lemon wedges and serve with Sour Cream-Dill Sauce.

SOUR CREAM-DILL SAUCE:

3/4 teaspoon salt
1 teaspoon grated lemon rind
3 tablespoons fresh dill or
  1 tablespoon dill weed

1/4 teaspoon pepper
2 cups sour cream

Blend all ingredients.

This mousse is very light and elegant. It is delicious served with a fresh fruit or vegetable salad and hot herb bread for luncheon. Serves 6-8.

Head Table Cooks

Baked Shad with Shad Roe Stuffing

4 tablespoons butter
1/4 cup onions, minced
1/4 cup bell pepper, minced
1/4 cup celery, minced
1/2 cup seasoned bread crumbs
8 ounces shad roe
1/2 cup mushrooms, chopped

1/2 teaspoon salt
1/2 teaspoon pepper
1 piece boneless roe shad
 (1-2 pounds)
3 pieces bacon cut in half
Juice from one lemon

Melt butter. Sauté onions, bell pepper, and celery until tender. Add bread crumbs. Break up roe and add mushrooms, salt, pepper; mix well and cook lightly.

Place shad in buttered baking dish, flesh side up. Stuff cavities of shad where bones were removed. Place halves of bacon across the top of boned stuffed shad with about 3 minutes of cooking time left to finish. Drip juice from one lemon on top. Cover and bake for 20-25 minutes in preheated 375° oven. Put a little water around edge to keep the shad from drying out. Serves 4-6.

For cooking in a microwave oven, cook without bacon 4-5 minutes per pound. Place bacon on top 3 minutes before finished. Allow one minute cooking time per slice of bacon. Cook covered. For extra treat, mix in pre-cooked shad roe with stuffing.

Vincent Russo's Seafood Cookbook

The Hotel Upson's
Seafood Thermidor Andrews

1 stick butter or margarine
2 cups chopped onions
2 cups chopped bell peppers
2 cups chopped celery
2 1/2 cups sliced mushrooms
2-3 cups medium shrimp,
  peeled and deveined
1 pound lump, white crabmeat
1 pound bay scallops,
  uncooked

1 pint cooking sherry
1 quart half-and-half
4 tablespoons cornstarch
1 cup water
1/2-3/4 cup grated Parmesan
  or Romano cheese
Dash of paprika

Melt the butter in a large skillet and sauté the onions, peppers and celery until almost done, being careful not to burn the onions. Add mushrooms, shrimp, crabmeat, and scallops, and continue to cook slowly until the shrimp turns pink. Douse the cooking sherry over entire ingredients while still cooking; then add the half-and-half. Do not allow the mixture to boil at any time. If you need more liquid to make sufficient sauce, add some more cream or a little whole milk. Stir several tablespoons of cornstarch into a cup of water, making a fairly thick paste; then stir this very slowly into the thermidor mixture to thicken it. Do not add the cornstarch all at once; add only what is necessary to get the consistency you desire.

Put the seafood mixture into a large casserole dish and sprinkle it generously with grated cheese. Put a dash of paprika on top of the cheese to add color. (If you're not ready to serve the dish, refrigerate it.) Place the dish in a 350° oven and bake until the cheese bubbles around the edges, usually about 30-40 minutes. Serves 6-8 generously.

Georgia's Historic Restaurants

Seafood Lasagna

1 pound sea trout fillets,
fresh or frozen
1/2 pound cooked, deveined
medium shrimp, fresh or
frozen
8 ounces lasagna noodles

1 1/2 cups prepared Italian
sauce
15 ounces low-fat ricotta
cheese
2 tablespoons grated
Parmesan cheese

Thaw seafood if frozen. Preheat oven to 400°. Poach fillets
and drain. (To poach: Bring small amount of water in
skillet to boiling point. Reduce heat and place fillets in
single layer in skillet. Simmer until fish flakes easily when
tested with a fork, taking care to retain shape of fillets.)

Cook lasagna noodles according to package directions.
Line bottom of a shallow 2-quart oblong well-greased baking dish with 1/3 of noodles. Carefully place sea trout
over noodles cover with 1/3 of sauce and half of ricotta
cheese. Add another layer of lasagna noodles. Place
shrimp over noodles and spread an additional 1/3 of
sauce. Top with remaining ricotta cheese. Add another
layer of noodles. Spread remaining sauce over noodles.
Sprinkle with Parmesan cheese. Bake at 400° for 10-15
minutes or until heated thoroughly. Yield: 8 servings.

Southern Seafood Classics

Ogeechee Mull

3 tablespoons butter,
divided
1 cup sliced fresh mushrooms
1/2 cup chopped onion
1/2 cup chopped green pepper
1/4 cup chopped celery
2 cups small shrimp, cooked,
peeled, and deveined
2 cups diced cured ham,
cooked
2 cups diced chicken or
turkey, cooked
1 (16-ounce) can tomatoes,
chopped

1/2 teaspoon salt
1/4 teaspoon freshly ground
black pepper
1 tablespoon sugar
Dash of Tabasco
1 tablespoon flour
1 cup chicken stock
1/2 cup olive oil or bacon
drippings
Chopped parsley for garnish
Lemon slices for garnish

CONTINUED

CONTINUED

Melt 2 tablespoons of the butter in a large, heavy sauce-pan and sauté the mushrooms, chopped onion, green pep-per and celery until limp. Add the shrimp, ham, chicken, tomatoes, and seasonings. Mix well and simmer over low heat for 15-20 minutes, or until the mixture thickens; stir occasionally to prevent sticking.

Mix the flour with a few tablespoons of liquid from the saucepan and stir until smooth. Stir into the mixture and add the remaining tablespoon of butter. Add the chicken stock and olive oil or bacon drippings and simmer for another 20 minutes. Taste and adjust seasonings. Serve over rice, garnishing with chopped parsley and lemon slices. Serves 4-6.

Recipes from The Olde Pink House

Seafood Pecan

2 tablespoons butter
2 tablespoons all-purpose
 flour
1 cup milk
1/4 teaspoon salt
1/2 cup grated sharp Cheddar
 cheese
1/2 cup sour cream
4 fish fillets, flounder,
 snapper, or other fish

1 cup crabmeat
1 cup uncooked scallops,
 rinsed
1 1/2 cups cooked rice or
 noodles
1/4 cup pecan pieces,
 toasted

Melt butter in saucepan over medium-low heat; blend in flour, then milk. Stir constantly until thickened. Add salt and cheese; stir until cheese melts. Set aside. When cool, add sour cream. Place fish fillets on bottom of greased, square, 1-quart casserole dish. Add crabmeat and scal-lops to cream sauce; pour over fish. Can be refrigerated at this point until ready to bake. Bake at 325° until fish is done, about 10-15 minutes. Serve over cooked rice or noodles. Sprinkle with pecan pieces. Serves 4.

Peachtree Bouquet

Shrimp Étouffée

1 stick butter
1/2 cup chili sauce
1/4 cup onions, chopped
1/4 cup celery, chopped
1/8 teaspoon salt
1/8 teaspoon pepper
2 pounds medium shrimp,
 peeled and deveined

1/4 cup white wine
1/4 cup fresh parsley,
 chopped
2 tablespoons shallot,
 minced
1 cup freshly cooked rice

Melt butter in a large skillet over a low heat. Add chili sauce, onion, celery, salt, and pepper; sauté until tender. Add shrimp and wine, sauté 3 minutes on each side. Add parsley and shallot, simmer 3 minutes. Serve hot over cooked rice. Serves 4.

Vincent Russo's Seafood Cookbook

Shrimp Creole

1 pound medium shrimp,
 shelled and deveined
1 tablespoon butter or
 vegetable oil
1 small red pepper
1 small green pepper
1 medium onion
1/4 pound medium mushrooms
1 stalk celery
1 clove garlic, pressed

1 can whole tomatoes
1/4 teaspoon salt
1 teaspoon sugar
1/4 teaspoon thyme
1 teaspoon chili powder
2 tablespoons all-purpose
 flour
3 cups cooked rice

Rinse and drain shrimp. Heat half of butter in large skillet over medium heat. Add shrimp and sauté, stirring until pink. Remove. Wash, drain and thinly slice peppers, onion, mushrooms and celery. Add remaining butter to skillet along with the sliced vegetables and garlic. Sauté, stirring until onions and garlic have browned slightly.

CONTINUED

CONTINUED

Pour off 1/4 cup of juice from tomatoes and set aside. Add remaining tomatoes and juice to sautéed vegetables and bring mixture to boiling over medium heat. Stir salt, sugar, thyme, chili powder, and flour into reserved tomato juice. Stir into vegetable mixture. Reduce heat and cook until thickened—about 3-5 minutes. Simmer until vegetables reach desired doneness—anywhere from 3-5 minutes. Add shrimp and heat through about 1 minute. Serve over rice.

Windsor Academy Cookbook

Broiled Rock Shrimp

2 1/2 pounds split, deveined
  rock shrimp, fresh or frozen
1/2 cup butter or margarine,
  melted

3/4 teaspoon salt
1/4 teaspoon white pepper
1/4 teaspoon paprika
Lemon-Butter Sauce

Thaw rock shrimp if frozen. Lay shrimp flat on a broiling pan with meat exposed. Baste with butter. Sprinkle with salt, white pepper, and paprika. Broil 4 inches from source of heat for approximately 2 minutes or until meat is opaque. Serve immediately with Lemon-Butter Sauce. Yield: 6 servings.

LEMON-BUTTER SAUCE:

1/2 cup butter or margarine,
  melted

2 tablespoons lemon juice

Combine butter and lemon juice. Heat. Yield: 1/2 cup.

Southern Seafood Classics

Frogmore Stew

Great for large casual dinner party!

3 pounds Polish sausage, cut
   in 1 1/2-inch pieces
2 large onions, chopped
2 lemons, sliced
2 tablespoons seafood
   seasoning

Salt and pepper to taste
15 ears of corn, shucked
1/2 cup butter
4 pounds raw, unpeeled
   shrimp
2 gallons water

Into 2 gallons of water, add sausage, onion, lemons, seafood seasoning, salt, and pepper. Bring to a boil and simmer 45 minutes. Add butter and let melt. Add corn and cook for 1 minutes. Add shrimp and cook about 5 minutes, or until shrimp are nice and pink. Drain water and serve on a large platter. Yield: 12 servings.

Georgia On My Menu

Cheese Fondue with Shrimp

1 3/4 cups grated Swiss
   cheese
1/4 cup grated sharp Cheddar
   cheese
1 1/2 tablespoons flour
2 tablespoons water

1 cup dry Chablis wine
1 teaspoon Worcestershire
2 tablespoons minced parsley
Salt to taste
40 medium-size cooked shrimp
Small chunks French bread

Place cheese in inset pan of chafing dish and place in water jacket containing boiling water. Stir and melt cheese. Beat flour and water with fork until smooth. Add to cheese and blend. Stir in 1/4 cup wine and stir until smooth. Keep adding wine, 1/4 cup at a time, and then add spices. When bubbly, add shrimp. Serve with French bread chunks.

Golden Isles Cuisine

Le Cruette St. John

1 pound shrimp, peeled and
  deveined
1/4 cup butter
2 tomatoes, peeled and diced
1 garlic clove, minced
1/2 cup chopped onions
10 large mushrooms, sliced
4 shallots or green onions,
  chopped

1/2 cup dry white wine
1/2 teaspoon tarragon leaves
Salt to taste
Red pepper to taste
1/4 teaspoon oregano
1/2 cup bread crumbs
1/2 cup grated Parmesan
  cheese

Peel and devein shrimp. Sauté tomatoes, garlic, onions, and mushrooms in butter. Remove and reserve mixture. Sauté shrimp. Add shallots, and when they are clear, add white wine and tarragon leaves. Return first mixture to skillet; simmer 5 minutes. Season to taste with salt, red pepper, and oregano. Place in 4 individual baking dishes and top with crumbs and cheese. Broil for 1-2 minutes to melt cheese. Yield: 4 servings.

Quail Country

Jekyll Stuffed Shrimp

CRABMEAT STUFFING:

2 tablespoons butter
2 tablespoons green pepper, finely chopped
1 tablespoon onion, minced
2 tablespoons flour
1/2 cup milk
1/2 cup soft bread crumbs

1 teaspoon Worcestershire
1/2 teaspoon seasoned salt
Dash cayenne
1 (7 1/2-ounce) can crabmeat
20 large raw shrimp
(1 1/2-pounds)

In hot butter, sauté green pepper about 2 minutes. Remove from heat; stir in minced onion, flour, and gradually stir in milk. Cook, stirring constantly, until very thick and mixture begins to boil. Remove from heat. Add bread crumbs, Worcestershire, salt, cayenne, and crabmeat; mix well. Set aside.

Shell shrimp, leaving on tails. Split each shrimp lengthwise along back being careful not to cut completely through. Devein, wash, and drain dry. Put 2 shrimp together, sandwich-style, using about a tablespoon of crabmeat stuffing as filling. Fasten with toothpicks; be sure tails are sticking up. Fill all shrimp, place in shallow baking pan and refrigerate 1 hour.

BARBECUE SAUCE:

1/4 cup salad oil
2 tablespoons vinegar
1/4 cup light brown sugar
2 (8-ounce) cans tomato sauce
1 tablespoon Worcestershire

1/2 teaspoon salt
Dash liquid hot pepper seasoning
Dash cayenne
4 cups hot cooked rice

Make barbecue sauce by combining all ingredients except rice. Bring to a boil, stirring. Reduce heat; simmer uncovered 5 minutes. Place shrimp in preheated 350° oven. Brush sauce lightly over shrimp. Cover pan lightly with foil; bake 20 minutes. Cook rice, spread on serving platter, and carefully arrange shrimp on rice (remove toothpicks). Reheat remaining sauce and pass separately. Serves 6-8.

Golden Isles Cuisine

Shrimp in "Wild Rice"

Everyone goes "wild" over this! Out of this world!

1/2 cup flour
1 cup melted butter or
  margarine (divided)
4 cups chicken broth
1/4 teaspoon white pepper
1 cup thinly sliced onions
1/2 cup thinly sliced green
  peppers

1 cup thinly sliced
  mushrooms
2 pounds cooked, peeled,
  deveined shrimp
2 tablespoons Worcestershire
  sauce
Few drops hot sauce
4 cups cooked wild rice

Gradually add flour to 1/2 cup melted butter and stir constantly over low heat until bubbly. Gradually add broth and stir until smooth and thickened. Add white pepper and simmer 2-3 minutes. Sauté onion, green pepper, and mushrooms in remaining 1/2 cup butter. Drain. Combine white sauce, sautéed vegetables, and remaining ingredients. Spoon into casserole and bake at 300° for 45-50 minutes. Freezes well.

Encore

Dooley's Bulldog Shrimp and Green Noodles

1/2 (8-ounce) package
  spinach noodles
2 pounds shrimp, peeled and
  deveined
1/2 cup clarified butter
1 can cream of mushroom soup
1 cup sour cream

1 cup mayonnaise
1 tablespoon chopped chives
1/2 teaspoon Dijon-style
  mustard
4 tablespoons dry sherry
1/2 cup sharp Cheddar
  cheese, grated

Cook noodles as directed on package. Line a 2-quart flat casserole with noodles. In a large frying pan, sauté the shrimp in butter until pink and tender (about 5 minutes). Cover noodles with shrimp. Combine soup, sour cream, mayonnaise and chives. Add mustard and sherry. Pour sauce over shrimp and sprinkle cheese over all. Bake at 350° for 30 minutes or until cheese has melted and is bubbly. Yield: 6 servings.

Traditionally Wesleyan

Seafood Vermouth with Pasta

1 (16-ounce) package
  fettucine
1/2 cup butter
2 tablespoons olive oil
1/2 cup chopped green onion
1 clove garlic, minced
1/2 pound sliced, fresh
  mushrooms
3 pounds raw seafood, any 1
  or a combination of shrimp,
  lobster, scallops, clams or
  oysters

2 teaspoons rosemary,
  crushed
1 1/2 tablespoons fresh
  lemon juice
1/4 cup vermouth
1/2 cup whipping cream
2 teaspoons chopped, fresh
  parsley
1 egg, optional
Salt and pepper to taste
Grated Parmesan cheese

Cook fettucine according to package directions. Drain. Melt butter and oil in heavy skillet. Add green onion, garlic, and mushrooms. Sauté until tender. Add seafood, rosemary, lemon juice, and vermouth. Cook 5 minutes. Add cream and parsley. Continue cooking on medium-high heat until sauce thickens, about 10-15 minutes. If sauce becomes too thin, add 1 beaten egg. If sauce is too thick, thin with additional cream. Add salt and pepper. Toss pasta with seafood mixture. Serve immediately with grated Parmesan cheese. Yield: 6-8 servings.

Second Round, Tea-Time at the Masters®

Seafood Casserole Melba

1/2 pound spaghetti, broken
  into short pieces
2 tablespoons grated onion
1/4 cup butter or margarine
1/4 cup flour
1 1/2 cups chicken stock
  (canned or bouillon cube
  broth may be used)
1 cup cream or undiluted
  evaporated milk
1/3 cup California dry
  sherry wine
1 teaspoon lemon juice

1/2 cup grated Parmesan
  cheese
1 teaspoon Worcestershire
  sauce
Salt, celery salt, pepper to
  taste
1 cup cooked or canned
  shrimp (whole if small, cut
  up if large)
1 cup flaked, cooked or
  canned crabmeat
Paprika

CONTINUED

CONTINUED

Cook spaghetti in plenty of boiling salted water just until tender; drain. Sauté onion gently in butter for 5 minutes. Blend in flour; add chicken stock and cream; cook, stirring until mixture boils and thickens. Add wine, lemon juice, 1/4 cup of cheese, and seasonings; gently stir in shrimp and crabmeat.

In greased casserole arrange alternate layers of spaghetti and seafood mixture, having a layer of seafood mixture on top; sprinkle with remaining cheese; dust with paprika. Bake in a moderately hot oven (400°) for 30 minutes or until bubbly and golden brown. Serves 6-8.

Head Table Cooks

Almond Crab Supreme

2 tablespoons butter	1-2 tablespoons sherry
2 tablespoons flour	1/2 cup sour cream
1/2 teaspoon paprika	1 pound lump crabmeat
1/2 teaspoon salt	2 tablespoons lemon juice
1/8 teaspoon pepper	1/2 cup chopped
1 cup whipping cream	almonds
1 tablespoon minced onion	1 package Pepperidge Farm
1 beaten egg yolk	patty shells

Melt butter over low heat and stir in flour, paprika, salt, pepper, cream, and onion. Cook, stirring constantly until sauce comes to a boil. Remove from heat. Stir in beaten egg yolk, sherry, and sour cream. Gently stir in crabmeat and heat through. Stir in lemon juice and half the almonds. Serve over patty shells and garnish with remaining almonds. Serves 4-6.

Frederica Fare

Lucille's Crab Savannah

2 tablespoons butter	1 can white asparagus
2 tablespoons flour	1 pound fresh lump crab
1 cup chicken stock	1/2 cup grated mozzarella
Salt to taste	cheese
White pepper to taste	4-6 egg whites, beaten
Dash of dry mustard	2-3 tablespoons mayonnaise
Dash of dry white wine	

Make a sauce by melting the butter in a small saucepan and stirring in the flour. Mix well and gradually add the chicken stock. Cook until thick, stirring constantly. Season to taste with salt and pepper. Stir in the mustard and wine. Preheat oven to 350°. Cover the bottom of a 1 1/2-quart baking dish with half of the sauce. Top with a layer of asparagus. Pick over the crabmeat to remove any shell; place the crab over the asparagus. Sprinkle with the grated cheese and top with the rest of the sauce. Bake at 350° for 20 minutes.

While the casserole is baking, prepare a meringue by beating the egg whites until stiff, gradually adding the mayonnaise. Take the casserole from the oven and spread the meringue evenly over the top. Place back in the hot oven and bake for another 5 minutes, or until the meringue is lightly browned. Serves 4.

Recipes from The Olde Pink House

Lillie's Crab Au Gratin

1/3 cup plain flour	1 pound lump crabmeat
Salt and pepper taste	12 Ritz crackers, crushed
2 cups milk	
1 1/2 cups grated sharp cheese	

Mix flour, salt and pepper with milk. Cook until smooth and thick. Add 1 1/4 cups of grated cheese (reserve 1/4 cup for topping). Blend well. In a casserole dish alternate thin layers of cheese sauce and crabmeat. Make sure to start layers with cheese sauce. Mix remaining cheese and crushed Ritz crackers together. Sprinkle on top. Bake at 400° until bubbly, about 30 minutes.

Crab Chatter

Old Plantation Deviled Crab

2 tablespoons chopped onion
3 tablespoons butter, melted
2 tablespoons flour
3/4 cup milk
1/2 teaspoon salt
Dash pepper
1/2 teaspoon dry mustard
1 teaspoon Worcestershire
  sauce

1/2 teaspoon sage
Dash of cayenne pepper
1 tablespoon lemon juice
1 egg, beaten
1 tablespoon chopped parsley
1 pound claw crabmeat
1 tablespoon butter, melted
1/4 cup dry bread crumbs

Cook onion in butter until tender. Blend in flour. Add milk gradually and cook until thick, stirring constantly. Add seasonings and lemon juice. Stir a little of the sauce into the egg; add to remaining sauce, stirring constantly. Add parsley and crabmeat. Place in 6 well-greased, individual shells or 5-ounce custard cups. Combine butter and crumbs; sprinkle over top of each shell. Bake at 350° for 15-20 minutes or until brown. Serves 6.

Crab Chatter

Devilishly Stuffed Soft-Shell Crab

8 soft-shell crabs, cleaned,
  fresh or frozen
1/4 cup chopped onion
1/4 cup chopped celery
2 tablespoons chopped green
  pepper
1 clove garlic, minced
1/4 cup butter or margarine,
  melted
1 cup finely crushed
  butter-flavored crackers

2 tablespoons milk
1 egg, beaten
1 tablespoon chopped parsley
1/2 teaspoon dry mustard
1/2 teaspoon Worcestershire
  sauce
1/4 teaspoon salt
1/8 teaspoon cayenne
1/4 cup butter or margarine,
  melted

Thaw crabs if frozen. Preheat oven to 400°. Wash crabs thoroughly; drain well. Cook onion, celery, green pepper, and garlic in butter until tender. In a medium bowl, combine mixture with the next 8 ingredients. Place crabs in a shallow, well-greased baking pan. Remove top shell from crabs and fill each cavity with 1 teaspoon stuffing mixture. Replace top shell. Brush crabs with melted butter. Bake at 400° degrees for 15 minutes or until shells turn red and crabs brown lightly. Yield: 4 servings.

Southern Seafood Classics

Sunny Crab Sandwich

12 ounces fresh crabmeat or
  2 (6-ounce) packages of
  frozen
1 cup sliced almonds
1/2 cup chopped celery
1/2 cup mayonnaise
2 tablespoons lemon juice

6 toasted, buttered English
  muffins
12 asparagus spears, cooked
6 (1-ounce) slices Cheddar
  cheese
Paprika
Tomato wedges

If frozen, thaw crabmeat; drain. Remove any remaining shell or cartilage. Combine almonds, celery, mayonnaise, lemon juice, and crabmeat. Arrange muffin halves on a cookie sheet. Place one or more asparagus spears on each muffin half. Cover asparagus and muffin with crab mixture. Cut each cheese slice diagonally into quarters. Place 2 triangles on each sandwich. Sprinkle with paprika. Bake at 400° for 15-20 minutes or until heated through and cheese is melted. Serve with tomato wedges. Makes 6 servings.

Golden Isles Cuisine

Vince's Crab Cakes

2 tablespoons chopped onions
2 tablespoons cooking oil
1 pound claw crabmeat
1 egg, beaten

1/2 teaspoon mustard
Salt and pepper to taste
1/2 cup seasoned bread
  crumbs

Sauté onions in oil until tender. Combine all ingredients except seasoned bread crumbs. Shape into 6 or 8 cakes, then roll in crumbs. Fry at moderate heat until golden brown on both sides, about 5-7 minutes. Drain on absorbent paper. Serves 3-4.

Vincent Russo's Seafood Cookbook

Sweet and Tangy Scallops

1 1/2 cups sliced celery
6 tablespoons chopped green
pepper
6 tablespoons chopped sweet
red pepper
18 ounces bay or sea scallops,
rinsed and drained
1 1/2 cups pineapple chunks,
canned in juice

2 cups pineapple juice
3/4 cup sliced water
chestnuts
6 tablespoons prepared
brown mustard
2 tablespoons arrowroot, mixed
with a little pineapple juice

Steam-fry celery and peppers in skillet with a small amount of water until crisp-tender. Add scallops, pineapple chunks, juice and water chestnuts. Simmer gently for about 3-4 minutes or until scallops turn an opaque white. DO NOT LET BOIL. Remove scallops with a slotted spoon to a warm bowl. Cover and set aside.

Stir mustard into the vegetable mixture and continue to cook until sauce begins to thicken and coats a spoon, about 1 minute. Return scallops to skillet and heat through slowly, again being careful not to boil. Serve over hot rice or warm chow mein noodles. Cooking time: about 15 minutes. Serves 6.

Cal.-185 Pro.-22g Fat-3g Carb.-19g Fib.-.7g Sod.-456mg Chol.-30m

Adventures in Healthful Cooking

Oysters Rockefeller

1 (15-ounce) can spinach
1 stick butter
1 tablespoon minced onions
1/4 teaspoon celery salt
Salt and pepper to taste
8 slices cooked bacon, chopped

2 bay leaves
1/2 cup seasoned bread crumbs
2 dozen oysters in half shell
Worcestershire sauce
Parmesan Cheese

Chop and drain spinach. Melt butter and add onions, celery salt, salt and pepper, chopped bacon, bay leaves, and cook over low heat for 5 minutes. Then add spinach and cook for 3 more minutes. Add bread crumbs and mix well. Spread mixture over oysters and add a few drops of Worcestershire sauce on top, then garnish with Parmesan cheese. Broil in oven until edges of oysters curl. Serve hot. Serves 4.

Vincent Russo's Seafood Cookbook

Oysters and Wild Rice Casserole

Excellent with turkey and dressing.

3 cups hot wild rice,
  drained (may substitute wild
  and long grain rice mixture)
1/2 cup chopped onions
2 cups chopped celery
1/2 stick butter or
  margarine
1/2 cup milk
3 tablespoons flour

1/2 teaspoon salt
1/4 teaspoon sage
1/4 teaspoon thyme
1/8 teaspoon black pepper
2 (8-ounce) cans fresh
  oysters, drained
1 stick butter, melted
Ritz cracker crumbs

While rice is cooking according to package directions, brown onions and celery in butter. Remove from heat and add milk, flour, salt, sage, thyme, and black pepper. Add well-drained rice to mixture. Pour into 2-quart casserole.

Drain oysters and let soak in lukewarm melted butter for 5-10 minutes. Pour oysters and butter over rice mixture and spread the oysters evenly. Top with Ritz cracker crumbs. Bake at 350° for 45 minutes or until the oysters curl. Yield: 8 servings.

A Taste of Georgia

Oysters with Salsa Verde

I served this as a dinner appetizer one night, and promptly had to go find the recipe to give to my guests. It's that good.

36 oysters, raw, in shell	1 tablespoon lemon juice
4 slices bacon	1/3 cup soft bread crumbs
1/4 cup butter or margarine, melted	Rock salt
	Salsa Verde
1/3 cup parsley, chopped	

Open oysters and wipe shells dry. Place oysters on deep halves of shells and rest shells in shallow pan that has been lined with rock salt. (Oysters are available on the half shell at some seafood markets.)

Cook bacon until crisp; drain, reserving drippings. Combine crumbled bacon, bacon drippings, margarine, parsley, and lemon juice. Top each oyster with approximately 1 teaspoon of the mixture; top with bread crumbs and bake at 450° for 10-12 minutes. Serve hot with Salsa Verde. Serves 6.

SALSA VERDE:

1 cup chopped parsley	2/3 cup mayonnaise
1/4 cup chopped green onion	2 tablespoons olive oil
2 tablespoons capers	1 tablespoon lemon juice
1 clove garlic, minced or pressed	1/2 teaspoon prepared mustard

Combine parsley, green onion, capers, and garlic in blender or food processor. Blend until finely chopped. Add mayonnaise, olive oil, lemon juice, and mustard. Blend. Chill. Serve with oysters as you would tartar sauce.

Savannah Collection

Tuna Casserole

2 (10 3/4-ounce) cans cream
  of mushroom soup
1 3/4 cups grated medium
  Cheddar cheese, divided
1 (12 1/2-ounce) can chunk
  light tuna, drained

3 cups cooked long-grain
  white rice
1 (17-ounce) can LeSueur
  early peas, drained
Salt and pepper to taste

Preheat oven to 350°. In large saucepan, heat soup and 1 cup of cheese until cheese is melted, stirring to mix. Add tuna and rice; mix well. Gently stir in peas. Salt and pepper to taste. Mix well. Pour mixture into lightly greased 2 1/2-quart baking dish. Sprinkle with remaining cheese. Bake uncovered for 30-35 minutes, or until hot and bubbly. Yield: 8 servings.

Guess Who's Coming to Dinner

Tuna Oriental

1/2 green pepper, cut in
  1/4-inch strips
1 small onion, thinly sliced
2 teaspoons oil
1/3 cup pineapple juice
1 1/2 teaspoons cornstarch
2/3 cup drained pineapple
  chunks (canned in juice)

1 tablespoon sugar
1 tablespoon vinegar
1 (6 1/2-ounce) can unsalted
  tuna, drained and flaked
1/8 teaspoon pepper
Dash Tabasco sauce

Cook green pepper and onion in oil, leaving slightly crisp. Mix pineapple juice with cornstarch and add to green pepper and onion mixture. Cook, stirring gently until thickened. Add remaining ingredients. Cook 5 minutes, stirring occasionally. May be served over rice. Makes 3 servings; 185 calories per serving.

Windsor Academy Cookbook

Cakes

The Henry W. Grady riverboat cruises the 365-acre Stone Mountain Lake.
Stone Mountain.

Five-Flavor Pound Cake

1 cup margarine	1 teaspoon baking powder
1/2 cup shortening	1 cup milk
3 cups sugar	1 teaspoon each coconut,
5 eggs	butter, rum, lemon, and
3 cups all-purpose flour	vanilla flavoring

Cream together margarine, shortening, and sugar. Add eggs 1 at a time, beating thoroughly after each addition. Sift together flour and baking powder; add alternately to batter with milk. Add flavorings last and beat well. Bake in a 10-inch tube pan at 325° for 1 1/2 hours. Cool in pan 10 minutes. Add Glaze, if desired.

GLAZE:

1/2 teaspoon each coconut,	1/2 cup sugar
butter, rum, lemon, and	1/4 cup water
vanilla flavoring	

Combine in heavy saucepan. Bring to a boil and stir until sugar is melted. Spoon half of hot mixture over cake before removing from pan. Keep remaining Glaze on low heat while Glaze soaks into cake, then turn out cake and spoon remaining Glaze over cake. Stays moist and freezes well.

Cooking with Tradition

Pineapple Pound Cake

2 cups butter
3 cups sugar
3 cups flour (all-purpose)
8 eggs

1 small can crushed
pineapple (drained)
1 teaspoon salt

Cream butter and sugar, adding sugar 1/2 cup at at time. Cream well. Add eggs 1 at a time alternately with 2 cups flour (1/2 cup at a time.) Add drained pineapple, along with remaining cup of flour and salt. Use greased and floured tube pan. Bake at 325° for 1 hour to 1 hour 15 minutes.

Good Cookin'

Candy Bar Pound Cake

1 cup butter
2 cups sugar
4 eggs
2 1/2 cups cake flour
1/4 teaspoon baking soda

1 cup buttermilk
8 Hershey bars
2 teaspoons vanilla
1 cup chopped pecans

Cream butter until light and fluffy, gradually adding the sugar. Add eggs, 1 at a time, beating well after each addition. Add sifted dry ingredients alternately with the buttermilk. Add melted Hershey bars, vanilla, and pecans. (Roll pecans in flour until lightly coated).

Grease and flour tube pan or Bundt pan and bake at 325° for 1 1/2 hours or until done.

A great favorite!

Country Cakes

The world's largest kitchen at the Central State Hospital in Milledgeville is capable of preparing 30,000 meals a day.

Cheesecake

A Savannah favorite. Easy, and the best anywhere.

1 pound cream cheese, at
  room temperature
2 tablespoons vegetable
  shortening
2/3 cup sugar
2 tablespoons all-purpose
  flour

1/2 teaspoon salt
1/4 teaspoon lemon extract
1/2 cup milk
3 eggs

Preheat oven to 350°. Grease and flour an 8-inch solid-bottom cheesecake pan (not springform). Beat cream cheese, shortening, sugar, flour, salt, and lemon extract on low speed until smooth, about 7 minutes. Beat in milk gradually. Beat in eggs 1 at a time, beating well after each addition.

Pour into prepared pan. Place in larger pan filled with hot water to come halfway up side of cheesecake pan. Bake until top is no longer liquid, but is still soft and golden brown, about 50-60 minutes. Cool on wire rack and refrigerate before turning out. Turn out on plate and flip back over so top is right-side-up. Cut with dental floss (not mint-flavored!). Serves 6-8.

Gottlieb's Bakery 100 Years of Recipes

The first golf course in Georgia, and possibly in the United States, was constructed in 1736 by once wealthy landowners from the Scottish Highlands who settled at the present site of Darien.

Kahlua Cheesecake

2 pounds cream cheese
1/4 cup flour
1/2 teaspoon salt
6 tablespoons cocoa
1 1/2 cups sugar
7 eggs, separated

6 fluid ounces whipping
  cream
2.5 fluid ounces Kahlua
3 cups graham cracker crumbs
5 1/2 tablespoons margarine

Blend cream cheese on low speed of electric mixer. When well blended, add flour, salt, cocoa, and half of the sugar. Separate egg whites and yolks. On low speed, blend whipping cream, egg yolks, and Kahlua. Blend well. Mix in cream cheese mixture.

On high speed in another bowl, beat egg whites with the remaining sugar until stiff. Fold into cheese mixture. Cover bottom of pan with aluminum foil. Grease sides. Make crust of graham crackers and margarine. Pat 1/2 inch thick into pan bottom. Carefully spoon cheese mixture into crust. Bake at 350° for 1 1/2 to 1 3/4 hours. From The Public House.

Somethin's Cookin' in the Mountains

Black Forest Cheesecake
(Microwave)

CRUST:

3 tablespoons butter
2/3 cup graham cracker
  crumbs

1 tablespoon sugar

In 7-inch pie plate microwave the butter on HIGH for 45 seconds. Stir in crumbs, 1 tablespoon sugar until moist. Press firmly against sides and bottom. Microwave on HIGH for 1-1/1/2 minutes. Set aside.

FILLING:

2 (3-ounce) packages cream
  cheese
1 beaten egg
1/3 cup sugar
1/3 cup dairy sour cream
3 tablespoons milk

2 squares semisweet
  chocolate, melted
1/4 cup cherry preserves
1 small jar maraschino
  cherries

In bowl, microwave cream cheese on 50 percent power for 1-1 1/2 minutes until soft. Stir in egg, 1/3 cup sugar, and sour cream until smooth. Add milk and chocolate. Mix well. Pour into crust.

Microwave on 50 percent power 8-10 minutes, turn quarter turn every 2 minutes, or use a micro-go-round. Test for doneness by inserting knife blade in 1-inch from side. Should come out clean.

In custard cup microwave the cherry preserves on HIGH 30-60 seconds until warm. Spoon over top of cheesecake. Dot with whole maraschino cherries, making a pretty pattern. Cool. Refrigerate at least 3 hours.

Cherries Galore

Milk Chocolate Cheesecake
with Custard Sauce

CRUST:

1 package plain chocolate
  wafers (may substitute 1 cup
  graham cracker crumbs)

1 tablespoon sugar
1/4 teaspoon cinnamon
1/2 cup butter, melted

CONTINUED

CONTINUED

Very lightly grease a 10-inch springform pan. Crush chocolate wafers and mix with sugar, cinnamon, and butter. Press into the springform pan; refrigerate.

FILLING:

3 (8-ounce) packages cream cheese, softened
4 eggs
1 cup sugar
1 (6-ounce) package milk chocolate morsels, melted

1 1/2 teaspoons vanilla extract
2 1/2 tablespoons cocoa
3 cups sour cream
1/4 cup unsalted butter, melted

Preheat oven to 350°. Beat cream cheese until fluffy; add eggs and sugar, mixing well. Add melted chocolate to egg mixture. Blend in vanilla, cocoa, and sour cream. Beat well and add melted butter. Mix well and pour into springform pan. Bake at 350° for 45-60 minutes. Cool. Refrigerate overnight. Remove from pan before serving. Serve with Custard Sauce.

CUSTARD SAUCE:

7 egg yolks
3/4 cup sugar
1 cup hot milk
2 cups heavy cream
1 1/2 teaspoons vanilla extract

4 tablespoons orange liqueur
Toasted slivered almonds, chopped finely (optional)

Beat yolks and sugar. Blend in milk and cream. Cook in a double boiler until thickened, stirring frequently. To keep from curdling, add some of the hot milk to egg mixture and mix well before adding other ingredients. Strain custard. When cool, add orange liqueur and vanilla extract. Refrigerate overnight.

To serve: Serve a small slice of cake on a dessert plate and spoon custard around the slice but not on top. Garnish the sauce with almonds. Yield: 16 servings.

Georgia On My Menu

Five Layer Banana-Split Cake

CRUST:

3 cups graham cracker crumbs   1 1/2 sticks margarine

FIRST LAYER:

1 box confectioners' sugar   4 eggs
2 sticks margarine   1 teaspoon vanilla

REMAINING LAYERS:

2 large cans crushed   2 large containers Cool Whip
  pineapple, drained   1 cup finely chopped pecans
3 or 4 bananas   Cherries

Mix first 2 ingredients and press into a large pan. Let stand 1 1/2 hours. Mix next 4 ingredients and beat 10 minutes. Pour over crust, spreading evenly. Pour pineapple over first layer. Slice bananas over pineapple. Spread Cool Whip over bananas. Sprinkle pecans over Cool Whip and top with cherries. Serves 6-8.

Encore

Grandma Rawson's Applesauce Cake

2 cups white sugar   3 cups plain flour
3/4 cup butter   2 cups raisins
2 cups apples cooked low   2 cups pecans
  without sugar   1 or 2 teaspoons allspice
2 teaspoons baking soda   and cloves

Cream butter and sugar. Add apples to which 2 teaspoons soda have been added. Add the rest of the ingredients. Cook at 325° for 1 1/2 hours. From Mark of the Potter.

Somethin's Cookin in the Mountains

Glazed Praline Cake

CAKE:

1 cup butter
1/2 cup shortening
16 ounces light brown sugar
1 cup white sugar
5 eggs
3 cups sifted all-purpose
 flour

1/2 teaspoon salt
1 teaspoon baking powder
1 cup milk
1 teaspoon vanilla extract
1 cup chopped walnuts

Preheat oven to 350°. In a large bowl, cream butter and shortening together. Gradually add both sugars to butter mixture. Cream until light and fluffy. Beat in eggs 1 at an time. Set aside.

Sift together flour, salt, and baking powder. Set aside. Mix together 1 cup milk and 1 teaspoon vanilla extract. Alternately add the flour mixture and the milk to the sugar mixture. Stir in walnuts. Blend well. Pour into a large greased and floured tube pan. Bake 1 hour and 15 minutes. While cake is baking, mix glaze ingredients together.

WALNUT GLAZE:

1 cup confectioners' sugar
2 tablespoons butter
6 tablespoons half-and-half

1/2 teaspoon vanilla extract
1/2 cup chopped walnuts

Cream confectioners' sugar and butter. Add cream and vanilla, mixing well. Add chopped walnuts, blending thoroughly. Cool cake 10 minutes then turn out of pan onto a plate. Evenly glaze. Keep covered in a cool, dry place.

Note: May substitute black walnuts for English walnuts. Serves 16.

Temptations

Pistachio Cake

Easy, pretty and so moist.

CAKE:

1 box white cake mix
  (2-layer size)
3/4 cup vegetable oil
3/4 cup water

4 eggs
1 (3-ounce) box pistachio
  instant pudding
1/2 cup chopped nuts

Combine cake mix, oil, water, eggs, and pudding mix. Beat about 4 minutes at medium speed. Pour into greased and floured 9x13x2-inch pan. Sprinkle top with nuts. Bake at 350° for 35-40 minutes.

GLAZE:

1/2 cup hot water
1 tablespoon butter, melted

2 cups powdered sugar
1/2 teaspoon vanilla

Place water, butter, powdered sugar, and vanilla in small bowl and beat with a fork. While cake is still hot, punch holes with a fork over the entire top. Spoon icing over cake allowing it to run down into holes. Pry holes open if necessary to insure that the icing runs into cake. Is a pretty green, stays moist, and is a real favorite.

A Taste of the Holidays

Higgins' Rum Cake

1 cup chopped pecans
1 cup firmly packed dark
 brown sugar
1/2 teaspoon cinnamon
1 package Duncan Hines deluxe
 yellow cake mix
1 (3 1/2-ounce) package
 Jello French vanilla instant
 pudding

4 eggs
1/2 cup cold water
1/2 cup vegetable oil
1/2 cup dark rum (80-proof)
1 (3 1/2-ounce) can coconut

Preheat oven to 350°. Grease a 10-inch tube pan or 12-cup Bundt pan. Do not flour pan. Using fingers, combine pecan pieces and dark brown sugar in small bowl. Sprinkle half the mixture over bottom of pan. Add cinnamon to remaining nut mixture and reserve. Combine cake mix, pudding mix, eggs, water, oil, and rum in mixing bowl. Beat on low speed until moistened. Scrape sides of bowl. Beat at medium speed for 2 minutes, scraping sides of bowl as needed. Beat in coconut on low speed.

Pour half of batter over nut mixture in pan. Sprinkle remaining nut mixture over batter. Pour remaining batter into pan and smooth top. Bake for 50-60 minutes, or until cake shrinks from sides of pan and a toothpick inserted in center comes out clean. Cool on wire rack. Turn out on serving plate. Glaze.

GLAZE:

5 tablespoons butter
1/4 cup water
1/2 cup granulated sugar

1/2 cup firmly packed dark
 brown sugar
1/2 cup dark rum

Melt butter in saucepan. Stir in water and sugars. Boil 3-5 minutes, stirring constantly. Remove from heat; stir in rum. Prick top of cake with a toothpick. Spoon glaze evenly over top and sides, allowing cake to absorb glaze before continuing. Repeat until glaze is used up.

Note: The glaze for this cake is extremely potent. If you want a more subtle rum taste, cut the glaze recipe in half.

The Pirates' House Cook Book

Million Dollar Bourbon Cake

A favorite of a French chef we know, from his wife's collection.

2 teaspoons nutmeg (freshly grated is best)
1 cup bourbon
4 cups pecans, coarsely chopped
2 cups raisins
3 cups flour, sifted

2 teaspoons baking powder
1 cup butter, softened
2 cups plus 4 teaspoons sugar
6-7 eggs (depending on size), separated
Dash salt

Soak nutmeg in bourbon at least 15 minutes. Put pecans and raisins in a bowl with 1 cup sifted flour. Combine remaining 2 cups flour with baking powder and sift twice more. Cream butter and sugar; add egg yolks 1 at a time and beat until smooth. Add flour and bourbon alternately; blend well. Fold in raisin-nut-flour mixture. Beat egg whites and salt until stiff. Gently fold egg whites. Put batter in a 9-inch tube pan which has been greased and lined with waxed paper. Bake at 325° for 1 hour and 15 minutes. Let stand 30 minutes before removing.

Puttin' on the Peachtree

Irish Whiskey Cake

Peel of 1 lemon
1 double jigger of Irish
6 ounces butter or margarine
6 ounces sugar
6 ounces flour

3 eggs separated
6 ounces sultanas
Pinch of salt
1 teaspoon baking powder

Put the lemon peel in a jar and pour the whiskey over it; leave overnight. Cream the butter and sugar until light. Sift the flour and add the egg yolks one at a time with a teaspoon of flour and mix well. Strain the whiskey from the jar into the mixture. Next add the sultanas with some more flour. Beat the egg whites until stiff and fold into the mixture with the salt, baking powder and the rest of the flour. Put into a cake pan greased and lined with waxed paper. Bake in a preheated oven at 350° for about 1 1/4-1 1/2 hours. Test for doneness before removing from the oven.

Cooklore and Recipes of Ireland

Southern Gingerbread
with Caramel Sauce

1/2 cup sugar	1/2 teaspoon salt
1/2 cup butter and lard, mixed	1 teaspoon ginger
	1/2 teaspoon cloves
1 egg	2 1/2 cups flour
1 cup dark syrup	1 1/2 teaspoons soda
1 teaspoon cinnamon	1 cup hot water

Cream sugar into butter. Add egg and syrup. Sift remaining dry ingredients. Add alternately with water. Pour into greased 9-inch square pan. Bake at 350° for 25-30 minutes. (Test for doneness with toothpick.)

CARAMEL SAUCE:

3 tablespoons butter	1 1/2 cups sugar
3 tablespoons flour	2 cups water

Cream butter and flour. Caramelize sugar by melting over low heat, stirring until browned. Add water slowly. Cook until bubbly. Add to butter and flour. Pour over Southern Gingerbread, to serve.

Betty Talmadge's Lovejoy Plantation Cookbook

Cherry Upside-Down Cake

1 (20-ounce) can pitted sour
  red cherries
2 1/2 tablespoons cornstarch
2/3 cup sugar
1 3/4 cups sifted cake flour
1/2 teaspoon salt
1/4 teaspoon baking soda
2 teaspoons baking powder

1/3 cup shortening
1 egg
1/2 cup all-bran
1 teaspoon grated orange
  rind
1/2 cup orange juice
1/4 cup milk
Whipped cream or hard sauce

Preheat oven to 375°. Grease 8-inch square baking pan. Drain cherries, reserve syrup. In small saucepan combine cornstarch and sugar; blend in reserved syrup to make a smooth paste. Cook over medium heat, stirring constantly, until thickened and clear. Stir in cherries; pour into pan.

Onto a piece of waxed paper sift together flour, salt, baking soda, and baking powder. In mixing bowl cream shortening, add egg; beat until smooth. Stir in all-bran and orange rind.

Add flour mixture alternately with orange juice and milk, beating well after each addition. Pour over cherries. Bake in preheated oven for 40-45 minutes. Cool for 5 minutes; invert onto serving dish. Serve warm with whipped cream or hard sauce, as desired.

Cherries Galore

Perfect Cake

1 cup butter	2 1/2 teaspoons baking
2 cups sugar	powder
5 eggs	1/4 teaspoon salt
1 teaspoon vanilla extract	1 cup milk
3 1/2 cups cake flour	

Cream butter and sugar until light and fluffy. Add eggs, one at a time, beating well after each addition. Blend in vanilla. Sift the flour, baking powder and salt together and then add alternately with the milk, blending thoroughly. Pour batter into 3 or 4 (9-inch) round greased and floured cake pans. Bake at 350° for 25-30 minutes or until cake tests done. Frost top, sides and layers with Perfect Cake Icing.

PERFECT CAKE ICING:

2 cups sugar	3 egg whites, stiffly beaten
1 cup water	1 teaspoon vanilla extract
1/4 cup white Karo syrup	

Boil sugar, water and syrup together until it spins a thread. Pour slowly and in a very thin stream over stiffly beaten, but not dry, egg whites, beating constantly. Beat until stiff enough to hold its shape. Blend in the vanilla extract and then add the following:

1 fresh coconut, grated	1 small bottle maraschino
1 small can pineapple,	cherries, chopped in small
crushed and well drained	pieces
1 cup chopped pecans	

After blending, spread immediately on cake. You may also use a Seven Minute Frosting instead of the cooked frosting; however, I prefer the cooked frosting since the frosting will hold its shape on the cake until it is all eaten.

A beautiful heirloom cake...and delicious!

Country Cakes

Rotten Cake

1 box yellow cake mix

FROSTING:

1 cup sugar
1 pint sour cream
1 teaspoon vanilla

1 (8-ounce) carton frozen
 whipped topping mix
2 large (12-ounce) packages
 frozen coconut

Bake cake as directed on box for 2-layer cake. Cool and slice each layer in half to make 4 thin layers. Combine sugar, sour cream, vanilla and coconut. (Reserve 1 cup of sour cream and a third of the coconut for side frosting.) Spread between layers. Combine 1 cup sour cream and whipped topping mix. Spread on top and sides of cake. Sprinkle with coconut. Refrigerate in tightly covered container for 3 days.

Boarding House Reach

Strawberry Cake

2 sticks butter
2 cups sugar
1 small package strawberry
 Jello
3 1/2 cups sifted cake flour

3 teaspoons baking powder
1 cup milk
6 egg whites, stiffly beaten
1/2 cup strawberries, cut up

Preheat oven at 350°. Cream together butter, sugar and Jello until well mixed and light and fluffy. Add sifted flour and baking powder alternately with the milk. Fold in the stiffly beaten egg whites. Stir in strawberries. Pour into 3 or 4 greased and floured (9-inch) round cake pans and bake around 25 minutes or until cakes test done. Spread layers, top and sides with Strawberry Icing.

STRAWBERRY ICING:

1 stick butter, softened
1/2 cup strawberries, cut up

1 box confectioners' sugar

Blend all ingredients well and spread on cake when cool. Appreciated more today than when developed so many years ago!

Country Cakes

Aunt Eileen's Peach Cake

4 eggs
2 cups sugar
1 cup vegetable oil
3 cups all-purpose flour
1 teaspoon salt
1 tablespoon baking powder
1/4 cup orange juice

2 1/2 teaspoons vanilla
 extract
2 cups sliced fresh peaches
1/4 cup sugar
2 teaspoons cinnamon
Confectioners' sugar

Preheat oven to 350°. Beat eggs and add sugar and oil, mixing well. Combine flour, salt, and baking powder; add to egg mixture alternately with orange juice. Add vanilla extract . In a separate bowl, toss peaches with sugar and cinnamon. Pour one-third batter into a greased, lightly floured tube pan. Layer one-half peach mixture over it. Cover with one-third batter and the remaining peach mixture. Spread remaining batter over all. Bake 1 hour. Cool cake 10 minutes before turning out onto a wire rack. Sprinkle with confectioners' sugar. Easy, can prepare ahead. Preparation time: 15 minutes. Serves 10.

Note: Two cups fresh blueberries or 2-3 large apples, peeled, cored, and thinly sliced, may be substituted for peaches.

Atlanta Cooknotes

Plum Cake

2 cups sugar
3 eggs, beaten
1 cup Wesson oil
1 teaspoon grated cloves

1 teaspoon cinnamon
2 cups self-rising flour
2 small jars baby food plums
1 cup chopped nuts

Mix in order given (not beating). Bake about 1 hour at 350° in greased, floured bundt or 2 loaf pans. Delicious!

Atlanta Natives' Favorite Recipes

Bavarian Apple Torte

1/2 cup butter
1/3 cup sugar
1/4 teaspoon vanilla
1 cup flour
1 (8-ounce) package cream cheese
1/4 cup sugar
1 egg

1/2 teaspoon vanilla
1/3 cup sugar
1/2 teaspoon cinnamon (or more)
6 peeled thin sliced apples
1 package almonds, ground in blender

Cream butter, sugar, and vanilla. Blend in flour. Spread dough into bottom and 2 inches on sides of 9-inch spring pan. Combine softened cream cheese and sugar. Mix well. Add eggs and vanilla. Mix well. Pour into pastry-lined pan. Combine sugar and cinnamon. Toss apples in sugar mixture. Spoon apple mixture over cream cheese layer. Sprinkle with nuts. Bake at 450° for 10 minutes. Reduce oven to 400° and continue baking for 25 minutes. Cool before removing.

The Holiday Hostess

Sunbury was the home of two signers of the Declaration of Independence: Button Gwinnett and Lyman Hall. The city, which was the state's second largest, was destroyed by a hurricane in 1824.

Fourteen Layer Chocolate Cake

This recipe is one of this cook's mother's, and its' especially good, she says.

1/2 cup margarine	1 cup milk
1/2 cup vegetable oil	3 cups self-rising flour,
2 cups sugar	sifted
6 eggs	2 teaspoons vanilla

Cream margarine, oil, and sugar well. Add eggs, 1 at a time. Alternate, adding milk and flour, beating at low speed. Add vanilla last. Put 3 tablespoons batter on iron griddle. Cook only a few minutes. Do not turn or flip.

FILLING:

2 cups sugar	Enough water to make paste
1 1/2 sticks margarine	1 1/2 cups evaporated milk
6 heaping tablespoons cocoa	

Cook until begins to thicken. Spread over layer—do not frost sides.

Good Cookin'

Chocolate Nut Torte

Very rich! Very elegant!

TORTE LAYERS:

7 eggs, separated
1/4 teaspoon salt
1 cup sugar
1 teaspoon vanilla extract
1 1/4 cups combination
  ground almonds and pecans

1/4 cup packaged dry bread
  crumbs
1 teaspoon baking powder
1/2 teaspoon salt

Preheat oven to 375°. Separate eggs and place whites in a large bowl, yolks in a small bowl. Let egg whites come to room temperature. Line bottoms of three 8-inch round layer pans with circles of waxed paper and grease lightly. With mixer on high speed, beat egg whites until stiff. Add salt and gradually add 1/2 cup sugar. Beat until stiff peaks form.

Beat yolks until thick and light. Gradually beat in the other 1/2 cup sugar until thick, about 3 minutes. Beat vanilla. Combine ground nuts, bread crumbs, baking powder, and salt. Fold this into yolk mixture with rubber spatula. Mix well with under-and-over motion. Fold this mixture into egwhites until combined. Divide evenly into 3 pans, smoothing the tops. Bake 25 minutes at 375°. Cool at least 1 hour.

FILLING:

1 cup whipped cream
1/2 cup confectioners' sugar

1 teaspoon vanilla extract

Pour whipping cream, confectioners' sugar, and vanilla into a medium bowl. Beat until stiff and refrigerate.

FROSTING:

4 (1-ounce) squares
  unsweetened chocolate
1/4 cup butter
3 cups sifted confectioners'
  sugar

1/2 cup hot coffee
1 1/2 teaspoons vanilla
  extract

CONTINUED

CONTINUED

Melt chocolate and butter over water in a double boiler. Remove from water. Mix in confectioners' sugar, hot coffee and vanilla until smooth.

Cake Assemblage: Loosen cake layers with a knife and turn out of pans. Remove waxed paper. Assemble layers with filling between. Reserve 1 cup of frosting mixture. Frost cake with remaining frosting. Put reserved frosting in a pastry bag fitted with a #2 star tip. Pipe 10-12 stars onto top of cake. Place pecan halves or almond slivers on stars to decorate. Refrigerate at least 1 hour. Serves 12.

Temptations

Luscious Chocolate Cake

4 ounces unsweetened
  chocolate
1/3 cup butter or margarine
1 3/4 cups unsifted
  all-purpose flour
1 1/2 cups sugar

1 1/2 teaspoons baking soda
1 teaspoon salt
1 1/2 cups dairy sour cream
2 eggs
1 teaspoon vanilla

Melt baking chocolate and butter in top of double boiler, or microwave 1 minute on HIGH. Stir to blend well; cool. Combine remaining ingredients in large bowl; blend in melted chocolate. Beat 3 minutes at medium speed. Pour batter into greased and floured pans. Bake at 350° for 30-35 minutes. Frost with Chocolate Caramel Frosting.

CHOCOLATE CARAMEL FROSTING:

1/3 cup butter
1 cup brown sugar, packed
1/3 cup light cream or
  evaporated milk

2 ounces semi-sweet
  chocolate
2 cups confectioners' sugar
1 teaspoon vanilla

Melt butter; add brown sugar and light cream. Bring to boil over low heat, stirring. Remove from heat. Add semi-sweet chocolate, blend until melted. Pour into bowl. Cool at room temperature. Beat in 10X sugar and vanilla. Beat until smooth. May add milk to thin. Be sure to cool cake and frosting completely before icing cake.

Foresters' Favorite Foods

Match-Making Cake
Cáca Cleamhnais

This is an Ulster cake since it was an accessory to match-making, it was baked by the intended bride's mother on the morning of the day that the final arrangements were made. The cake was cut and passed around the assembled people as soon as an agreement was reached regarding the dowry and date.

4 ounces butter
8 ounces flour
4 ounces oatmeal
8 ounces brown sugar
Pinch each of salt and
 baking soda

1 cup water
8 ounces pitted dates
4 ounces brown sugar

Rub the butter into the flour, add oatmeal, 8 ounces brown sugar, soda and salt. Mix well together. Put 1 cup water in pan, add 4 ounces brown sugar, pitted dates and bring to boil, let cool. Line a greased cake pan and put in half of the dry flour mixture. Spread the date mixture on top of this, top with remainder of the dry flour mixture and bake in a moderate oven for about 30 minutes. Let cool in pan before removing.

Cooklore and Recipes of Ireland

Hot Fudge Sauce

3/4 cup sugar
3 tablespoons cocoa
2 tablespoons water
Dash of salt

1 small can evaporated milk
2 tablespoons butter
1 teaspoon vanilla

Put first 4 ingredients in saucepan and blend until cocoa dissolves. Add evaporated milk; bring to boil gently (3-4 minutes) stirring constantly. Do not use high heat. Remove from heat and stir in butter and vanilla. Pour over cake or ice cream while sauce is still hot.

Dee-licious!

Country Cakes

Kahlua Angel Food

Great way to liven up a bought cake.

1 angel food cake
2 tablespoons Kahlua
1/4 cup cream

1/4 cup Kahlua
1 (16-ounce) tub Cool Whip

Purchase angel food cake. Poke holes all over top of cake with thin knife or skewer. Combine 2 tablespoons Kahlua and 1/4 cup cream and pour half of it into holes. Place cake in refrigerator for 2 hours. Pour the rest of Kahlua and cream mixture into holes and refrigerate 2 more hours. Combine Cool Whip, 1/4 cup Kahlua and spread on top and side of cake—serve.

A Taste of the Holidays

Chocolate Buttercream Icing

1/4 cup water
1 pound powdered sugar
1 tablespoon light corn
  syrup
1 pound unsalted butter, at
  room temperature

1 egg white
3-6 ounces semisweet
  chocolate chips, melted

Combine water, powdered sugar, and corn syrup and heat in double boiler until warm. Place in bowl of electric mixer and beat in butter 1 tablespoon at a time until light and fluffy. Beat in egg white and melted chocolate. Refrigerate if necessary to reach good spreading consistency.

Note: Vary amount of chocolate depending on taste and color of icing desired.

Gottlieb's Bakery 100 Years of Recipes

Cookies
and
Candies

Georgia's Agrirama has a living history farm and town of rural Georgia prior to 1900. Tifton.

Almond Florentines

A Savannah favorite.

2 1/2 cups sliced almonds
1 cup sugar
1/2 cup unsalted butter,
  melted
5 tablespoons unbleached
  all-purpose flour

2 egg whites, slightly
  beaten
Pinch salt
1/2 teaspoon vanilla extract

Preheat oven to 350°. Line cookie sheets with parchment paper—no substitute! Toss almonds and sugar together. Stir in melted butter. Stir in flour, egg whites, salt, and vanilla until well blended. Drop by spoonfuls onto sheets, or pick up a blob of batter in your hand and squeeze out 1 cookie's worth at a time, scraping off onto sheet with your other thumb. Space about 2 inches apart. Bake 1 sheet at a time for 10 minutes, or until golden brown on bottom and edges. Makes 6 dozen 2-inch cookies.

Gottlieb's Bakery 100 Years of Recipes

Apple and Cheese Pleasers

3/4 cup flour
2/3 cup margarine, softened
1/3 cup brown sugar
1 egg
1 teaspoon vanilla
1/2 teaspoon cinnamon
1/2 teaspoon baking powder

1/2 teaspoon salt
1 1/2 cups Quaker Oats
1 cup shredded Cheddar
  cheese
3/4 cup raisins
1 cup chopped apple

Combine flour, margarine, sugar, egg, vanilla, cinnamon, baking powder, and salt in large bowl. Mix well. Add oats, cheese and raisins. Mix well. Stir in apples. Drop by tablespoonfuls onto ungreased cookie sheet. Bake at 375° for 15 minutes or until golden brown. Store in tightly covered container in refrigerator. Yield about 24 cookies. Children love these high-protein breakfast cookies.

Educated Taste

Coconut Krisps

1 cup shortening
1 cup sugar
1 cup brown sugar
2 eggs
2 cups flour
1/2 teaspoon salt

1 teaspoon soda
1 tablespoon vanilla
1 cup coconut flakes
1 cup quick oatmeal
1 cup Rice Krispies

Mix together to make stiff batter. Drop by teaspoonsful onto cookie sheet. Bake at 350° until light brown.

Country Cupboard Cookbook

Country Store Soft Ginger Cookies

Once your family smells these cooking, they won't let you give them away!

1 pound unsalted butter
3 cups sugar
1 cup unsulphured molasses
3 large eggs
8 cups all-purpose flour
1 teaspoon salt

1 1/2 tablespoons baking
  soda
1 1/2 tablespoons ginger
1 tablespoon ground cloves
1 tablespoon ground cinnamon
Sugar (to roll cookies in)

Preheat oven to 350°. In a very large bowl, cream butter. Beat in sugar until light and fluffy. Beat in molasses. Add eggs 1 at a time, beating well after each one.

Sift dry ingredients together. Stir into butter mixture and blend well.

Roll into 1 1/2-inch balls and roll in sugar. Place 2 inches apart on ungreased cookie sheet. Bake for 13-15 minutes. Yield: 6 dozen.

Temptations

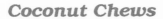

Coconut Chews

1 1/2 sticks margarine
1 cup brown sugar
1 egg
1 teaspoon vanilla
1 1/2 cups graham cracker
  crumbs

1 cup flour
1 teaspoon baking soda
3/4 cup flaked coconut

Melt margarine. Add sugar, egg, vanilla, and crumbs; stir until smooth. Mix flour and soda together. Gradually add flour mixture and stir until smooth. Mix in coconut. Cover and chill at least 1 hour. Drop by teaspoonfuls on greased cookie sheet. Bake at 350° 8-12 minutes. Yield: 6 dozen.

A Taste of the Holidays

Oatmeal Cookies

1 cup butter
1 cup brown sugar (packed)
1 cup white sugar
2 eggs
1 teaspoon vanilla
2 cups flour

1 teaspoon baking soda
1 teaspoon baking powder
1/4 teaspoon salt
2 cups oatmeal
1 cup chopped nuts

Cream butter and sugars. Add eggs 1 at a time beating well. Add other ingredients and beat until well blended. Bake for 10 minutes at 350°.

Note: 1/2 cup raisins, 1 cup gum drops or 1 cup coconut may be added for variation.

Country Cupboard Cookbook

Benne Cookies

As southern as you can get.

1 1/2 cups firmly packed	1/4 cup water
light brown sugar	2 cups all-purpose flour
1/4 cup vegetable shortening	(White Lily preferred)
1/4 cup creamy peanut butter	1/2 teaspoon salt
1 tablespoon vegetable oil	1 teaspoon baking soda
3 eggs	1 cup sesame (benne) seeds

Preheat oven to 350°. Throw everything into the bowl of an electric mixer and beat until smooth. Pipe quarter-sized dots through 1/2-inch top onto parchment-lined (or very well greased and floured) cookie sheets. Bake 1 sheet at a time for 8-10 minutes, remove from sheet with metal spatula and cool on wire racks. Makes about 300 little cookies. Store in an airtight container.

Note: Please don't buy umpteen little jars of sesame seeds at the grocery store to get a cup of seeds. Buy them in bulk at a health food store.

Gottlieb's Bakery 100 Years of Recipes

Benne Seed Wafers

1 cup sesame seed	2 eggs
2 1/2 cups light brown sugar	1 1/4 cups self-rising flour
1 cup salad oil	2 teaspoons vanilla extract

Place sesame seeds in heavy skillet over low heat and stir till golden. Set aside. Mix sugar, salad oil, and eggs in electric mixer at medium speed till light and fluffy. Add flour and mix thoroughly. Stir in vanilla and sesame seeds. Drop by teaspoons on greased baking sheets and bake at 325° for about 10 minutes or until golden. Let stand on cookie sheet for 2 minutes before removing from pan. When cool, store in a covered container.

Fancy Foods & Flowers

Date Nut Fingers

1 stick margarine
1 cup sugar
1 (8-ounce) package pitted
  dates

1 cup rice crispies
1 cup chopped nuts
1 teaspoon vanilla extract

Dissolve first 3 ingredients over low heat. Stir and mash. Remove from heat and add next 3 ingredients. Roll into finger shapes or balls and then roll in sifted powdered sugar. Delicious!

Country Cakes

Alice's Date-Filled Cookies

Children love them and they are fun to make!

1 pound dates, chopped
3/4 cup water
1/2 cup sugar
1 1/2 cups brown sugar
1 cup butter or margarine
2 eggs
3 cups all-purpose flour

1 1/2 cups minute rolled
  oats
1 teaspoon vanilla
1 teaspoon cream of tartar
1 teaspoon soda in 1
  tablespoon water
Confectioners' sugar

Boil dates, water, and 1/2 cup sugar about 5 minutes (until mixture is smooth). Set aside to cool. Mix next 8 ingredients with electric beater. Dough will be quite thick. Chill for better handling. Divide dough in half. Roll each half into a rectangle 1/8-inch thick. Using 2-inch cookie cutter, cut as many rounds as possible. Place half the rounds on greased cookie sheet. Make small mounds of date mixture on this half. Place remaining rounds over date mixture and gently seal around sides with fork. Bake 10-12 minutes at 375° (until light brown). Roll in confectioners' sugar while warm, not hot. Cookies keep well. Yield: 2-3 dozen.

The Historic Roswell Cook Book

Cherry Wink Cookies

2 1/4 cups flour
1 teaspoon baking powder
1/2 teaspoon soda
1/2 teaspoon salt
3/4 cup shortening
1 cup sugar
2 eggs
2 tablespoons milk
1 teaspoon vanilla

1/3 cup chopped maraschino
  cherries, drained
1 cup chopped pecans
1 cup chopped dates
2 1/2 cups crushed
  cornflakes
1/3 cup maraschino cherries,
  halved

Sift dry ingredients together and set aside. Cream shortening and sugar and blend in eggs. Add milk and vanilla. Mix in chopped cherries. Blend in sifted dry ingredients; mix well.

Shape dough into balls using a level tablespoon for each. Crush 2 1/2 cups cornflakes. Roll each ball of dough in the crushed cornflakes. Place on greased baking sheet; top each cookie with 1/2 maraschino cherry. Bake 10-12 minutes at 350°.

Cherries Galore

Macon is the home of over 70,000 Yoshino Cherry Trees and the award-winning Cherry Blossom Festival held every March.

Chocolate-Pistachio Cookies

2 cups sifted flour
1 1/2 teaspoons baking
  powder
1/2 teaspoon salt
2/3 cup butter, at room
  temperature
1 cup sugar
1 egg
1 teaspoon vanilla extract

1/2 teaspoon almond extract
1 cup finely chopped
  pistachio nuts or almonds,
  divided
Green food coloring
  (optional)
1 (6-ounce) package
  chocolate chips, melted

Sift flour with baking powder and salt and set aside. In a large bowl, beat butter, sugar, egg, and extracts until fluffy. Slowly add flour mixture. Take out 3/4 cup of the batter, and combine with 1/4 cup chopped nuts and 2 or 3 drops green food color, if desired. Mix well. Fold into 2 long thin rolls. Wrap in plastic and refrigerate.

Form remaining dough into two rectangles. Unwrap first rolls from refrigerator and place on top of these. Roll lengthwise and wrap. Refrigerate 8 hours, or freeze.
Preheat oven to 375°. Cut dough with a sharp kinfe into slices 1/8-1/4-inch wide. Place on ungreased cookie sheets and bake 8-10 minutes. When cool, roll edges first in melted chocolate chips and then in remaining nuts. Let set well before serving or storing. Store in airtight box in cool place. Yield: about 6 dozen.

Georgia Entertains

Chocolate Kiss Cookies

1 cup butter, softened
2/3 cup sugar
1 teaspoon vanilla extract
1 2/3 cups unsifted
  all-purpose flour
1/4 cup cocoa

3/4 cup finely chopped
  pecans
1 (9-ounce) package milk
  chocolate kisses
Powdered sugar

Cream butter, sugar, and vanilla in large mixing bowl. Combine flour and cocoa; blend into creamed mixture. Add pecans; blend well. Chill dough 1 hour. Unwrap kisses. Shape a scant tablespoon of dough around each kiss, covering completely. Shape into balls.

CONTINUED

CONTINUED

Place on ungreased cookie sheet. Bake at 375° for 10 minutes. Cool slightly; remove to wire rack; cool completely. Roll in powdered sugar. Yield: 4 1/2 dozen.

Peachtree Bouquet

Love Notes
(Lemon Cookies)

CRUST:

2 cups sifted plain flour   1 cup butter
1/2 cup 4X powdered sugar

Cut flour and powdered sugar into butter until mixture clings together. Press dough into 13x9-inch baking pan. Bake at 350° for 25 minutes. Cool to room temperature before putting on the topping. This is essential for a crisp crust.

TOPPING:

4 eggs, slightly beaten   1 teaspoon baking powder
2 cups granulated sugar   1/4 cup plain flour
6 tablespoons lemon juice

Mix eggs, sugar, and lemon juice together. When well blended, add remaining ingredients. Mix well. Pour over baked crust. Bake at 350° for 25 minutes. Sprinkle with powdered sugar. Cool completely, then cut into bars. Yields 2 1/2 dozen. From Mrs. Tom Watson, wife of 1977 Masters' Champion.

Tea-Time at the Masters®

Toll House Marble Squares

1/2 cup butter or margarine,
  softened
1/4 cup plus 2 tablespoons
  granulated sugar
1/4 cup plus 2 tablespoons
  brown sugar, packed
1/2 teaspoon vanilla
1 egg

1 cup flour, unsifted
1/2 teaspoon soda
1/2 teaspoon salt
1/2 cup coarsely chopped
  walnuts, optional
1 (6-ounce) package
  semi-sweet chocolate morsels

Heat oven to 375°. Grease oblong pan (13x9x2-inch). Mix butter, sugars, and vanilla thoroughly. Beat in egg. Blend in flour, soda, and salt. Mix in walnuts. Spread in prepared pan. Sprinkle chocolate morsels over top of dough. Place in oven about 2 minutes. Remove from oven and run knife through dough to marbelize. Return to oven; bake 12-14 minutes. Cool. Cut into squares.

Windsor Academy Cookbook

Chocolate Chip Pizza

1/2 cup sugar
1/2 cup firmly packed brown
  sugar
1/2 cup margarine, softened
1/2 cup peanut butter
1/2 teaspoon vanilla extract
1 egg

1 1/2 cups flour
2 cups miniature
  marshmallows
6 ounces semi-sweet chocolate
  chips
1/2 cup pecan halves
  (optional)

Preheat oven to 375°. In large bowl combine sugar, brown sugar, margarine, peanut butter, vanilla, and egg. Blend well. Add flour and stir until soft dough forms. Press dough evenly over bottom of 12 to 14-inch pizza pan, forming rim along edge. Bake at 375° for 10 minutes. Remove from oven. Sprinkle with marshmallows, chocolate chips, and pecans. Continue baking for 5 minutes or until marshmallows are puffy and lightly browned. Cool and cut into wedges. (May store in tightly covered container.) Must do ahead. Serves 15-20.

Perennials

Lemon Bars

2 cups sifted all-purpose flour	4 beaten eggs
1/2 cup sifted confectioners' sugar	2 cups granulated sugar
1 cup butter or margarine	1/3 cup lemon juice
	1/4 cup all-purpose flour
	1/2 teaspoon baking powder

Sift 2 cups flour and confectioners' sugar together. Cut in butter or margarine until mixture clings together. Press in 13x9x2-inch baking pan. Bake in 350° oven for 20-25 minutes or until lightly browned. Beat together eggs, granulated sugar, and lemon juice. Sift flour and baking powder; stir into egg mixture. Pour over baked crust. Bake in 350° oven for 25 minutes longer. Sprinkle with additional confectioners' sugar, if desired. Cool. Chill in refrigerator for several hours or overnight. Cut in bars. Yield: 2 1/2-3 dozen.

The Stuffed Griffin

Peanut Butter Squares
(Microwave)

1/2 cup graham cracker crumbs	1 cup melted butter
2 1/2 cups powdered sugar	1 cup chunky peanut butter
	2 cups milk chocolate chips

Mix crumbs, sugar, butter, and peanut butter. Spread in a 9x13-inch dish. Shield ends of dish with foil. Microwave on HIGH 2 minutes to set. Melt chocolate by microwaving on 5% power for 3-4 minutes. Spread on above mixture while warm. Chill and cut in squares. If you like Reese's Peanut Butter Cups, you'll love these.

Simply Scrumptious Microwaving

Chocolate Caramel Bars

1 package (50) Kraft
  caramels
1/3 cup evaporated milk
1 box German chocolate cake
  mix

1/3 cup evaporated milk
3/4 cup melted butter
1 cup chopped nuts
1 cup chocolate chips

Melt caramels and evaporated milk, stirring often. Mix German chocolate cake mix with 1/3 cup evaporated milk, melted butter, and nuts. Put half of this mixture in bottom of 9x13-inch pan. Bake at 350° for 6 minutes. Remove from oven. Sprinkle 1 cup chocolate chips over warm crust. Pour melted caramel mixture over chips. Spread remaining crust mixture over top. Bake at 350° for 15-20 minutes. Cut into bars.

Country Cupboard Cookbook

Chocolate Sherry Cream Bars

4 ounces baking chocolate	1 cup flour
1 cup margarine	1/2 teaspoon salt
4 eggs	1 teaspoon vanilla
2 cups sugar	

Melt chocolate and margarine over hot water—cool slightly. Beat eggs until light. Gradually cream in sugar. Add remaining ingredients. Beat 1 minute. Pour into greased and floured 10x14-inch pan. Bake 25 minutes in moderate oven. Cool!

FILLING:

1/2 cup butter	1/4 cup sherry
4 cups powdered sugar	1 cup chopped nuts
1/4 cup coffee cream	

Beat butter and sugar together while gradually adding cream and sherry. Mixture should be light and fluffy...mix in walnuts. Spread over base and chill.

TOPPING:

1 (6-ounce) package	4 tablespoons water
semi-sweet chocolate pieces	4 tablespoons butter

Melt chocolate pieces with water and butter over hot water. Mix well. Dribble over filling. Chill until firm. Cut into 1x2-inch bars. Store in refrigerator. Yield 5 dozen bars.

Note: I have copied this over so many times because they are absolutely out of this world. I am hoping this will be circulated enough so that I'll never have to copy it again. Amen!

Frederica Fare

Bourbon Brownies

1 (23-ounce) package Duncan
 Hines brownie mix
3 eggs
1 cup chopped walnuts
6 tablespoons bourbon
1/2 cup softened butter

2 cups confectioners' sugar
3 tablespoons rum
6 ounces semi-sweet
 chocolate
4 tablespoons butter

Preheat oven to 350°. Omitting water called for on package, combine brownie mix, eggs, and walnuts. Bake according to package directions. Remove from oven and immediately sprinkle with bourbon. Cool thoroughly. Combine butter, confectioners' sugar, and rum. Spread evenly over brownies.

Chill about 1 hour. Melt chocolate and butter. Drizzle over brownies. Chill an additional hour or until chocolate hardens. With a warm knife, cut into small brownies. Easy, must prepare ahead, can freeze. Preparation time: 45 minutes. Makes 4 dozen.

Atlanta Cooknotes

Golden Eggnog Brownies

2 1/4 cups vanilla wafer
 crumbs, lightly packed
1 teaspoon nutmeg
1 (14-ounce) can sweetened
 condensed milk
2 tablespoons golden rum
1/2 teaspoon rum extract

2 egg yolks, beaten
1/2 cup chopped golden
 raisins
1/2 cup finely diced walnuts
Extra nutmeg
Powdered sugar

Preheat oven to 350°. Butter an 8-inch square pan. In medium-size bowl, stir together vanilla wafer crumbs and nutmeg. Thoroughly blend in sweetened condensed milk. Stir in rum, rum extract, and beaten egg yolks. Mix well. Fold in raisins and walnuts. Spread batter evenly in pan. Sprinkle generously with extra nutmeg. Bake for 20-25 minutes or until toothpick comes out clean. Cool in pan. Lightly sift powdered sugar over top and cut into squares. Makes 16 brownies.

The Holiday Hostess

Bran Brownies

Satisfy that chocolate craving and get some bran at the same time.

3 tablespoons cocoa powder
1 tablespoon instant coffee
1 tablespoon water
2 very ripe bananas
2 cups sugar (less if you prefer)
6 egg whites

1 teaspoon vanilla
1 cup oat bran cereal
1/4 teaspoon salt (optional)
1 cup chopped nuts (or substitute raisins to cut fat further)

Heat oven to 350°. Spray 9x9-inch baking pan with non-stick pan primer; set aside. Combine the cocoa, coffee, water and bananas, and mix in blender or bowl of mixer. Add the sugar, egg whites, vanilla and mix well. Mix together the oat bran cereal and salt; add to cocoa mixture. Fold in the nuts or raisins. Pour into baking pan. Bake 45 minutes. Cut into individual squares, cool and serve. Yield: 16-20.

Lasting Impressions

Crème de Menthe Brownies

4 ounces unsweetened baking
  chocolate
1 cup margarine
4 eggs

2 cups sugar
1/2 teaspoon salt
1 teaspoon vanilla
1 cup flour, sifted

In double boiler, melt chocolate and margarine over water; cool slightly. In mixing bowl, beat eggs until light and fluffy. Beat in sugar gradually. Add remaining ingredients including chocolate mixture. Beat 1 minute. Pour into greased 13x9-inch pan. Bake at 350° for 25 minutes. Do not overbake. Cool. Base will be fudge.

FILLING:

1/2 cup margarine
4 cups confectioners' sugar
 sifted

1/4 cup whipping cream
1/4 cup crème de menthe

Beat together margarine and sugar while gradually adding milk and creme de menthe. Mixture will be light and fluffy. Spread over base and chill 1 1/2 hours.

TOPPING:

6 ounces chocolate chips
4 tablespoons margarine

3 tablespoons water

Melt chocolate chips and margarine over water. Mix and spread over filling. Chill. Store in refrigerator. Freezes well. Yields approximately 5 dozen.

Savannah Style

 A Cherokee Indian named Sequoyah invented the Cherokee alphabet at New Echota, near Calhoun, now a State Historical Site.

Georgia Peanut Brittle

Use a candy thermometer and the brittle will be perfect!

3 cups sugar	3 cups raw Georgia peanuts
1 cup white corn syrup	3 teaspoons margarine
(Karo)	1 teaspoon salt
1/2 cup water	2 tablespoons soda

Grease 2 long pieces of aluminum foil and have them ready on counter top. Combine sugar, syrup, and water in heavy 5-6-quart pan. On medium heat, stir until sugar melts, then add peanuts. Leave on medium to medium-high heat and stir occasionally. Cook until candy thermometer reaches 300—hard crack stage. Syrup will be golden and peanuts will "pop" because they have roasted. Remove from heat and add margarine, salt, and soda, stirring well. Candy will "puff up." Pour candy on pieces of prepared, greased aluminum foil. Pour candy quickly and stretch, using a fork or hands, when cool enough. Cool and break into pieces. Yield: 2 1/2 to 3 pounds.

A Taste of Georgia

Syrup Candy

This cook remembers as a child as she and her friends stood around the kitchen table pulling syrup candy.

1 1/2 cups cane syrup	1 teaspoon vinegar
1 cup sugar	1 big teaspoon butter

Cook until forms ball in a cup of water and will crack on side of cup. Pour candy on buttered plate. When cool enough to handle, pull until very light.

Good Cookin'

Smoothest Divinity

Never try to make this on a rainy day or without a candy thermometer.

1/2 cup Karo syrup (red label)	1/2 cup water
2 1/2 cups sugar	2 large egg whites
1/4 teaspoon salt	1 teaspoon vanilla
	1 cup chopped nuts

Combine first 4 ingredients in saucepan. Cook over medium heat stirring constantly, until sugar is dissolved. Cook, without stirring, to firm ball stage (248°). Be sure to use candy thermometer. Just before syrup reaches 248° beat egg whites until stiff, not dry. Pour about 1/2 of the syrup over the egg whites, beating constantly. Cook the remainder of the syrup to soft crack stage (272°). Add syrup slowly to first mixture, beating constantly. Continue beating until mixture holds shape. Add vanilla and nuts; drop from spoon onto wax paper or tin foil. Makes about 1 3/4 pounds.

The Hors d'Oeuvre Tray

Marshmallow Fudge

4 cups sugar	1 (12-ounce) package chocolate chips
1 (14 1/2-ounce) can evaporated milk	1 teaspoon vanilla
1 cup butter	1 cup chopped nuts
1 pint marshmallow cream	

Bring sugar, milk, and butter to a boil. Cook to medium-soft stage (236°), stirring. Remove from heat. Add marshmallow cream, chips, vanilla, and nuts. Stir. Pour into pan, at least 9x9-inch. Cut into squares when cool. Makes 3 pounds.

The Stuffed Griffin

Grandma's Microwave Fudge

Wonderfully delicious—remarkably easy!

1 box powdered sugar	1/4 cup milk
1/2 cup cocoa	1 teaspoon vanilla
1 stick butter	Chopped nuts

Blend together sugar and cocoa in a glass bowl; add milk. Place butter on top of mixture and microwave 2 minutes. Stir; add vanilla and nuts and mix well. Spread onto foil or waxed-paper-lined pan (for easier removal from pan) and refrigerate for 1 hour. Cut into squares, remove from pan, and serve.

Ramblin' Chefs From Georgia Tech

Pecan Log Roll

1 (6-ounce) package	1/2 cup chopped pecans
butterscotch morsels	1 egg white, slightly beaten
1/3 cup condensed milk	(optional)
1/2 teaspoon vanilla	Additional chopped pecans

Melt morsels over hot (not boiling) water. Remove from heat. Stir in condensed milk, vanilla, and pecans. Chill until firm enough to handle. Roll tightly on waxed paper to form 12-inch roll. Brush with egg whites (if desired), and roll in additional chopped pecans. Chill and slice.

Boarding House Reach

Easy Toffee

This is an amazing recipe from a friend of my mother's.

1 stack of Saltine crackers
1 cup butter or margarine
1 packed cup light-brown
sugar

1 (12-ounce) package
semi-sweet chocolate morsels

Line a large cookie sheet with foil. Lay crackers on foil in a solid cover, crackers touching. Boil butter and brown sugar for 3 minutes, stirring constantly. Pour over crackers, spreading to cover them all. Bake at 400° for 5-7 minutes; do not allow sugar mixture to burn. Remove from oven and allow to sit about 3 minutes. Sprinkle chocolate chips evenly over candy and spread with a spatula as chocolate begins to melt. Refrigerate. Chocolate will harden in about 30 minutes to an hour and candy can be broken into pieces.

Savannah Collection

Pies and Desserts

The Jekyll Island Millionaires' Club.

Charlotte's Peanut Butter Pie

1 cup confectioners' sugar
1/2 cup crunchy peanut
 butter

1 pie shell, baked

Blend peanut butter and confectioners' sugar. Spread all but 3 tablespoons on bottom of pie shell. Save remainder for topping.

FILLING:

2/3 cup sugar
1/4 cup cornstarch
1/4 teaspoon salt
2 cups milk, scalded

3 egg yolks, beaten
2 tablespoons butter
1 teaspoon vanilla

Blend sugar, cornstarch, and salt. Slowly add scalded milk. Place over medium heat. Cook, stirring constantly. Slowly add yolks and butter. Continue stirring until thickened. Set aside and stir in vanilla. Pour over peanut butter mixture.

MERINGUE:

3 egg whites
3 tablespoons sugar

1/8 teaspoon cream of tartar

Beat egg whites, sugar, and cream of tartar until fluffy. Spread over filling. Top meringue with the remaining peanut butter mixture. Place in 300° oven until meringue is lightly browned. Serve at room temperature or chilled. Makes 6-8 servings.

Betty Talmadge's Lovejoy Plantation Cookbook

Chantilly Peanut Pie

1 (10-inch) chocolate crumb
  crust
1 quart vanilla ice cream,
  slightly softened
3/4 cup creamy peanut butter

1 cup chopped unsalted
  peanuts
1 tablespoon vanilla
Whipped cream (sweetened)
Hot fudge sauce

Combine ice cream, peanut butter, 1/2 cup peanuts and vanilla in bowl. Mix well. Pour into prepared crust. Sprinkle with remaining nuts. Freeze. Remove from freezer about 10 minutes before serving. Garnish with whipped cream and serve hot fudge sauce drizzled over each slice.

Educated Taste

German Chocolate Pie

1/3 cup brown sugar
1/3 cup coconut
1/3 cup chopped pecans
1/3 cup butter
1 prebaked pastry shell
1 cup sugar
1/3 cup flour

Dash of salt
2 cups milk
2 squares unsweetened
  baker's chocolate
3 egg yolks
2 tablespoons butter
1 teaspoon vanilla

Place first 4 ingredients in pan and melt, stirring constantly. Pour into bottom of prebaked pastry shell and put in oven till bubbly. Remove and cool.

In a saucepan place sugar, flour, salt, milk, and chocolate; stir over medium heat till mixture comes to a boil. Continue stirring for 3 minutes. Pour half of hot mixture into beaten egg yolks and stir; remove mixture to pan and cook for 2 additional minutes. Remove from heat and stir in butter and vanilla. Pour hot mixture over caramel-pecan layer in pantry shell and cover with waxed paper. Cool in refrigerator and serve with whipped cream. Garnish with pecans, toasted coconut, and shaved chocolate. From the Calico Cafe.

Somethin's Cookin' in the Mountains

Rum Cream Pie

Simply scrumptious! Good light Thanksgiving or Christmas dessert!

CRUST:

2 1/4 cups graham cracker
  crumbs
1/2 cup butter, melted

2 tablespoons sugar
1/2 teaspoon ground cinnamon
1/2 cup chopped pecans

FILLING:

1 envelope unflavored
  gelatin
1/2 cup cold water
5 egg yolks
1 cup sugar

1/3 cup Myers dark rum
1 1/2 cups whipping cream,
  whipped
Unsweetened chocolate,
  shaved for garnish

Combine crust ingredients and press in a 9-inch pie plate. Microwave on HIGH 3 minutes. Chill. Soften gelatin in water. Microwave on HIGH 45 seconds to 1 minute to dissolve gelatin. Beat egg yolks and sugar until very light. Stir gelatin into egg mixture. Cool. Gradually add rum, beating constantly. Fold whipped cream into egg mixture. Cool until mixture begins to set, then spoon into crust. Chill until firm. Top with grated chocolate.

Note: Try substituting other liquors or liqueurs for rum. For example: bourbon, praline liqueur, Kahlua, amaretto.

Simply Scrumptious Microwaving

The Okefenokee Swamp Park near Waycross has a museum, wildlife exhibits, nature walks, lectures, and a reconstructed homestead. Boat rides show the denseness and beauty of the swamp; a 90-foot observation tower affords a panoramic view.

Caribbean Fudge Pie

Chocolate flavored with a hint of coffee and rum.

1/4 cup margarine, softened (1/2 stick)	1 teaspoon rum extract
3/4 cup brown sugar, packed	1/4 cup flour
3 eggs	1 1/2 cups pecans, chopped (divided)
1 (12-ounce) package chocolate chips, melted	1 unbaked (9-inch) pastry shell
2 teaspoons instant coffee	Whipped cream for topping

Heat oven to 375°. In bowl of mixer cream margarine and sugar until light and fluffy. Add eggs, 1 at a time, beating well after each addition. Add melted chocolate chips, instant coffee, and rum extract; mix well. Stir in flour and 1 cup pecans; blend well. Pour into pie shell; sprinkle remaining pecans over top. Bake 25 minutes or until filling is set. Cool and serve topped with whipped cream. Yield: 1 pie.

Lasting Impressions

Black Bottom Pie

CRUST:

1/2 package Nabisco Famous chocolate wafers, crushed	1/4 cup butter or margarine, melted

Preheat oven to 350°. Combine cookie crumbs and butter. This can be done in a food processor. Press onto bottom and sides of a 9-inch pie pan. Bake for 7-8 minutes, until set. Cool.

FILLING:

1 envelope unflavored gelatin	1/2 cup all-purpose flour
1/4 cup cold water	2 ounces baking chocolate
4 cups cold water	1 teaspoon vanilla extract
4 cups milk	1/2 cup Myers dark rum
5 eggs, separated	1/4 teaspoon cream of tartar
3/4 cup sugar	1/4 cup sugar

Dissolve gelatin in cold water and set aside to soften. Bring the milk to a rolling boil in a heavy saucepan. Be careful that it doesn't boil over. Meanwhile, beat the egg yolks and 3/4 cup sugar with a wire whisk until thick. Beat in the flour until smooth. When the milk boils, pour it slowly and carefully into the egg mixture, whisking constantly. Whisk until smooth, pour the mixture back into the milk pan, and return to heat. Bring to a boil over medium heat, whisking constantly. Reduce heat and cook for 2-3 minutes, stirring constantly to prevent scorching.

Place the chocolate in a bowl. Pour 2 1/2 cups of hot custard over the chocolate. Immediately place a piece of plastic wrap directly onto the surface of the custard to prevent a skin from forming. If you fail to do this, you will have lumps in your pie. Let sit until chocolate is melted, add vanilla extract, and stir to blend. Replace plastic wrap. Cool to room temperature and fill pie crust, spreading chocolate custard up to edge of crust. Refrigerate.

Add gelatin to remaining hot custard to melt. Cover

CONTINUED

CONTINUED

with plastic wrap as for chocolate custard. Cool. Add rum. Refrigerate, stirring occasionally, until custard begins to thicken to about the consistency of unbeaten egg whites. Beat egg whites and cream of tartar until they form soft peaks. Beat in sugar; continue beating until peaks are stiff but not dry. Fold thickened rum custard into egg whites and mound on top of chocolate custard. If the rum mixture does not set up—highly possible in a hot kitchen—refrigerate, stirring frequently with a rubber spatula, until it thickens enough to mound. Refrigerate uncovered 4-6 hours or overnight. Garnish with whipped cream and tiny chocolate chip—and a cherry! Serves 8.

The Pirates' House Cook Book

Mince Pie

1 pie crust
2 boxes prepared mincemeat
4 cups water
1 cup chopped nuts
2 cups chopped apple
1 cup raisins

1/2 cup sherry
Sugar
Butter
Whipped cream, ice cream, or
    cheese, to serve

Prepare pie crust. Preheat oven to 350°. Chop mincemeat into water and put on to boil until water is absorbed. Add to this chopped nuts, chopped apple, raisins, and sherry. Put mixture into uncooked pie crust. Make crisscross strips across pie, sprinkle with sugar, dot with butter, and bake about 30 minutes. Top with whipped cream, ice cream, or a sliver of cheese. Oh boy, am I hungry! I can smell it now! Serves 6-8.

From Mother with Love

Southern Pecan Pie

Orange flavor makes the difference.

3 large eggs
1 cup white corn syrup
3/4 cup sugar
1 tablespoon orange juice
2 tablespoons grated orange
  rind

2 tablespoons butter, melted
1 cup pecans, coarsely
  chopped
1 pie shell, unbaked
Whipped cream, optional

Beat eggs slightly. Add syrup, sugar, juice, and rind. Stir in butter. Spread pecans over unbaked pie crust and pour filling over. Bake approximately 45 minutes at 350°. Serve topped with whipped cream, if desired. Yield: 1 (8 or 9-inch) pie.

A Taste of Georgia

Ritz Pecan Pie

At Callaway Gardens there are so many good things served to eat...it's hard to decide what you like best...but one dessert you'll always enjoy is this delicious pie.

2/3 cup egg whites
1 cup sugar
1/2 teaspoon baking powder

16 Ritz crackers, crumbled
1/4 pound chopped pecans

Beat the egg whites. Mix sugar and baking powder. Add to egg whites. Beat until stiff peaks form. Fold in nuts and cracker crumbs. Bake in buttered pie pan 45 minutes at 300°. When cooled, top with whipped cream. Garnish with extra cracker crumbs and pecans.

Country Cookin'

 Dougherty County has about 250,000 pecan trees, more than any other U.S. county. First planted in Baconton in 1872, pecans have become Georgia's second leading crop.

Pecan Cheesecake Pie
(Microwave)

PIE SHELL:

1 1/2 cups graham cracker crumbs

1 stick butter/margarine

1/3 cup finely chopped pecans

Melt butter/margarine for 2-3 minutes on Full Power in a glass measuring cup. Blend butter/margarine into cracker crumbs and 1/3 cup pecans. Press into a 9-inch glass pie pan. Cook in microwave on Full Power for 1 1/2-2 minutes. Allow crust to cool before filling.

FILLING:

1 (8-ounce) package cream cheese

1 cup sugar

3/4 cup chopped pecans

Blend softened cream cheese with 1 cup sugar in food processor or blender until smooth and creamy and no longer "grainy." Add 3/4 cup chopped pecans toward the end of the processing. Spread filling evenly into cooled pie shell. Cook on 70% power for 5-6 minutes or until filling is "set."

TOPPING:

2 tablespoons sugar

2 teaspoons vanilla

1/2 pint commercial sour cream

Pecan halves, to garnish

Add 2 tablespoons sugar and vanilla to sour cream. After filling has cooled, spread filling evenly over top of pie. Return pie to microwave and cook on 70% power for 2-3 more minutes. Allow to cool then garnish with chopped pecans or pecan halves. Chill about an hour before serving. Flavor of pie is best if allowed to "sit out" at room temperature 30 minutes before serving. Serves 6-8.

The Dapper Zapper

Incredible Peach Pie

2 eggs
1/2 cup milk
1/2 cup light corn syrup
1/4 cup melted butter
1/4 cup sugar
1 teaspoon vanilla

1/2 cup self-rising flour
1 cup shredded coconut
2 1/2 cups chopped peaches
1/2 cup chopped pecans
Nutmeg or cinnamon

In large bowl beat eggs Add next 6 ingredients; mix until smooth. Stir in peaches and coconut. Pour into a greased and floured pie plate. Sprinkle generously with nutmeg or cinnamon. Top with pecans. Bake at 350° for 40-50 minutes, or until custard is set. Let stand for awhile before cutting. This pie makes its own crust and needs to set awhile to make the crust firm.

Head Table Cooks

Peach Cream Pie

Delicious made with Georgia peaches, fresh or from the freezer.

2 cups vanilla wafer crumbs
1 stick margarine, melted
1 (14-ounce) can sweetened
 condensed milk
1/2 cup lemon juice

1 (1-pint) carton frozen
 peaches (or 2 cups)
1 (9-ounce) carton frozen
 whipped dessert topping,
 thawed

Make crust of 2 cups vanilla wafer crumbs and 1 stick melted margarine. Press into 9-inch pie plate and chill.

Blend condensed milk and lemon juice until thick. Partially thaw frozen peaches; put them into blender and blend for a few seconds until smooth. Pour peaches into milk mixture and blend well. Fold in dessert topping with spoon and pile into crumb crust. Yield: 1 (9-inch) pie.

A Taste of Georgia

Peach Crisp
(or cherry)

1 (16-ounce) can peach pie
  filling
1 (7 1/2-ounce) box yellow
  mix (1-layer size)

1 stick margarine
1/2-1 cup chopped pecans

Turn oven on to preheat to 350°. Pour can of pie filling into 8x8-inch baking pan. Sprinkle dry cake mix over pie filling. Cut margarine into small slices and lay on top of cake mix. Sprinkle chopped nuts on top. Bake at 350° for 30-35 minutes.

Great with ice cream or Cool Whip served on top while warm.

Look Mom, I Can Cook

Southern Peach Cobbler

1/2 cup sugar
1/2 cup water

6 or 7 peaches, peeled
4 tablespoons margarine

Mix together sugar and water and boil for a few minutes to make syrup. Slice peaches into syrup. Put margarine into Pyrex dish. Melt in 375° oven.

CRUST:

1/2 cup sugar
1 1/2 teaspoons baking
  powder

1/2 cup milk
1/2 cup plain flour
1/2 teaspoon salt

Mix all ingredients together. Pour into Pyrex dish over melted butter. Pour peaches and syrup over this. Bake at 375° 30-40 minutes until brown. The crust will rise.

Traditionally Wesleyan

Georgia is the third largest peach-producing state. Most peaches are harvested between mid-May and mid-August. They are high in Vitamins A and C as well as containing calcium and iron. One medium peach contains 38 calories.

Peach Buckle

Some say this recipe should be called "Peach Unbuckle," since that's what a lot of it could do to your waistline...

2 pounds peaches (about 6 medium), or to taste	**1 teaspoon vanilla extract**
1 tablespoon lemon juice	**1 egg, lightly beaten**
3/4 cup sugar, divided	**1 cup flour**
4 tablespoons butter or margarine, at room temperature	**1/4 teaspoon salt**
	1 teaspoon baking powder
	1/3 cup milk

Preheat oven to 375°. Slice peeled peaches thinly, and toss with lemon juice and 1/4 cup sugar. Set aside. Cream butter or margarine with remaining sugar, and add vanilla and egg. Blend well. Sift together 1 cup flour, salt, and baking powder. Add dry ingredients alternately with milk to the creamed mixture, beating well after each addition. Pour batter into greased 10-inch baking dish. Spoon peaches over batter.

CRUMB TOPPING:

1/3 cup sugar	**1/4 cup butter or margarine**
1/3 cup flour	

Combine crumb topping ingredients to form coarse crumbs, and sprinkle over fruit. Bake about 40-50 minutes, or until top is golden brown. Serve warm, with sweetened whipped cream or ice cream as desired. Yield: 8-10 servings.

Note: Apples or blueberries are also good in this recipe, with cinnamon and nutmeg added to taste, say 1 teaspoon cinnamon and 1/4 teaspoon nutmeg for the apple batter, and a dash of each in the topping.

This same Crumb Topping recipe is also excellent instead of a top crust for fruit pies, and has fewer calories. For extra nutrition, 1/4 cup wheat germ may also be added to the mixture, either plain or the honey variety.

Georgia Entertains

Sweet Potato Pie

1 1/2 cups sugar
3 eggs
1 1/2 cups mashed sweet
 potatoes
1 teaspoon vanilla extract

1 stick butter, melted
1/2 cup milk
1 deep (9-inch) pie shell,
 unbaked

Beat together sugar and eggs. Add potatoes, vanilla extract, and melted butter. Mix, then add milk. Cook in unbaked pie shell for 1 hour at 350°. Yield: 1 (9-inch) pie.

A Taste of Georgia

The Georgia Peach Commission says when buying Georgia peaches, look for a creamy gold to yellow under-color. The red or "blush" is an indication of variety rather than ripeness. The crease should be well-defined and run from the stem end of the peach to the point. It should smell "peachy" and be soft to the touch. Refrigerate peaches and use within a week. To keep them from darkening after slicing, treat with lemon juice or ascorbic acid powder. To peel a peach, simply dip into boiling water for 30 seconds, then in cold water--the peeling should slide off easily.

Angel Pies

MERINGUE:

5 egg whites
1/4 teaspoon salt
1/2 teaspoon cream of tartar

1 1/2 cups sugar
1 teaspoon vanilla

Beat egg whites until peaks form, then add salt and cream of tartar. Add the sugar gradually, beating until egg whites are stiff, then add vanilla. Pour into a greased and floured 9-inch pie pan. Spread meringue on bottom, pulling it high around the edges, scooping out the center to form a shell. This can be poured on cookie sheet lined with waxed paper and formed into a circle, pulling sides up like a pie shell. Place meringue in a 400° oven, then turn oven off at once. Leave meringue in oven for 4-5 hours or overnight.

PEACH ANGEL FILLING:

2 packages frozen peaches
1 1/2 cups heavy cream
1/2 teaspoon almond
  flavoring

1 tablespoon sugar

Drain thawed peaches. Just before serving, whip cream and add flavoring and sugar. Spread a layer of whipped cream over meringue shell, then a layer of peaches, another layer of cream, and top with rest of peaches. Serve at once. Serves 8.

ANGEL LEMON OR KEY LIME FILLING:

1 (9-ounce) carton Cool Whip
1 (6-ounce) can frozen
  lemonade

1 can condensed milk

Fold milk, Cool Whip, and lemonade together. Spread over cold meringue and chill. Limeade can be substituted for lemonade to make Key Lime pie.

CONTINUED

CONTINUED

ANGEL CHOCOLATE CHIFFON FILLING:

2 tablespoons sugar
1 cup chocolate semi-sweet
  morsels

3 tablespoons milk
4 eggs, separated
1/2 pint whipping cream

Melt together sugar, chocolate bits, and milk. Stir and cook. Add egg yolks one at a time to chocolate mixture, beating after each addition. Beat egg whites until stiff. Fold chocolate filling into the beaten egg whites. Put filling into the meringue shell and chill. Top each serving with whipped cream which has been slightly sweetened. This pie can be made a day ahead, holds up quite well.

Golden Isles Cuisine

Bob Hope's Favorite Lemon Pie

1 cup sugar plus 2
  tablespoons
3 tablespoons cornstarch
1 cup boiling water
4 tablespoons lemon juice

2 teaspoons butter
4 egg yolks (reserve 3
  whites)
Pinch of salt
Grated rind of 1 lemon

Combine cornstarch and 1 cup sugar. Add water slowly, stirring constantly until thick and smooth. Add slightly beaten egg yolks, butter, lemon rind, juice and salt. Cook 2-3 minutes. Pour into baked pie shell. Cover with meringue made from 3 egg whites beaten stiff and 2 teaspoons sugar. Bake in slow oven for 15 minutes or until light brown.

Cool to room temperature before refrigerating to keep meringue from "weeping."

Atlanta's Pet Recipes

Muscadine Pie

1/2 gallon ripe muscadines	2-2 1/2 cups sugar
Juice from 1/2 lemon	Dots of butter
1/4 cup flour	

Mash muscadines. Separate hulls from pulp. Strain so as to get juice, leaving pulp and seed. Cook hulls in juice until tender, adding a little water if needed. Let cool, then add lemon juice, flour, and sugar. Put this mixture in a 9-inch unbaked pie shell and dot with butter. Place lattice crust across top. Bake in 400° oven for approximately 10 minutes—then reduce heat to 375° and bake another 30 minutes. Serve with topping of whipped cream.

Country Cookin'

Sour Cream Cherry Pie

PIE CRUST:

1 1/2 cups enriched flour (spooned into cup)	1/2 cup shortening
1 teaspoon orange peel	3-6 tablespoons cold water
3/4 teaspoon salt	2 tablespoons ground almonds, toasted

Sift together flour, orange peel, and salt. Cut in shortening until pieces are size of small peas. Sprinkle with water, a tablespoon at a time, mixing lightly until dough begins to stick together. Press into ball. Roll out 1/8-inch thick on lightly floured surface; fit loosely into 9-inch pie pan. Trim and flute edge. Press almonds into bottom.

FILLING:

1 (21-ounce) can cherry pie filling	3 eggs
1 tablespoon lemon juice	1/3 cup sugar
1 teaspoon grated orange peel	1 teaspoon vanilla extract
	1/2 teaspoon almond extract
	3/4 cup dairy sour cream

CONTINUED

CONTINUED

In small bowl, stir together cherry pie filling, juice, and peel; spoon over nuts in crust. Beat eggs, sugar, vanilla, and almond extracts until thick and lemon-colored, about 10 minutes. Stir in sour cream. Pour cream mixture over cherries. Bake at 350° on lowest rack for 45 minutes or until crust is brown. Serve chilled.

Cherries Galore

Spiked Apple Crisp

5 cups apples, peeled and diced	3/4 cup sugar
1/2 teaspoon ground cinnamon	1/4 cup light brown sugar
1 teaspoon grated lemon peel	3/4 cup flour
1 teaspoon grated orange peel	1/4 teaspoon salt
1 ounce Grand Marnier	1/2 cup butter, softened
1 ounce amaretto	Vanilla ice cream or whipped cream

Preheat oven to 350°. Arrange apples in a greased 2-quart casserole. Sprinkle cinnamon, lemon and orange peels, Grand Marnier and amaretto on top of apples. Combine sugars, flour, salt and butter until crumbly. Spread this mixture over apples. Bake 1 hour or until apples are tender and top is brown. Serve warm with vanilla ice cream or whipped cream. Yield: 8 servings.

Georgia On My Menu

Fried Pies
A Southern specialty!

1 teaspoon salt
1 teaspoon baking powder
2 cups all-purpose flour,
  sifted
2 tablespoons solid
  shortening

1 egg yolk
4 tablespoons sugar
1/2 cup milk
Dried fruit, cooked and
  sweetened

Sift salt and baking powder with sifted and measured flour. Blend in shortening. Combine egg yolk, sugar, and milk. Stir into flour mixture.

Roll out on a floured board to 1/4-inch thickness. Cut into circles 4-5 inches in diameter. Spread a small amount of cooked and sweetened dried fruit on half of each round. Fold the other half of crust over filling. Seal edges with a fork dipped in flour. Fry in deep fat at 360 until browned. Drain on absorbent paper and sprinkle with powdered sugar.

A Taste of Georgia

Apricot Squares

Jam-filled squares dusted with confectioners' sugar.

1 cup butter, softened (2
  sticks)
1 cup sugar
2 egg yolks

2 cups flour (all-purpose)
1 cup walnuts, chopped
1/2 cup apricot jam
Confectioners' sugar

Heat oven to 325°. Lightly grease an 8x8-inch baking dish; set aside. In bowl of mixer cream butter; add sugar gradually, beat until light and fluffy. Add egg yolks; blend well. Add flour, a little at a time; mix thoroughly. Fold in nuts. Spoon 1/2 of dough into prepared baking dish; spread evenly. Spread jam over top. Carefully spread remaining doughover top. Bake 1 hour until lightly browned. Cool and cut into squares. Dust with confectioners' sugar. Yield: 16-20.

Lasting Impressions

Praline Cookie Cups
with Raspberry Sauce

CUPS:

1 cup all-purpose flour
1 cup finely chopped pecans
1/4 cup butter
1/4 cup shortening
1/2 cup light corn syrup

2/3 cup firmly packed light
 brown sugar
2 oranges to form cups
Vanilla ice cream
Fresh strawberries, sliced

Combine flour and pecans. In heavy saucepan, melt butter and shortening. Add syrup and sugar. Bring to a boil. Remove from heat. Add flour mixture and blend well. Drop by heaping tablespoons onto greased cookie sheet, allowing only 2 cookies for each sheet. Bake at 325° for 8-10 minutes. Cool 1 minute, then remove with spatula and place over orange to form cup. Allow to cool and harden. Cups may be made in advance and stored in Zip-lock freezer bags. Cups are delicate. To serve, fill praline cups with ice cream and strawberries. Top with Raspberry Sauce.

RASPBERRY SAUCE:

2 (10-ounce) packages frozen
 raspberries, thawed
1 tablespoon cornstarch

2 tablespoons fresh lemon
 juice
2 tablespoons kirsch

In blender, purée raspberries. Press mixture through sieve into saucepan. Combine cornstarch and lemon juice. Add to raspberry mixture. Bring to a boil and cook until slightly thickened. Add kirsch. Chill before serving. (Sauce may be stored in refrigerator.)
Yield: 24-30 cups.

Second Round, Tea-Time at the Masters®

Each April the Augusta National Golf Club hosts the Masters Golf Tournament, one of professional golf's most prestigious events.

Exhibition Dessert

1 quart milk	3 tablespoons crème de cacao
6 eggs, separated	or 3 teaspoons vanilla
4 tablespoons sugar	extract
1 tablespoon cornstarch	1 quart water

Make your Exhibition Dessert in the morning so that it will have plenty of time to chill. Start with 1 quart of milk, the yolks of 6 eggs (put whites in a bowl and put in ice box to chill), sugar, cornstarch. Heat milk. Beat sugar, cornstarch, and egg yolks together. Add to milk. Stir constantly over low heat until thick. Remove from stove and let cool about 20 minutes, then add crème de cacao or 3 teaspoons vanilla extract.

Now the scary part! Put 1 quart of water on to boil. Beat the egg whites until they stand up in peaks. Now (don't be frightened) with a big kitchen spoon, dip up the boiling water and pour slowly over the whites until all water has been poured through the egg whites. You see you'll need to do this in a large mixing bowl. Don't stir the whites. They will float. Cover the bowl about 10 minutes so the steam from the hot water can finish cooking the egg whites.

Get out your prettiest glass bowl and pour the custard in. Now (using a ladle, a spoon with holes in it, or a slotted spatula) scoop up great heaps of egg white and put on top of custard. Then dip up some custard over the egg whites. Put the last drained egg whites piled up in the center of the bowl. Leave these white. Put it in icebox. Serves 8-10.

From Mother with Love

Pink House Trifle

1 1/2 quarts milk
1 1/2 cups sugar
2 tablespoons cornstarch
6 eggs
1/2 cup sherry

2 cups cream, whipped
1 1/2 pounds pound cake, sliced
Raspberry or strawberry preserves

Pour the milk into the top of a double boiler. In a mixing bowl, beat together the sugar, cornstarch and eggs until smooth. Add to the milk and heat until the mixture is thickened, stirring constantly. Set aside to cool. Add sherry to the cooled custard. Whip the cream and set aside.

Arrange the cake slices in a 13 x 9 1/4 x 2-inch baking pan. Spread with preserves, then top with a layer of custard and a layer of whipped cream. Repeat until all of the ingredients are used. Chill and serve. Serves 6-8.

Recipes from The Olde Pink House

Chocolate Bread Pudding

My children request this! Men love it!

2 squares unsweetened baking chocolate
4 cups milk
2 eggs

2/3 cup sugar
1 teaspoon vanilla
1/4 teaspoon salt
2 cups bread crumbs

Melt chocolate in milk. Beat eggs and add sugar. Combine with chocolate and milk and add vanilla and salt. Pour over bread crumbs and stir until all are soaked. Bake in greased Pyrex 1 1/2-quart casserole. Set in pan of hot water and bake at 350° for 1 hour.

SAUCE:

1/3 cup soft butter
1 cup brown sugar (light)

3 tablespoons milk

Cream butter with sugar. Gradually add milk, drop-by-drop, beating all the time. Alternate: whipped cream.

Frederica Fare

Great Grandmother's Chocolate Mousse

This recipe is over 100 years old.

1/2 pound sweet chocolate	**2 1/2 dozen lady fingers**
2 tablespoons sugar	**Sherry**
3 tablespoons water	**Vanilla**
4 eggs, separated	

Melt chocolate in a double boiler, add sugar and water. Add slightly beaten egg yolks. Stir while thickening. Remove from heat to cool. Beat egg whites until stiff and gently fold into the chocolate mixture. Put waxed paper or foil in bottom of cake pan or springform pan. Line the bottom of pan with some of the split lady fingers. Pour some chocolate filling over them and continue layers of lady fingers and chocolate until pan is filled. Chill until set. Unmold and garnish with whipped cream flavored with sherry and vanilla. Yield: 6-8 servings.

Cooking with Tradition

Lemon Mousse with Raspberry Sauce

MOUSSE:

1 (1/4-ounce) envelope	**3 eggs, separated**
unflavored gelatin	**8 tablespoons sugar, divided**
2 tablespoons white wine	**1 cup heavy cream, whipped**
1/3 cup lemon juice	
1 1/2 tablespoons grated	
lemon rind	

Soften gelatin in wine in top of double boiler. Add lemon juice and lemon rind. Stir over simmering water until gelatin dissolves. Beat egg yolks with 3 tablespoons sugar. Slowly add to gelatin mixture, stirring constantly. Cool. Fold in whipped cream. Beat egg whites until stiff, gradually adding 5 tablespoons sugar. Fold into lemon mixture. Pour into a 6-8 cup mold; chill at least 2 hours.

CONTINUED

CONTINUED

SAUCE:

1 (10-ounce) package frozen   1 tablespoon lemon juice
  raspberries, thawed   1 tablespoon Grand Marnier
2 tablespoons sugar

Drain raspberries and reserve juice. Combine raspberries, sugar, and lemon juice; purée in processor or blender. Strain. Add liqueur and as much raspberry juice as needed for desired consistency. Unmold mousse and serve with sauce.

Macon Sets a Fine Table

Banana Mousse

1 teaspoon plain gelatin   4 egg whites
1/4 cup cold water   1/2 cup crushed ice
1 package non-instant banana
  pudding mix

Dissolve the gelatin in the cold water, then add the pudding mix, blending well. Simmer the mixture slowly, stirring constantly until it thickens. Let the mixture cool to room temperature. Beat the egg whites until frothy and add the crushed ice slowly while beating. Continue beating until the egg whites hold a peak. Fold the egg whites gently into the pudding mixture, combining well. Spoon into sherbet glasses and chill. Serves 5.

Cal. per serving 17 - Pro. 3.6gm. - Carb. 0gm. Fat 0gm. - Sod. 38.4gm.

Southwind Cuisine

 Berry College's 28,000 acres make it the largest campus in the world.

Strawberry Cloud

1 (8-10-ounce) package
  frozen sliced, sweetened
  strawberries
2 large egg whites, unbeaten
1/2 cup sifted granulated
  sugar

1 tablespoon strained fresh
  lemon juice
1 cup very cold light
  whipping cream

Place partially thawed strawberries, egg whites, sugar, and lemon juice into a large mixing bowl with high sides. Beat at high speed of electric mixer for about 5 minutes or until thick and fluffy. Whip cream. Fold whipped cream into strawberry mixture. Freeze in molds or baked pie shell. (Nutritional information does not include food values for pie shell.) Serve directly from freezer. (May be served with toasted almonds, lady fingers, or whipped topping.) Serves 12. No cooking required.

Cal.-121 Pro.-1g Fat-6g Carb.-16g Fib.-trg Sod.-1 6mg Chol.-23mg

Adventures in Healthful Cooking

Scalloped Apples

3/4 cup sugar
1/4 teaspoon salt
1/8 teaspoon cinnamon
1/8 teaspoon nutmeg
6 apples, peeled and sliced
  thin (or 1 can pie apples)

3/4 stick butter
3 cups soft bread crumbs (6
  slices)

Mix sugar and seasonings and pour over apples. Stir well and put in casserole dish. Mix bread crumbs with melted butter and put on top of apples. Bake in moderate oven (350°) about 40 minutes, until crumbs are brown and apples are bubbly.

Educated Taste

Orange Charlotte
A scrumptious orange cloud for dessert!

1 1/3 tablespoons unflavored
  gelatin
1/3 cup cold water
1/3 cup boiling water
1 cup sugar
3 tablespoons fresh lemon
  juice

1 cup fresh orange juice
1 cup heavy cream
2 teaspoons vanilla
  flavoring
3 egg whites
Cherries and nuts, if desired
  for garnish

Soften gelatin in cold water. Dissolve in boiling water.
Add sugar and stir until dissolved over low heat if necessary. Add lemon juice and orange juice to mixture. Chill
in refrigerator until mixture begins to congeal slightly.
Whip cream, flavor with vanilla, and fold into juice mixture. Fold in beaten egg whites. Return to refrigerator
until firm. Garnish with cherries and nuts. May be served
in individual dishes or crystal bowl.

Note: Use a sweet and juicy orange for the best taste.

Hint: Frozen concentrate may be used in place of fresh
orange juice. Makes 6-8 servings.

Puttin' on the Peachtree

Sherman Strikes Again

4 large peaches (peeled and sliced)
1/2 cup white wine

2 ounces of peach or apricot brandy
1 quart peach ice cream

Put peaches in pan, add wine; heat just before serving, add brandy and heat. Ignite and serve flaming over ice cream. Serves 4.

Puttin' on the Peachtree

Strawberries Romanoff

A simple but elegant dessert that is almost no trouble to prepare.

1 quart fresh strawberries
1/2 cup Grand Marnier
4 tablespoons sugar
2 orange rinds, grated
2 tablespoons melba sauce (commercially available)

2 cups heavy cream, lightly sweetened and whipped stiff
4 scoops vanilla ice cream, softened

Wash strawberries and remove stems. Place in bowl and add Grand Marnier, sugar, orange rind, and melba sauce. Toss a few minutes to blend, and cover with a plate. Chill in refrigerator for 1 hour. Remove strawberries from refrigerator, add whipped cream and mix. Add ice cream and stir just enough to blend all ingredients. Divide mixture into individual sherbet glasses or dessert dishes. Serve immediately.

The Abbey Cookbook

Bananas Nourries

A dramatic flamed banana dessert, this is surprisingly simple to make.

4 bananas	1/4 cup rum (151 proof)
8 tablespoons butter	1 pint vanilla ice cream
3/4 cup light brown sugar	1/2 cup roasted chopped
1/2 cup banana liqueur	hazelnuts

Slice bananas lengthwise. Heat butter in 1 large or 2 smaller skillets. Add brown sugar, and stir over medium to high heat until sugar dissolves and a caramel glaze is formed. Stir in banana liqueur. Lay bananas in the caramel glaze; cook, turning occasionally, for 2 minutes. Add rum and flame. Serve each person 2 banana halves over 2 scoops of ice cream. Sprinkle with nuts.

The Abbey Cookbook

Cantaloupe Supreme

2 cantaloupes	2 egg whites
1 1/2 pints strawberries	1/2 cup sugar
1 pint vanilla ice cream	Dash kirsch

Cut bottoms off melons so they sit easily on a cookie sheet. Cut in half and remove seeds. Using a grapefruit knife, loosen fruit from rind. Cut fruit into fairly small pieces and put back in rind. Cut strawberries in half and add just enough sugar to sweeten. Add these to the melons and put a dash of kirsch over all.

Make a meringue from egg whites and add sugar slowly. Turn on broiler and put rack on the second level. Put 1 scoop of ice cream on each melon and cover well with meringue. Put in oven to brown lightly.

Blueberries can be used in place of strawberries and amount of meringue can be doubled. Serves 4.

Savannah Style

Frosty Cranberry Pie

1 1/4 cups crushed
  cornflakes
1/4 cup butter, melted
1 (8-ounce) package cream
  cheese, softened

1 cup whipped topping
1 (16-ounce) can whole berry
  cranberry sauce
Additional whipped topping

Combine cornflakes and butter. Press mixture into lightly greased 9-inch pie pan. Bake at 350° for 8 minutes. Cool. Beat cream cheese; fold in whipped topping. Mash cranberry sauce. Fold into cream cheese mixture. Spoon mixture into crust. Freeze. Remove from freezer 15-20 minutes before serving. Garnish with whipped topping.

The Holiday Hostess

Frozen Almond Ring with Raspberries

8 ounces whole blanched
  almonds
1/2 cup plus 4 tablespoons
  sugar
1/2 teaspoon almond extract

4 tablespoons kirsch
2 1/2 cups whipping cream,
  divided
1 (10-ounce) package frozen
  raspberries, thawed

In a food processor or blender grind almonds with 1/2 cup sugar until fine. Add 1/2 cup cream, almond extract, and kirsch. Process until puréed. Strain mixture through fine sieve to remove any large particles. Whip 1 cup of the remaining cream with 2 tablespoons sugar until stiff peaks are formed. Fold into almond mixture. Pour into a 3-cup ring mold and freeze. Purée raspberries in a food processor or blender, strain and chill. Whip the remaining cup of cream with 2 tablespoons sugar and chill. When ready to serve, unmold ring by dipping in hot water for several seconds. Spoon some of the raspberry sauce around, but not on it. (The almond ring should remain white.) To serve, slice mold and add remaining sauce and whipped cream. Serves 6.

Temptations

Toffee Ice Cream Pie

PIE:

12 (3/4-ounce) Heath bars
1 1/4 cups chocolate wafer
 crumbs

1/4 cup butter, melted
1/2 gallon vanilla ice cream

Put Heath bars in freezer to harden. Mix crumbs and butter. Line 9x13-inch pan. Press mixture evenly. Put into refrigerator to harden. Crush Heath bars and mix with softened ice cream. Put in crust and freeze overnight.

SAUCE:

1 stick butter
1 (12-ounce) package
 chocolate chips
2 cups 10-X powdered sugar

1 (13-ounce) can evaporated
 milk
2 teaspoons vanilla

Melt butter and chocolate chips. Add sugar and milk. Cook about 8 minutes or until thick, stirring constantly. Add vanilla. Serve warm over pie. The sauce can be made early in day and heated at last minute. Serves 8-10.

Oreos may be substituted for chocolate wafers if the filling is scraped off.

Tea-Time at the Masters®

Aunt Pittypat's Homemade Peach Ice Cream

2 cups sugar
2 tablespoons flour
4 eggs, slightly beaten
2 cups half-and-half
2 cans undiluted evaporated
 milk

12 overripe peaches, peeled,
 crushed, and sweetened with
 1 cup sugar

Mix sugar and flour. Add eggs and half-and-half. Cook in double boiler, stirring constantly, until mixture steams. Remove from heat. Add evaporated milk. Pour into ice cream freezer. When mixture reaches mushy consistency, add peaches. Continue freezing until firm. To serve, place scoops of ice cream in large bowl. Let guests help themselves.

Betty Talmadge's Lovejoy Plantation Cookbook

The Attic's Almond Amaretto Ice Cream

1/2 gallon vanilla ice cream
8 tablespoons amaretto
 liqueur

Almond Crunch Topping
(recipe follows)

Freeze parfait or wine glasses. Just before serving spoon in ice cream, splash with amaretto and sprinkle with Almond Crunch Topping. Serves 8.

ALMOND CRUNCH TOPPING:

2 ounces sliced almonds
2 tablespoons butter

1 cup sugar
1 tablespoon water

Spread sliced almonds in a buttered pan. In a small, heavy saucepan, stir together the sugar with a tablespoon of water over low heat until the sugar has melted. Then pour it over the almonds and let harden. When the topping is completely cold, break it up with your fingers or a kitchen hammer and grind it in a blender into smaller bits. Store the topping in a covered jar in the refrigerator.

Georgia's Historic Restaurants

Coffee Ice Cream

4 eggs
1 1/2 cups sugar
1/2 cup sweetened condensed
 milk
1/4 teaspoon salt
2 quarts heavy cream,
 divided

2 cups milk
1 teaspoon vanilla extract
1/4 cup instant coffee
 crystals

Whisk eggs, sugar, condensed milk and salt together until thick and smooth. Heat 2 cups cream with milk to a full rolling boil. Slowly pour into egg mixture, whisking constantly. Return to milk pan; cook, stirring with a wooden spoon, until mixture thickens slightly and a finger drawn across the spoon leaves a clear trail. Strain into a bowl; whisk in coffee until dissolved. Add vanilla and remaining cream. Cool; freeze in ice cream churn according to manufacturer's instructions.

CONTINUED

CONTINUED

FUDGE SAUCE:

4 ounces unsweetened baking
  chocolate
1 1/2 cups sugar
1 cup cream or evaporated
  milk

4 tablespoons butter
1 teaspoon vanilla extract

Combine chocolate, sugar and cream in a heavy sauce-pan. Cook, stirring constantly, over medium heat until chocolate is melted. Raise heat, bring to a boil, and boil 5 minutes, stirring constantly. Remove from heat; beat in butter and vanilla. Serve hot or cold. Keeps indefinitely in the refrigerator. Reheat in a bowl or pan over hot water, or in a microwave oven.

Note: Easy to make, and a lot better than store-bought.

The Pirates' House Cook Book

Muscadine Ice

2 1/2 gallons muscadines
Water

Sugar
Lemon juice

Wash and mash muscadines. Strain the juice and set aside. Put the muscadine hulls and pulp with a little water in a kettle and boil 20 minutes. Remove from heat and strain through a sieve or cloth jelly bag. Add this juice to that which was saved from the mashed muscadines. Sweeten to taste (being careful not to oversweeten!) Add a little lemon juice. Put in ice cream freezer and freeze as you would ice cream.

Country Cookin'

Thomasville is the city of roses and host of the Annual National Rose Festival. With a population of 20,000, the city has more roses than people.

Banana Pop Freeze

3 or 4 bananas
Wooden or plastic sticks
2-3 tablespoons orange juice
1 (6-ounce) bag chocolate
  chips

1 tablespoon margarine
Finely chopped pecans or
  coconut

Peel bananas and cut in half crosswise. Insert wooden or plastic sticks in cut end. Brush bananas with orange juice. Place on waxed paper on cookie sheet and freeze until firm. Put chocolate chips and margarine in top of double boiler. Cook until chocolate melts. Allow to cool slightly. Spoon chocolate over frozen bananas. Roll at once in chopped nuts. Eat at once or wrap in waxed paper and keep in freezer.

Look Mom, I Can Cook

Yippee Yogurt Pops

Cool, refreshing, and nutritious. Even so, kids love it!

2 (8-ounce) cartons vanilla
  yogurt
1 (6-ounce) can frozen juice
  concentrate (apple, pink
  lemonade, pineapple, or
  grape)

10 (3-ounce) paper cups
10 wooden sticks

In small bowl combine yogurt and thawed concentrate; stir to blend. Fill cups 1/2-2/3 full. Place in freezer until partially frozen, about 1 hour. Insert sticks, freeze completely. To serve, peel off paper cups. For larger pops, use 5 (5-ounce) paper cups and 5 wooden sticks. Must do ahead. Yield: 10.

Perennials

Index

The Georgia State Capitol, one of two U.S. capitols whose dome is sheeted in gold. The gold was brought from Georgia's own gold mine in Dahlonega in the northeast Georgia mountains. Atlanta.

INDEX

Catalog of Contributing Cookbooks

The World Congress Center is the second largest convention center in the United States. Atlanta.

CATALOG OF CONTRIBUTING COOKBOOKS

All recipes in this book have been submitted from the Georgia cookbooks shown on the following pages. Individuals who wish to obtain a copy of any particular book may do so by sending a check or money order to the address listed. Prices are subject to change. Please note the postage and handling charges that may be required. State residents add tax only when requested. Retailers are invited to call or write to same address for discount information. Some of these contributing cookbooks may have gone out of print since the original publication of this book. Quail Ridge Press is proud to preserve America's food heritage by keeping many of their recipes in print.

THE ABBEY COOKBOOK
by Hans Bertram
The Harvard Common Press
535 Albany Street
Boston, MA 02118   617/423-5803

Visitors to the church on Piedmont and Ponce de Leon Avenues in Atlanta go there to be inspired, but not to pray—because one of the city's most famous churches is also a restaurant. European chef Hans Bertram serves up a breathtaking continental cuisine and shares 155 of his gourmet recipes in this handsome book. Illustrated; comb bound.

$10.95 Retail Price
$ .77 Tax for Georgia residents
$ 3.00 Postage and handling
Make check payable to Harvard Common Press
ISBN 0-916782-26-3

ADVENTURES IN HEALTHFUL COOKING
by Peggy Rhodes Scribner
Stone Mountain, GA

These recipes are elegant, fast and simple; each shows the calories, fat, cholesterol, sodium, protein, carbohydrates and fiber content. Includes nutritional information, charts and dietary guidelines. Has been featured on radio and TV shows and on the American Dietetic Assn.'s Good Nutrition Reading list. Currently out of print.

ATLANTA COOKNOTES

The Junior League of Atlanta, Inc.
P.O. Box 53428
Atlanta, GA 30355-1428   404/233-4767

Mouth-watering memories of the old and new south, this book has 440 pages packed with 750 kitchen tested recipes. Featuring renowned Jack Sheild's watercolors along with durable tabs for easy reference. "Cooknotes" refers to historical facts or specific cooking advice plus new "Healthy Health Notes" section. Proceeds go to sponsor community projects.

$19.95 Retail price
$ 1.40 Tax for Georgia residents
$ 4.00 Postage and handling
Make check payable to *Atlanta Cooknotes*
ISBN 0-960-79142-6

ATLANTA NATIVES' FAVORITE RECIPES
Roswell, GA

Atlanta Natives' Favorite Recipes is a historic book filled with 438 rercipes for all occasions, 13 pages of Atlanta history, 13 large illustrations of noted landmarks, almost 100 small illustrations of native plants and 2 pages of Jus' Cookin'. Each recipe is a family favorite of many years and generations. Currently out of print.

ATLANTA'S PET RECIPES
The Atlanta Humane Society
Atlanta, GA

Atlanta's Pet Recipes has 280 pages containing approximately 800 recipes. Most of the recipes are from the tried and true kitchens of our Atlanta Humane Society Auxiliary, but our book also contains the favorite recipes from internationally known men and women—from President and Nancy Reagan to Cher. Currently out of print.

311

THE BACHELOR'S COOKBOOK

Dot Gibson Publications
P.O. Box 117
Waycross, GA 31502   912/285-2848

A real winner! Unique theme; outstanding cover. Great for college students, working bachelors, the single-agains, married guys sharing K.P. Duty, and the bachelorettes. Simple but good food with easy step-by-step directions. 96 pages; 144 recipes; comb binder. Reissued as *Out On Our Own.*

$ 7.95 Retail price
$ .56 Tax for Georgia residents
$ 1.25 Postage and handling
Make check payable to Dot Gibson Publications

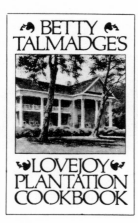

BETTY TALMADGE'S LOVEJOY PLANTATION COOKBOOK

by Betty Talmadge
Atlanta, GA

Southern hospitality has been a tradition at Lovejoy Plantation (the home of the former Georgia First Lady) since the 1830's. Whether it's dinner for two in front of the fireplace or the author's famous barbecue on the lawn, the food and the ambiance create an unforgettable dining experience. Currently out of print.

BOARDING HOUSE REACH

Dot Gibson Publications
Waycross, GA

Southern cooking at its finest! Recipes from a famous boarding house whose table has become a legend—The Smith House. No gourmet cooking, just old-fashioned terrific food—like eating at grandmother's house! Banana Fritters, Chestnut Souffle, Out-Of-This-World Rolls, and the famous Rotten Cake. 192 pages; 278 recipes; comb binder. Currently out of print.

CHERRIES GALORE
Edited by Clara Eschmann
Macon, GA

This book was published as a souvenir for our annual Cherry Blossom Festival held in Macon. All of the recipes contain cherries as an ingredient, and it has some great ones—old fashioned ideas and a wide variety—in this lovely book. Comb bound hard cover; 206 pages. Currently out of print.

COOKING IN THE NEW SOUTH
by Anne Byrn Phillips
Peachtree Publishers, Ltd.
494 Armour Circle
Atlanta, GA 30324   404/876-8761

The more than two hundred tested recipes assembled here reveal that southern cooking, while retaining its regional flavor, is far from being dependent on fatback and lard. Southerners are expanding their style of cookery with the availability of once hard-to-find ingredients. Cooking that has never been better—-from the Food Editor of the Atlanta newspapers.

$13.95 Retail price
$ .98 Tax for Georgia residents
$ 2.75 Postage and handling (.80 each additional)
ISBN 0-931948-52-5
Make check payable to Peachtree Publishers, Ltd.

COOKING WITH TRADITION
Woodward Academy Parents Club
P.O. Box 87190
College Park, Georgia 30337   404/765-2018

This lovely 402-page ring-bound book is filled with over 700 family recipes, carefully selected, thoughtfully organized, and attractively presented for interesting cooking. Includes a microwave section, holiday and party menus, and helpful cooking and housekeeping hints. Proceeds go to the Academy (formerly Georgia Military Academy) for student use.

$17.95 Retail price
$ 1.26 Tax for Georgia residents
$ 1.55 Postage and handling
Make check payable to Woodward Academy Parents Club

COOKLORE AND RECIPES OF IRELAND
by Christiana Courtenay
Adrian, GA

A unique cornucopia of authentic Irishness. Many of these traditionally ancient recipes and dishes were handed down by word-of-mouth. Laced with twenty stories, legends, and sagas of Ireland with illustrations. It makes excellent reading and reference material, even if you aren't Irish and even if you never cook. 240 pages; 220 recipes. Currently out of print.

COUNTRY CAKES
by Bevelyn Blair
Columbus, GA

Country Cakes is a new and enticing collection of over 600 treasured cake and cookie recipes, including heirloom recipes never before published. Beautiful, durable covers that can be wiped with a damp cloth. An exceptional cookbook...one you'll treasure using, and a gift truly worth giving! 240 pages—629 recipes. Fourth printing, 40,000 copies in print. Currently out of print.

COUNTRY COOKIN': RECIPES FROM CALLAWAY GARDENS
The Gardens Country Store
45 Highway 27   800/280-7524
Pine Mountain, GA 31822   706/663-2281

These truly southern recipes—including many from Callaway Gardens restaurants—were collected and tested by Columbus TV personality, Rozell Fabiani, with artwork by Clydetta Fulmer of Montgomery. Enticing chapter titles (The Pickle Crock, The Pie Safe, The Soup Kettle) indicate the country flavor of the book.

$10.95 Retail price
$ .77 Tax for Georgia residents
$ 4.95 Postage and handling
Make check payable to Callaway Gardens

314

COUNTRY CUPBOARD COOKBOOK

Central High School Athletic Club
c/o Ponders Inc.
117 North Madison Street
Thomasville, GA 31792   912/226-3341

Over 600 recipes on 300 plus pages, the *Country Cupboard* has recipes suited for every occasion...from elegant dinner entrees to basic country cooking. Scrumptious, naughty and irresistible desserts, enticing, traditional Southern recipes, creative casseroles, country sho'nuff section, fully indexed, spiral bound, original country illustrations.

$11.95 Retail price
$ .84 Tax for Georgia residents
$ 2.50 Postage and handling
Make check payable to Ponder's Inc.

CRAB CHATTER

by Mildred and Gennie Lewis
c/o Carol Lewis Spriggs
103 Blackbeard Island Circle
Brunswick, GA 31520   912/264-4210 (night)

Crab Chatter is a unique collection of 167 delectable crabmeat recipes. Many of these recipes have been handed down from generation to generation by families who have lived along the seashore and harvested bounties of our coastal waterways.

$10.00 Retail price (includes postage)
Make check payable to *Crab Chatter*

CULINARY CLASSICS

The Circle for Tallulah Falls School
Roswell, GA

A flavorful collection of favorite Georgia recipes from the kitchens of some of Georgia's favorite cooks. Featured are recipes for delicious appetizers, tasty main course dishes, scrumptious desserts and much more. All recipes include level of difficulty and preparation time. Over 500 recipes and 297 pages. Spiral bound. Currently out of print.

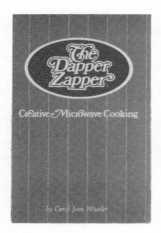

THE DAPPER ZAPPER
by Carol Jean Wheeler
Alpharetta, GA

Become a creative microwave cook using *The Dapper Zapper* by home economist Carol Jean Wheeler. It contains easy but unique and interesting recipes. You'll be creating memorable meals, including scrumptious appetizers and desserts, plus scores of tips on successful microwaving. Try these specials: Shrimp Remoulade, Curried Fruit, or English Trifle. 190 pages; ring bound. Currently out of print.

EDUCATED TASTE
LaGrange College Alumni Association
LaGrange, GA

Educated Taste contains over 700 recipes from alumni and members of the LaGrange College family, photographs of the campus and interesting reminiscences. The cover is a photograph of the restored college arch and gateposts in four colors. It is a first-time-out publication of the LaGrange College Alumni Association. Currently out of print.

ENCORE
Dot Gibson Publications
Waycross, GA

A good-looking book printed in brown and packed with every type recipe from Berry Good Breakfast Drink, Drunkenweenies, to the $25,000 winning Candy Bar Cookie. Sections for microwave, food processors, and low-calorie cooking. 301 pages; 693 recipes; comb binder. Currently out of print.

FAMOUS RECIPES FROM
MRS. WILKES BOARDING HOUSE

by Mrs. L. H. Wilkes
107 West Jones Street   912/232-5997
Savannah, GA 31401   or 925-3464

My cookbook is used by Sumpter County Career Center School, Sumpter, South Carolina, to teach food service to groups from area high schools. People describe it as a guide to plain and simple good cooking. 122 pages, over 275 basic recipes, 75,000 in print, and sales increase as years go by. May, 1989, 16 pages were added with over 50 more recipes.

$12.00 Retail price
$ 3.00 Postage and handling
Make check payable to Mrs. L. H. Wilkes
ISBN 0-939114-72-0

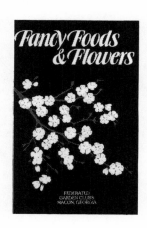

FANCY FOODS AND FLOWERS

Federated Garden Clubs of Macon, Inc.
Macon, GA

Menus of historical and interesting places in Macon, Georgia. Recipes for special events, flower arrangement suggestions, artwork and serving details. Helpful hints, canning section, no cholesterol and dietetic foods. Heavy plastic cover. 306 pages. Currently out of print.

FEAST AND FELLOWSHIP

St. Francis Guild, Cathedral of St. Philip
Atlanta, GA

Feast and Fellowship is a collection of recipes from the largest Episcopal parish in the United States. Recipes range from the simple to the extravagant and are interspersed with blessings, scripture verses and architectural features of the cathedral of St. Philip. 302 pages. Currently out of print.

FLATLANDERS COOK BOOK

by Helen L. Strickland
P.O. Box 125
Lakeland, GA 31635   912/482-3463 (home)
                          386-3266 (office)

This 280-page book is a homey, folksy kind of cookbook representative of the Southcentral region of Georgia. It contains recipes for foods that real people eat and enjoy because they taste good. The third edition offers recipes contributed by men and women of Lanier County. Index of recipes and contributors. Reissued as *Flatlanders Celebrate Cookbook.*

$14.00 Retail price
$ .98 Tax for Georgia residents
$ 2.50 Postage and handling
Make check payable to Helen Strickland

FORESTERS' FAVORITE FOODS

Pine Forest United Methodist
Women's Organization
400 Woods Avenue
Dublin, GA 31021   912/272-2441

The proceeds of this cookbook are committed to mission works. 288 tasty recipes, many which are prize winners, are represented in our book. We are also proud to have Mrs. Luella Rowland, wife of U.S. Congressman J. Roy Rowland as one of our contributors.

$ 6.50 Retail price
$ 1.50 Postage and handling
Make check payable to Pine Forest UMW

THE FRANCES VIRGINIA TEA ROOM COOKBOOK

by Mildred Huff Coleman
2065 Spring Lake Drive NW
Atlanta, GA 30305   404/351-1313

The Frances Virginia Tea Room—where ladies wore white gloves, the atmosphere was elegant and the food sumptuous—no longer exists. But in this volume, its secret recipes do. Recipe inventions such as "War Pies" made without sugar, reducing fat without losing flavor, and stories about Atlanta before the wrecking ball are all included in this fascinating cookbook of southern memories and recipes.

$14.95 Retail price
$ 1.05 Tax for Georgia residents
$ 2.50 Postage and handling
Make check payable to Mildred Coleman
ISBN 0-9653416-0-7

FREDERICA FARE
The Parents Association of Frederica Academy
200 Hamilton Road
St. Simons Island, GA 31522   912/638-9981

Frederica Fare was organized by parents and friends of Frederica Academy as a reflection of love for our area, "a unique place beneath the sun and for those who love this way of life, wherever they live." *Frederica Fare* contains 285 pages with 600 tested recipes along with historical comments and sketches of St. Simons and the Golden Isles of Georgia.

$ 8.95 Retail price
$ .63 Tax for Georgia residents
$ 1.00 Postage and handling
Make check payable to *Frederica Fare*

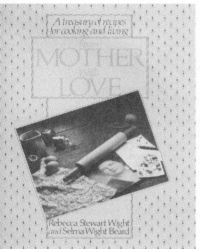

FROM MOTHER WITH LOVE
by Rebecca Stewart Wight and Selma Wight Beard
Atlanta, GA

A year long series of letters from a mother to her daughter, a young World War II bride who found herself a stranger in her own kitchen—with advice that was not always just about cooking. Currently out of print.

GEORGIA ENTERTAINS
Edited by Margaret DeBolt
with Emma Rylander Law and Carter Olive

Georgia Entertains is the best of old and new Georgia recipes. Presenting Georgia's rich legacy of fine food and gracious hospitality, it contains traditional as well as modern Georgia specialties. Also included are helpful cooking hints. 322 pages; 614 recipes; illustrated with line drawings of famed Georgia residences and places of historical interest. Currently out of print.

GEORGIA ON MY MENU

Junior League of Cobb-Marietta
P.O. Box 727
Marietta, GA 30060   770/422-5266

Georgia on my Menu is a 350-page medley of over
650 tested recipes in bold, easy-to-read print.
Washable cover with locking comb binding. Special section featuring recipes from Georgia celebrities and Georgia's finest restaurants. Each section is individually indexed. A composition of culinary delights...a symphony of Southern favorites.

$14.95 Retail price
$ .75 Tax for Georgia residents
$ 2.00 Postage and handling
Make check payable to League Publications
ISBN 0-9619983-0-X

GEORGIA'S HISTORICAL RESTAU-
RANTS AND THEIR RECIPES

by Jean Spaugh and Dawn O'Brien
John F. Blair, Publisher
1406 Plaza Drive   336/768-1374
Winston-Salem, NC 27103   800/222-9796

This book features fifty Georgia restaurants that
are housed in buildings at least fifty years old.
Each entry includes an illustration of the restaurant, a brief description, and one or more recipes
from that restaurant.

$16.95 Retail price
$ 5.00 Postage and handling
Make check payable to John F. Blair, Publisher
ISBN 0-89587-056-8

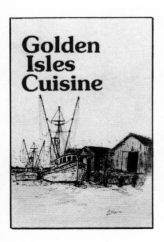

GOLDEN ISLES CUISINE

Dot Gibson Publications
Waycross, GA

A beautiful book! Eye-appealing cover and terrific
recipes. Though it is filled with outstanding seafood recipes, it is a complete 14-section cookbook
with local photographs dividing the chapters.
These are indeed culinary gems from the Golden
Isles of Georgia. 256 pages; 584 recipes; comb
binder with hard cover. Currently out of print.

GOOD COOKIN'

by Virginia B. Snell
P.O. Box 8
Metter, GA 30439   912/685-6566

When Virginia Snell started a weekly newspaper
December 1977, she started a weekly column,
"Good Cookin." This cookbook contains the recipes of the first three years of publication, the best
recipes of the best cooks of the community. (Volume 2 will follow June 1989, with volume 3 published by Christmas.) *Good Cookin'* is also good
readin'. 304 pages.

$14.95 Retail price
$ 1.05 Tax for Georgia residents
$ 2.00 Postage and handling
Make check payable to *Metter News and Advertiser*

GOTTLIEB'S BAKERY
100 YEARS OF RECIPES

by Isser Gottlieb
305 Johnston Street
Savannah, GA 31405   912/352-8354

Gottlieb's Bakery began in 1884 in a small base-
ment, when Isadore peddled his baked goods on
foot, then by horse and wagon. Through the
years, the family-owned and operated business
has expanded to several stores, with Isadore's
grandson, Isser, in charge, still serving their wonderful bakery goods as they have done for over 100
years. 132 pages; ring binder.

$11.95 Retail price
$ 1.50 Postage and handling
Make check payable to Ava Gottlieb
ISBN 0-939114-90-9

GUESS WHO'S COMING TO DINNER

by Mary Beth Busbee with Jan Busbee Curtis
Atlanta, GA

Mary Beth Busbee and daughter Jan Busbee Curtis let us in on what it was like playing hostess to
famous personalities at the Georgia Governor's
Mansion and share with us the recipes they
served. 209 pages; hardcover. Currently out of
print.

HEAD TABLE COOKS

American Camellia Society
100 Massee Lane   912/967-2358
Fort Valley, GA 31030   Fax 912/967-2083

Favorite recipes from around the world presented
by members and friends of The American Camellia
Society, Inc. which is engaged in research in all
aspects of camellia culture and maintains a 10-
acre garden, a landscaped greenhouse, Japanese
and rose gardens, gallery of Boehm porcelains and
an Education-Museum Building. Hard cover, spiral bound; 402 pages.

$10.00 Retail price
$ .70 Sales tax for Georgia residents
$ 2.50 Postage and handling
Make check payable to The American Camellia
Society
ISBN 0-910185-00-X

THE HISTORIC ROSWELL COOKBOOK

The Roswell Historical Society
P. O. Box 1636
Roswell, GA 30077   770/992-1665

These recipes cover a period in Roswell's history
from open-hearth to microwave cooking. Included
are highlights of Roswell's history and pen and ink
drawings of its historic structures. Anecdotes are
also included. The proceeds go toward the preser-
vation of historic Roswell. A bit of the South
shines through in its recipes and its history. 229
pages; 470 recipes.

$12.95 Retail price
$ .91 Tax for Georgia residents
$ 3.00 Postage and handling
Make check payable to Roswell Historical Society

THE HOLIDAY HOSTESS

Valdosta Junior Service League
Valdosta, GA

A collection of 300 "special" holiday recipes. These
recipes are traditions in our homes and we know
they'll soon be traditions in yours, too! The book
includes recipes for all major holidays with a special emphasis on Christmas "goodies." Also included are menus to make your holidays memorable. Currently out of print.

THE HORS D'OEUVRE TRAY

Valdosta Junior Service League
P.O. Box 1582
Valdosta, GA 31603 912/244-8575

This book is a "must" if you are planning a special event. It is jam packed with 266 recipes for all the hors d'oeuvres, party foods and beverages to make your next party a huge success. Spiral bound with full color cover.

$ 6.00 Retail price
$ 1.50 Postage and handling
Make check payable to Valdosta Junior Service League

LASTING IMPRESSIONS

Saint Joseph's Hospital of Atlanta Auxiliary
Atlanta, GA

Whether you're entertaining guests or your family, you'll find fresh, new ideas in *Lasting Impressions* as well as international recipes. For people who don't do a great deal of cooking or who run into problems, Special Helps aids in all categories. The Food for Fitness section has tempting, delicious low cholesterol and low sodium recipes. 467 recipes; 328 pages. Currently out of print.

LITTLE BIT DIFFERENT!

St. John's Episcopal Church
P.O. Box 1657
Moultrie, GA 31767 912/985-3676

Little Bit Different! is a lot different! The 296-page spiral bound cookbook includes drawings of Moultrie's loveliest homes along with party and menu ideas. It includes notable regional recipes reflecting the hunting and seafood of the area, as well as those ranging from California to Paris.

$ 9.50 Retail price
$ .48 Tax for Georgia residents
$ 1.50 Postage and handling
Make check payable to *Little Bit Different!*
ISBN 0-939-114-61-5

LOOK MOM, I CAN COOK

Dot Gibson Publications
P.O. Box 117
Waycross, GA 31502   912/285-2848

A delightful "first cookbook" for children. Attractive cover and interior art. Basic recipes for the little beginner—Spider Candy, Jello Squares, Cinnamon Toast, Chocolate Chip Cookies. A clever, colorful book. 71 pages; 93 recipes; comb binder.

$ 7.95 Retail price
$ .56 Tax for Georgia residents
$ 1.25 Postage and handling
Make check payable to Dot Gibson Publications

MACON SETS A FINE TABLE

Middle Georgia Historical Society, Inc.
935 High Street
Macon, Georgia 31201   912/743-3851

Macon, Georgia, is noted for beautiful historic as well as new homes; for good food and gracious entertaining. Pictured in this book are sixteen homes with tables set for various affairs. Eighty recipes appropriate for the occasions include some family favorites enjoyed for generations and shared for the first time.

$ 4.95 Retail price
$ .35 Tax for Georgia residents
$ 4.00 Postage and handling
Make check payable to Middle Georgia Historical Society

THE MARKET PLACE

Augusta Junior Woman's Club, Inc.
Augusta, GA

A unique blend of the past and present. Contemporary recipes with the flavor of the old markets of the South. The delightful dishes are equaled only by the appealing pen and ink drawings detailing the vanishing corner markets which dot the urban areas of a distinctive Southern city, Augusta, Georgia. Currently out of print.

THE ORIGINAL VIDALIA ONION COOKBOOK

Vidalia Chamber of Commerce
2805 E. First Street
Vidalia, GA 30474   912/537-4466

Compiled by Mrs. Pam Thompson for the Vidalia Chamber of Commerce, the book contains 76 pages of recipes using those delicious Vidalia Sweet Onions. This cookbook shows how to prepare the Vidalia Onion in ways that you have never thought before, including salads, soups, main dishes, desserts, and many microwave recipes.

$ 5.30 Retail price (includes tax)
$ 2.00 Postage and handling
Make check payable to *Vidalia Onion Cookbook*

PEACHTREE BOUQUET

Junior League of DeKalb
P. O. Box 183
Decatur, GA 30030   404/377-2973

Peachtree Bouquet features over 600 recipes in 13 sections, including designations for quick and easy, children and gift recipes and wine suggestions with entrees. Easy-to-read format with recipe preparation guides. Beautiful 5-color artist-designed laminated hard cover with durable plastic comb binding.

$14.95 Retail price
$ 1.05 Tax for Georgia residents
$ 3.00 Postage and handling
Make check payable to JLD Publications
ISBN 0-9618508-1-7

PERENNIALS

Junior Service League of Gainesville, GA, Inc.
P.O. Box 1472
Gainesville, GA 30503   770/535-1951

A southern celebration of food and flavors. Tastemaker Award Finalist. *Perennials* features over 700 triple-tested recipes, microwave adaptations, menu and wine suggestions, a children's section, and more. Hard cover, with full-color original artwork of native wildflowers and quotations from southern writers throughout each of the twelve sections.

$19.00 Retail price
$ 3.00 Postage and handling
Make check payable to Junior League
ISBN 0-9612234-0-5

THE PIRATES' HOUSE COOKBOOK
The Pirates' House Restaurant
20 East Broad Street
Savannah, GA 31401   912/233-5757

"What Foods These Morsels Be"...so states the slogan The Pirates' House has been using for years to describe the masterpieces created by its wonderful chefs. Their new 339-page cookbook contains over 400 classic recipes...many never before published. All have been tested in a home kitchen for practically fool-proof results.

$15.95 Retail price
$ 1.12 Tax for Georgia residents
$ 3.20 Postage and handling
Make check payable to *The Pirates' House Cookbook*
ISBN 0-939-11461-5

POTLUCKS AND PETTICOATS
Appalacian Cultural Center
P.O. Box 129
Dillard, GA 30537   706/746-2134

Potlucks and Petticoats pairs the history of square dancing with over 500 recipes chosen for variety, ease of preparation and portability to potluck dinners. Original artwork and amusing anecdotes bring dance history to life throughout the 336 colorful pages. Part of the proceeds benefit Habitat for Humanity.

$11.95 Retail price
$ 2.50 Postage and handling
Make check payable to *Potlucks and Petticoats*
ISBN 0-96177157-0-7

PUTTIN' ON THE PEACHTREE
Junior League of DeKalb
P. O. Box 183
Decatur, GA 30030   404/378-4536

Puttin' on the Peachtree, with over 100,000 copies in print, contains 346 pages with 650 plus recipes. Durable stacon cover with spiral binding. Comprehensive index, bonus section with international fare, microwave and cooking tips throughout.

$16.95 Retail price
$ 1.18 Tax for Georgia residents
$ 3.00 Postage and handling
Make check payable to JLD Publications
ISBN 0-918544-69-6

QUAIL COUNTRY

Smith House Publications
Albany, GA

For over a century the abundance of wild game, fruits and vegetables grown in the pleasant climate of South Georgia, with riverboats bringing oysters from the Gulf has made for truly bountiful tables. The Junior League of Albany preserves the heritage of this Southern hospitality in their beautiful hardcover 372-page book. Currently out of print.

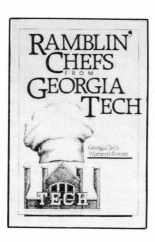

RAMBLIN' CHEFS FROM GEORGIA TECH

The Georgia Tech Women's Forum
Atlanta, GA

Ramblin' Chefs from Georgia Tech is the first Georgia Tech cookbook and is a fundraising project of the Georgia Tech Women's Forum. The book contains 193 pages and has over 275 recipes. All proceeds from the sale of the cookbook are used for scholarships for outstanding women students. Currently out of print.

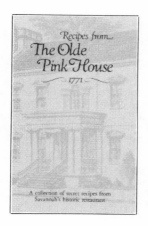

RECIPES FROM THE OLDE PINK HOUSE

4 Season Development
23 Abercorn Street
Savannah, GA 31401   912/232-4286

To dine at the historic Olde Pink House in Savannah (built in 1771) is to live for a few hours in the beautiful and refined world of yesteryear that yet endures in this most gracious of Southern cities. Secret recipes are shared in this cookbook. 190 pages, wire bound, laminated pink cover.

$10.95 Retail price
$ .55 Tax for Georgia residents
$ 1.50 Postage and handling
Make check payable to Pink House
ISBN 0-938072-01-3

327

SAVANNAH COLLECTION

by Martha Giddens Nesbit
215 Grimball Point Road
Savannah, GA 31401   912/355-5049

Savannah Collection, written by the former food editor of the *Savannah News-Press*, contains recipes from some of the city's finest cooks, as well as personal favorites and family treasures. This cookbook has become a staple in Savannah kitchens. "The recipes are easy, and everything I've tried is delicious!" 224 pages; hard cover; spiral bound.

$15.00 Retail price
$ .90 Tax for Georgia residents
$ 2.00 Postage and handling
Make check payable to *Martha Nesbit Cookbook*
ISBN 0-9617126-0-0

SAVANNAH STYLE

Junior League of Savannah
P.O. Box 1864   912/352-4999
Savannah, GA 31402   Fax 352-0406

Savannah Style features 435 tried and true recipes combined with delightful glimpses into Savannah's past. This regional cookbook has captured the city's warmth and charm in recipes that are truly an education in good eating and entertaining...uniquely Savannah Style. Over 400 recipes; hard-bound with hidden spiral; over 75,000 copies sold.

$12.95 Retail price
$ .78 Tax for Georgia residents
$ 1.75 Postage and handling
Make check payable to *Savannah Style*
ISBN 0-9613411-0-6

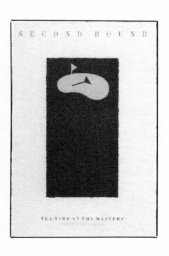

SECOND ROUND,
TEA-TIME AT THE MASTERS®

Junior League of Augusta
P.O. Box 3232
Augusta, GA 30904-3232   706/736-0033

Over 650 triple tested recipes on over 330 pages. Accent is on today's cooking direction toward fresh and healthy foods. Selections of recipes from golf celebrities and famous resort chefs. Hard cover with unique and colorful design. Nutritional information aids. Colorful divider pages.

$16.95 Retail price
$ 1.19 Tax for Georgia residents
$ 4.00 Postage and handling
Make check payable to Tea-Time Publications
ISBN 0-9621062-0-8

SIMPLY SCRUMPTIOUS MICROWAVING
Kitchen Classics
Stone Mountain, GA

Simply Scrumptious Microwaving is filled with almost 600 recipes that have never been so simple or so scrumptious—a practical and creative approach to microwaving that can revolutionize the way you cook. It is the most widely sold cookbook for answering microwave questions in the United States and United Kingdom, having sold over 250,000 copies. Currently out of print.

SOMETHIN'S COOKIN' IN THE MOUNTAINS
by Jay Bucek
Clarkesville, GA

The ideal way to get introduced to the mountains including 386 recipes, 86 John Kollock sketches, information on motels, restaurants, shops and services, seven maps, and page after page of information about our lakes, rivers, waterfalls, campgrounds, hiking trails, fairs and festivals and much more. Spiral bound. Currently out of print.

SOUTHERN SEAFOOD CLASSICS
Peachtree Publishers, Ltd.
Atlanta, GA

This is the official cookbook of the Southeastern Fisheries Association. Fish consumption is rising dramatically in America—seafood is plentiful, nutritious and reasonably priced—and cooks from coast to coast are looking for new and creative ways to prepare it. This is the answer—a first-class cookbook! Currently out of print.

SOUTHWIND CUISINE
Southwind Health Resort
Cartersville, GA

By following the dietary instructions mentioned in this book, you will reduce your cholesterol, lose weight and significantly reduce the sodium in your diet. These dietetic gourmet recipes are among those served at the Southwind Health Resort. 108 pages; laminated cover; ring bound. Currently out of print.

THE STUFFED GRIFFIN
The Utility Club of Griffin
P.O. Box 711
Griffin, GA 30224

The Stuffed Griffin has been a nationwide favorite for over twelve years. Its 370 pages contain over 650 classic southern recipes. Special sections on menus, parties, and cooking hints make entertaining a pleasure. Proceeds are used to provide cultural and educational enrichment for the citizens of Griffin and Spalding Counties.

$19.95 Retail price
$ 1.40 Tax for Georgia residents
$ 2.50 Postage and handling
Make check payable to *The Stuffed Griffin*
ISBN 0-9607584-0-2

A TASTE OF GEORGIA
Newman Junior Service League
P.O. Box 1433
Newman, GA 30263   770/251-0113

This large "one-of-a-kind" volume contains carefully tested, superior rated recipes...extensive, unique, kitchen charts...hundreds of culinary hints...and valuable illustrated guides for the novice and the expert. All designed to bring the flavor and tastes of the South to the discriminating cook and hostess. 619 pages; 808 recipes; spiral bound.

$18.95 Retail price
$ 1.33 Tax for Georgia residents
$ 3.00 Postage and handling
Make check payable to *A Taste of Georgia*
ISBN 0-9611002-0-6

A TASTE OF THE HOLIDAYS

Dot Gibson Publications
P.O. Box 117
Waycross, GA 31502   912/285-2848

A new book for the holidays! Perfect for a "stocking stuffer," teacher's gift, or remembrance for the lady down the street. Great price, outstanding, full-color cover, terrific recipes. 96 pages; paperback.

$ 3.95 Retail price
$ .28 Tax for Georgia residents
$ 1.25 Postage and handling
Make check payable to Dot Gibson Publications

TEA-TIME AT THE MASTERS®

Junior League of Augusta, Inc.
P.O. Box 3232
Augusta, GA 30904   706/733-9098

Tea Time at the Masters® is an absolute must for the serious collector of cookbooks. Scattered throughout the books are recipes submitted by PGA golfers and their wives, famous golfing resorts, Native Augustans and other "masters" of the culinary arts. 292 pages; ring bound.

$16.95 Retail price
$ 1.19 Tax for Georgia residents
$ 4.00 Postage and handling ($2.00 each add'l)
Make check payable to Tea-Time Publications
ISBN 0-918544-38-6

TEMPTATIONS

Junior Service League of Rome, Inc.
Rome, GA

Temptations is a special collection of treasured recipes shared by active and sustaining members of the Junior Service League of Rome, Inc. More that 1000 recipes were submitted with 124 selected after thorough testing. These recipes are sure to tempt anyone who enjoys preparing and eating delicious cuisine. Currently out of print.

TRADITIONALLY WESLEYAN

Wesleyan College Business Club
Wesleyan College
47060 Forsythe Road
Macon, GA 31297   912/757-5172

Traditionally Wesleyan is composed of superb recipes from Wesleyan Alumni. There are recipes from
hors d'oeuvres and beverages to entrees and delicious desserts. A description of the rich heritage,
sisterhood, and fellowship separate the sections.
A wonderful addition to southern cooking!

$ 9.95 Retail price
$ .40 Tax for Georgia residents
Make check payable to Wesleyan College Business
Club

TULLIE'S RECEIPTS

Kitchen Guild of Tullie Smith House Restoration
Museum Shop
130 W. Paces Ferry Road NW
Atlanta, GA 30305   404/814-4075

A historical document of 19th century life, this
book was created through research in unpub-
lished manuscripts and family receipts handed
down from generation to generation. Also included in the intriguing documentation are house-
hold goods, hints and wisdoms, dyeing, and rem-
edies.

$15.95 Retail price
$ 1.12 Tax for Georgia residents
$ 3.00 Postage and handling
Make check payable to Atlanta Historical Society
Museum Shop

UNBEARABLY GOOD!

Americus Junior Service League
P.O. Box 92
Americus, GA 31709   912/924-2327

You can't bear to miss this undeniably fun cookbook with 352 pages of 567 outstanding, beary
special recipes. Special features on the back of divider pages are Bearing Gift ideas and Bear Essen-
tials for Entertaining, helpful hints to make serving more fun. Bear theme used throughout the
book. Sold 10,000 copies in bearly a year.

$13.95 Retail price
$ .84 Tax for Georgia residents
$ 2.00 Postage and handling
Make check payable to *Unbearably Good!*
ISBN 0-9617759-0-4

VINCENT RUSSO'S SEAFOOD COOKBOOK

by Vincent Russo
802 Perry Cove
Savannah, GA 31418   912/897-7944

Good looking book from Savannah's most famous seafood caterer. Great recipes and pictures showing steps to clean, fillet, shuck and pickle your seafood, oysters, mussels, clams, scallops, lobster, crab and shrimp. 128 pages; 113 recipes; comb binding.

$ 9.95 Retail price
$ .60 Tax for Georgia residents
$ 2.25 Postage and handling
Make check payable to Vincent Russo's Catering
ISBN 0-9618071-0-5

WINDSOR ACADEMY COOKBOOK

Windsor Academy
Thomasville, GA

From the kitchens of middle Georgia, this 112-page cookbook is divided into 10 sections ranging from meat and poultry, casseroles, cookies and candies to seafood, diet, microwave and salads. Included is also a small selection of foreign fare which includes some very special recipes from various foreign countries. Currently out of print.

YOU ARE THE BOSS IN THE KITCHEN!

by Ursula Knaeusel
Ursula's Cooking School
1764 Chesire Bridge Road Northeast
Atlanta, GA 30324   404/876-7463

Ursula's cooking school (Cooking Around the World with Ursula) is the largest independent cooking school in the nation, with 540 students attending each quarter. In over 16 years of teaching, she has not used the same recipe twice. Here she presents some of her favorite recipes interspersed with some of her anecdotes and kitchen hints. 268 pages; ring bound.

$ 9.95 Retail price
$ .70 Tax for Georgia residents
$ 3.20 Postage and handling
Make check payable to Ursula's Cookbook

Preserving America's Food Heritage

BEST OF THE BEST STATE COOKBOOK SERIES

Cookbooks listed below have been completed as of December 31, 2000.

Best of the Best from
ALABAMA
288 pages, $16.95

Best of the Best from
ARIZONA
288 pages, $16.95

Best of the Best from
ARKANSAS
288 pages, $16.95

Best of the Best from
CALIFORNIA
384 pages, $16.95

Best of the Best from
COLORADO
288 pages, $16.95

Best of the Best from
FLORIDA
288 pages, $16.95

Best of the Best from
GEORGIA
336 pages, $16.95

Best of the Best from the
GREAT PLAINS
288 pages, $16.95

Best of the Best from
ILLINOIS
288 pages, $16.95

Best of the Best from
INDIANA
288 pages, $16.95

Best of the Best from
IOWA
288 pages, $16.95

Best of the Best from
KENTUCKY
288 pages, $16.95

Best of the Best from
LOUISIANA
288 pages, $16.95

Best of the Best from
LOUISIANA II
288 pages, $16.95

Best of the Best from
MICHIGAN
288 pages, $16.95

Best of the Best from
MINNESOTA
288 pages, $16.95

Best of the Best from
MISSISSIPPI
288 pages, $16.95

Best of the Best from
MISSOURI
304 pages, $16.95

Best of the Best from
NEW ENGLAND
368 pages, $16.95

Best of the Best from
NEW MEXICO
288 pages, $16.95

Best of the Best from
NORTH CAROLINA
288 pages, $16.95

Best of the Best from
OHIO
352 pages, $16.95

Best of the Best from
OKLAHOMA
288 pages, $16.95

Best of the Best from
PENNSYLVANIA
320 pages, $16.95

Best of the Best from
SOUTH CAROLINA
288 pages, $16.95

Best of the Best from
TENNESSEE
288 pages, $16.95

Best of the Best from
TEXAS
352 pages, $16.95

Best of the Best from
TEXAS II
352 pages, $16.95

Best of the Best from
VIRGINIA
320 pages, $16.95

Best of the Best from
WISCONSIN
288 pages, $16.95

Note: All cookbooks
are ringbound except
California, which is
paperbound.

Special discount offers available!

(See previous page for details.)

To order by credit card, call toll-free **1-800-343-1583** or send check or money order to:
QUAIL RIDGE PRESS • P. O. Box 123 • Brandon, MS 39043
Visit our website at **www.quailridge.com** to order online!

- -